Runaway Daughters

Runaway Daughters

Seduction, Elopement, and Honor in Nineteenth-Century Mexico

❧

KATHRYN A. SLOAN

UNIVERSITY OF NEW MEXICO PRESS ❧ ALBUQUERQUE

Library of Congress Cataloging-in-Publication Data

Sloan, Kathryn A., 1961–

  Runaway daughters : seduction, elopement, and honor
in nineteenth-century Mexico / Kathryn A. Sloan.

      p. cm.

  Includes bibliographical references and index.

ISBN 978-0-8263-4477-9 (pbk. : alk. paper)

1. Seduction—Mexico—Oaxaca (State)—History—19th century.

2. Young women—Mexico—Oaxaca (State)—History—19th century.

I. Title.

HV6587.M49R86 2008

364.15´3—dc22

                        2008021674

Book design and type composition by Melissa Tandysh

Composed in 10/13.75 ScalaOT

Display type is ITC Legacy Serif Std

To the loves in my life—
Jerry, Ian, and Orion

Contents

Maps and Figures

Acknowledgments

WHERE DO I BEGIN? There are so many people and organizations to thank because the book began taking form during my graduate education at the University of Kansas. Indeed, the research for it sprang from a chapter of my dissertation, and the encouragement of many colleagues along the way has brought it to fruition.

First, I would like to acknowledge the impact of two advisers at the University of Kansas—Elizabeth Kuznesof and Anton Rosenthal. I met Tony my first day of class as a Masters student in Latin American Studies. It was his enthusiasm and excellent teaching that inspired me to pursue a doctorate in Latin American history. Betsy deserves my sincerest gratitude for her encouragement while I wrote the dissertation, and perhaps more importantly, for her mentoring after its completion, as I went out into the job market and subsequently took a tenure-track position at the University of Arkansas. Having passed from student to colleague, I am pleased that our relationship has also grown beyond that of mentor and student. Her example as a scholar, teacher, and friend has inspired me to strive hard in those capacities as well. I would also like to thank the other members of my committee—Mehrangiz Najafizadeh, Rita Napier, and Lorraine Bayard de Volo—for their comments and critiques. Finally, I had the good fortune of meeting Bill Beezley in Oaxaca while doing field research. He included me in his fine Oaxaca Summer Institute in 2000 and continues to take an interest in my scholarship and career.

How fortunate that I had a group of fellow graduate students who became close friends. Our shared meals and discussions added levity to our hectic schedules. Sterling Evans, Kirk Shaffer, Mary Rose Shaffer, Sam Sommerville, Laura Herlihy, and Chris Brown were a supportive community of colleagues. Adriana Natali Sommerville helped to translate some of the love letters discussed in this volume. Nancy Chaison, then affiliated with the Center of Latin American Studies, helped me out in every way, even babysitting my infant son when I attended classes! I especially appreciate the friendship of my then-office mate and now dear friend, Cynthia Ingham, who has been both a sounding board and source of support through graduate school and my years as an assistant professor.

I would never have been privy to the lives discussed herein without the diligent archivists who endeavored to preserve their public records for posterity. I would like to thank the various directors and employees of the Archivo Histórico Municipal de la Ciudad de Oaxaca (the Oaxaca Municipal Historical Archive) in particular, as I gleaned most of my research from that fine repository. First, Dr. Carlos Sánchez Silva introduced me to the archive and ensured that competent archivists were available to assist me, including Aarón Martínez García and Gloria Irma Méndez. Gloria, in particular, showed a keen interest in my research, and we shared an afternoon at the Festival de Mescal during the city's annual Guelaguetza celebration in July. I worked in that archive over four successive summers and then again in 2005 to expand the scope of the project. By then, its new director Lic. Nora Olivia Sedeño Torres had initiated a reorganization of the criminal documents, classifying them by court rather than type of crime. When I decided to expand the time frame of the study, I had to plod through each court's numerous boxes once again. Although I was initially overwhelmed, the reorganization worked to my favor in that I discovered several rapto cases that had been previously misfiled. I would also like to thank the archivists and librarians of the Archivo General del Estado de Oaxaca (Oaxaca State General Archive) as well as the Hemeroteca (Periodicals Library) of Universidad Nacional de México (UNAM) in Mexico City. On this side of the border, I owe a debt of gratitude to the Nettie Benson Library at the University of Texas, as well as the fine Mexican and Oaxacan collections at the University of New Mexico (UNM) Libraries, especially the collections of the Center for Southwest Research. Librarians Nancy Brown-Martínez and Ann Massmann facilitated my research into the Mexican Broadsides and Van de Velde Collections at UNM during the summer of 2006.

Funding for this project has come from numerous sources. As a graduate student, I benefited from fellowships and stipends from the Tinker Foundation as well as the Department of Education's Foreign Language and Area Studies Fellowship program. My research trips were also supported by two James B. Pearson fellowships, which are named in honor of a former Kansas senator who believed in international education and experience. I was also fortunate to receive an Oppenheimer Fellowship, named after Robert Oppenheimer, the renowned late Latin Americanist. A summer stipend, travel grant, and Connor faculty fellowship from the Fulbright College at the University of Arkansas funded two additional trips to Oaxaca's archives. A generous stipend from Barbara and Mitch Singleton, under the auspices of the Singleton fellowship from the Department of History at the

University of Arkansas, also helped fund final trips to Mexico. Finally, a visiting scholar award from University of New Mexico's Division of Iberian and Latin American Resources and Services (DILARES) and the Latin American and Iberian Institute (LAII) allowed me to investigate the Center of Southwest Research's vast collection of Mexican chapbooks and broadsides. Vicky Madrid Nelson, Senior Program Manager at LAII, and Carolyn Mountain of DILARES made my visit a pleasant and productive one.

I also have several debts to colleagues at the University of Arkansas. Lynda Coon and Tricia Starks read different parts of the manuscript and provided encouraging and critical advice. Their collegiality and, more importantly, friendship have been invaluable to me. I have also shared numerous meals, laughs, and kvetching with other colleagues, including Beth Barton Schweiger, Mike Pierce, Kirstin Erickson, Kim Sexton, and Jo Ann D'Alisera. All of their good cheer, sarcasm, and mirth has made life and work more fun.

In the production of the book, I also have several people to thank. Working with the UNM Press staff has been a pleasure. Patricia Rosas also deserves my appreciation. Not only does she know a lot about Mexican history, she is a superb copy editor.

Last, but certainly not least, are my personal debts. I jokingly call my two sons the Masters baby and the PhD baby. They were literally with me the entire way, as the first day of school as a Masters student, I found out I was pregnant with my oldest, Ian. Indeed, he was born on Cinco de Mayo during finals week! Orion was born the year I took comprehensive exams, and I have been fortunate to have both with me on various research trips to Oaxaca. While motherhood may have lengthened my graduate career, I do not think I would have finished without the balance that role gave to my task as teacher and scholar. Jerry McCormick—my partner, my best friend, the love of my life—cajoled me constantly not to take myself too seriously, to have fun, and to shun the self-absorption that exists in academia. He has been my biggest ally, and the research trips on which he accompanied me were certainly my happiest and most productive.

Introduction

❧

IN 1886, CIPRIANA VÁSQUEZ, A THIRTY-SIX-YEAR-OLD SINGLE MOTHER, WHO lived alone with her daughter, Petrona, opened her door to a neighbor bearing shocking news. The woman had heard gossip that Cipriana's daughter had been forcibly abducted by a certain Mariano Cruz. Horrified, Cipriana sprang into action and rushed a mile to Oaxaca City to file a criminal complaint. The mother prevailed upon the court to charge Mariano with rapto de seducción (abduction by seduction) and to send police officers to apprehend the couple. The 1871 Mexican Penal Code defined rapto as the abduction of a woman against her will by the use of physical violence, deception, or seduction in order to satisfy "carnal desires" or to marry.[1] Rapto also occurred when a woman under sixteen years of age went voluntarily with a man—a situation more akin to elopement than abduction. The law had two main intentions: to protect young virgins from seduction in order to guard their honor and that of their family and to promote civil marriage.

Once police took the couple into custody, the judge collected a battery of depositions. Petrona spoke first, explaining that she was fourteen years old and had had "no sort of relations" with any man before Mariano. Every day she walked from her mother's home in El Marquesado[2] to the center of Oaxaca City, where she served in the house of Don Vicente. Three days earlier, while walking back to El Marquesado, Mariano had confronted her in the street and ordered her to follow him. When she refused, he grabbed her by the arm and took her to a room in San Juanito where, according to Petrona, they had sex twice. The young girl claimed that Mariano had not given her gifts or money, but he did offer to marry her.

In this calculated move, Petrona was publicly laying claim to honor and respectability by stressing Mariano's proper proposal of marriage and the fact that she did not accept money for sex. That a promise of marriage informally sanctioned the beginning of sexual relations was a custom that had been condoned for centuries in Hispanic society.[3] Petrona also told the judge that her mother routinely mistreated her, perhaps another calculated admission since this charge resonated with nineteenth-century jurists. According to the law, a judge had the right to nullify the parental rights of an abusive mother or father and even to emancipate a minor child.[4] In the present study, minors wishing to marry without parental consent frequently insisted that mistreatment or child abuse, in addition to love and a promise of marriage, had compelled them to elope with their sweethearts. This set nineteenth-century runaway daughters apart from their colonial sisters, since now a judge might rule in favor of the minor couple, in effect emancipating them, and the minors no longer necessarily needed parental sanction to marry.

The judge gave Mariano equal space to tell his story. Claiming to be of "majority" (at least twenty-one years of age) and a farmhand from the same working-class neighborhood, Mariano confessed to having had "amorous relations" with Petrona for five months. He also admitted to writing her several love letters to prove his honorable intentions in the liaison and subsequent elopement.[5] Mexican society viewed love letters or small gifts as *prendas* (love tokens) that solidified a promise to marry. Indeed, in various testimonies recorded during rapto trials, there are references to prendas, given to prove the suitor's serious intentions. Mariano further swore that Cipriana neglected Petrona, by depriving her of food and forcing her to serve as a maid in Don Vicente's home. He contended that Petrona willingly fled with him to San Juanito and agreed to sexual intercourse after he promised to marry her. Mariano also told the judge that he intended to fulfill his promise of marriage even though he claimed she was not a virgin at their first sexual encounter. The judge continued the investigation and called in family members and witnesses to testify about the sequence of events.[6] Witnesses also vouched for Mariano's honorable conduct and lack of a prison record to prove that he was not a criminal or someone devious.

By claiming that Petrona had not been not a virgin when they first had sexual intercourse, Mariano implied that she was unworthy of legal protection. At the same time, he professed that he still wanted to marry her. Petrona endeavored to convince the judge that Mariano had forcibly abducted her. As a defenseless and deceived virgin, the court was mandated to shelter her. Their testimonies contradict each other initially, but the goal of their narratives was clear: to convince the judge of their innocence in the crime and of their rights as honorable citizens to be protected by the law. By initially lying and claiming that Mariano had forcibly abducted her, Petrona played on prevailing gendered scripts that required her to be a victim who would never disobey her parents by running off with her suitor. It is also possible that Petrona knew that her mother did not have a birth certificate to prove that she was under sixteen years of age. Were the judge to deem her to be older, she would only be worthy of protection under the law if she could prove that Mariano employed force to seduce her.[7] Petrona had to claim force in order to be taken seriously by the judge. If the judge believed that she had wantonly gone with Mariano to have sex, the law would not protect her. She did not want Mariano to be incarcerated. She likely understood that rapto trials rarely led to jail time for male defendants. Her end goal was to assert her honor and begin life with Mariano.

Few scholars have systematically analyzed nineteenth-century rapto cases in Latin American countries. *Runaway Daughters* is the first to mine these rich court records in order to understand intergenerational conflict and interactions among working-class Mexicans and the state in a provincial capital city.[8] The prosecution of rapto, in the case of Petrona and Mariano as well as those of other couples, underscores the importance of the category of "family" for understanding gender, youth, and ethnicity. Investigating family quarrels reveals more than just the seeds of conflict. The testimonies of the antagonists speak to cultural norms, the social history of everyday life, and the negotiations between families and state officials concerning the law and behavioral norms. Runaway daughters in Oaxaca, some of them of indigenous background, found themselves at the nexus of family-state conflict over their rights and responsibilities as minor children. Their voices, largely muted in official documents, are loud and compelling in the elopement dramas, as they provided testimonies that detailed their love lives and tribulations with their mothers and fathers.

This project is also one of the few comprehensive studies of gender relations and honor among young working-class couples and their families in post-colonial Mexico. Based on 212 rapto cases, it places the spotlight on older children, those between thirteen and twenty-one years of age—a social group that has lamentably left few traces in the historical record. An examination of the court testimonies of parents, their children, and witnesses, as well as a reading of the love letters included as evidence of a relationship or promise of marriage, highlights courtship practices, generational conflict, and the negotiation of honor. These materials provide an indication of how individuals, like Petrona and Mariano, understood their gender identities. Additionally, they reveal the significant role that the working class played in refashioning accepted codes of conduct and honor as well as the state's role in shaping the terms of civil marriage and adjudicating power struggles between family members and between "citizens" and the nation. The state, in this case, is represented by the cadre of liberal civil servants that sought to shape Oaxaca's civil and political life in the nineteenth century.

Consider the tale of Mariano and Petrona. Their elopement had implications both for their families and for the state officials who ruled on the actions and the futures of these two young people. Petrona had lost her honor by running off with Mariano and that would have been the case even if she had not engaged in sexual relations. Mariano faced a possible prison term. Both faced a public airing of their courtship and exploits, actions that could damage their reputations in the community. Yet, for many eloping youngsters, the risks were worth the benefits of forging an autonomous life together. Cipriana, who sent Petrona daily to work in the home of an elite gentleman, rejected Mariano as a son-in-law for reasons unknown to us, but a motivation might have been the fear of losing Petrona's financial contribution to the family economy. For the historian more than a century later, the testimonies are a veritable goldmine that reveals norms, mores, and tidbits of everyday life of working-class Mexicans. The crime of rapto itself is not the focus of this book. Whereas for some couples, rapto was simply a dramatic courtship ritual that originated centuries earlier, rapto in nineteenth-century Mexico was a personal and political act. Intergenerational conflict figured prominently because in these cases, minors like Petrona employed the drama of rapto as a strategy to defy parental authority and sometimes earn legal emancipation to make independent choices about their sexual or conjugal arrangements. In more than 90 percent of the 212 cases that were examined, the girls voluntarily ran away with their suitors, and some even engineered the entire escapade. Few girls claimed to have been tricked or raped, and of those who did, some, like Petrona, eventually recanted and admitted their consent to eloping and having sexual intercourse. Parents either demanded marriage to restore family honor or the suitor's punishment and their daughter's return home. Witnesses, at times, complicated the dialogue by weighing in on honor or reputation and the sequence of events. Their testimonies could either substantiate the sexual honor of the girl or impugn the boy's reputation by noting his previous conduct with other young girls. Court officials also offered their opinion, with defense attorneys particularly contributing discourses on love, marriage, honor, and the proclivities of the working class. In many ways, judges played a silent role in that they rarely explained their verdicts, offering little to elucidate their decisions. However, their conclusions spoke volumes about their view of the "order of families" and "public morality." Rapto was just the crime, but the testimonies reveal much about courtship practices, attitudes toward marriage, the boundaries of parental authority and filial obedience, and the relationship between the state and its lower-status citizens.

The cases from the capital city, Oaxaca de Juárez (today, Oaxaca City), also present vivid contrasts with other studies of conflict between parents and children over marriage and elopement in Latin America. Oaxaca City provides a unique setting to explore the social history of gender ideologies and family relations in nineteenth-century Mexico. Between 1857 and 1891, indigenous groups, such as the Zapotec, Mixtec, and Triqui, were between 77 percent and 87 percent of the state's population.[9] Indigenous women played important social and economic roles throughout Oaxaca's history. Many scholars have gathered evidence that attests to their remarkable litigiousness seen in their vigorous contesting of property rights and conjugal disputes in the state's courtrooms.[10] Their penchant for legal wrangling aside, scholars have rightly argued that a notion of complementarity infused gender relations among the indigenous Oaxacans. Certainly women felt the brunt of patriarchal structures that oppressed; however domestic quarrels occurred on a more level playing field with positive outcomes for the women involved in them.[11] For example a Zapotec or Mixtec woman who suffered domestic abuse could strategically lobby other men and also mobilized female allies to censure her violent husband. A firm belief in contingent rights informed the negotiation of these disputes. Individuals who violated them, male or female, were held accountable by their peers. Men were supposed to contribute economically to the household and eschew extraordinary violence in their relations with wives and children. In contrast, women cooked, cleaned, cared for the children, and behaved decorously and modestly in the presence of other men and in public spaces. The desire for social peace, a core community value of these indigenous cultures, sometimes resulted in community sanction of men who displayed excessive violence or swagger. The assorted legal complaints stressed the very collective nature of familial strife. It was in the best interests of the community to resolve family conflict, whether between husbands and wives or parents and children. Minor daughters sometimes engineered their own elopements, but at the very least, they claimed their nascent rights as minor children. Men did not abandon nonvirgins, and Oaxacans of both sexes possessed a keen sense of conditional rights and responsibilities between lovers and parents and children. That Zapotec and Mixtec women parlayed conjugal disputes on more equal footing suggests an alternative structure of gender relations in Oaxaca that acknowledged female assertiveness and power—an assertiveness that will be revealed in the rapto dramas.[12]

In colonial Mexico, young couples turned to church courts if their parents denied them permission to marry. In these cases, there is less evidence that they eloped to overturn their parent's decision. Committed to the norm of free will in a person's decision to marry, ecclesiastical jurists, disregarding parental objections, sanctioned the marriage of willing minor children. Later, sexual honor rather than parental authority was the top priority for ecclesiastical jurists.[13] Priests performed secret marriages in many cases. It was not until the late-eighteenth century that the Church began to support the parents when they could prove that their inexperienced sons and daughters had made unequal love matches—meaning that one of the betrothed lacked the same social status of the intractable parents.[14] After Mexicans won their independence from Spain in 1821, civil courts, like their ecclesiastical predecessors, favored the free will of children to choose a spouse over parental opposition. While the colonial Church had supported parents for economic reasons, the civil courts in Oaxaca City in post-Independence Mexico consistently supported children over parents unless insurmountable obstacles to marriage, such as consanguinity, force, or violence, existed. Siding with children against parents promoted social order by protecting female sexual honor, which was the foundation of family honor. Allowing a deflowered minor girl to marry satisfied the goals of seduction laws: to uphold sexual honor and promote civil marriage. Yet, 96 percent of the complaints materialized from working-class families, and the elite were blind to the internal hierarchies within this social group. Therefore, siding with parents against children for economic reasons was not an outcome manifested in the Oaxacan examples. But, clearly, some parents opposed the love matches of their runaway daughters because they perceived that the suitor lacked sufficient social or economic status. In addition, supporting working-class minors against their parents had two results in post-Independence Mexico: it sanctioned love and reason as sufficient proof of maturity and will to marry, but it also opened a window for the state to scrutinize and subvert the paternal authority of lower-class parents.

Supported by the Royal Pragmatic on Marriage (1778), which upheld parental power over their children's marriages, parents in colonial Argentina and Cuba could successfully block a marriage if they could convincingly charge that the their child's betrothed was of African descent.[15] Afro-Cubans, furthermore, accepted the white-imposed ideology and spurned individuals who could not "whiten" the lineage.[16] Afro-Cuban parents desired that their children "marry up," by choosing light-skinned, free partners. Race or ethnicity played a different role in Oaxaca than in Cuba since there were few cases of an Indian marrying a non-Indian, and none in which the issue of African heritage was mentioned. However, ethnic and gender relations in Oaxaca certainly informed the dialogue between lovers and their families and their negotiations with court officials. The alternative gender ideology in indigenous Oaxaca placed women under the dominion of male family members but also allowed them legitimate space to effectively contest abuse and assert female power with better results than their mestiza counterparts.[17] Of the 212 rapto cases examined here, 203 involved working-class individuals who married within their own social class (endogamous), at least in the minds of elite judges.[18] Litigants never mentioned the color of skin but did refer to a person's work habits and comportment in public. Those sources of reputation were more important to this social group.

When court cases involved lower-status Mexicans the goal shifted from securing the financial networks of the elite to ensuring the social order, an order that was dependent on family stability and the regulation of female sexuality. It is no wonder that family relationships and comportments figured prominently in rapto cases. During the Porfiriato—the era of President Porfirio Díaz from 1876–1911—the family was not a clone of the colonial Mexican family, which had been epitomized by a strong patriarch who ruled over his home like a lord reigned over his fief. A new, ephemeral figure emerged, the state, which purloined the paternal role, especially in the lives of working-class Mexicans.[19] Indeed, intellectuals, charity organizations, and politicians sought to control and influence poor families, which they viewed as breeding grounds of vice and immorality, two conditions that imperiled Mexico's development and enlistment in the rank of modern nations. As in Argentina, the Mexican state increasingly wielded influence over domestic matters, such as childrearing, marriage, and the limits of parental rule.[20] In both nations, the state reified mothers for their role in bearing and nurturing the next generation of hardworking and patriotic citizens. State officials regularly displaced the patriarchal head in working-class families to momentarily rule in his stead, especially in matters pertaining to his offspring.[21]

This study supports the argument that gender and family were key concepts in nation-building, but it also looks more closely at how minors and their parents discussed love and childrearing within the larger and changing discourses of liberalism. Mexican liberals embraced reason, science, and technology as tools to modernize a society that they considered hamstrung by religious and colonial authoritarianism and the "communal traditions of Mesoamerica."[22] Thus liberals sought secular solutions, first by divesting the Catholic Church of its power and property, and secondly, by focusing a microscope on society. An evangelical belief in "progress" seduced Mexican liberals as well. They believed that Mexican society desperately needed renovation in order for the country to join the ranks of developed nations. Liberalism entailed a commitment to democratic values including equality of opportunity and individual liberty, values that permeated all strata of society. Working-class and indigenous Oaxacans had a keen understanding of not only the law but also prevailing discourses of proper family life and childrearing and how they intersected with liberal values. With the assistance of court officials, people from the lower strata of society effectively invoked these sentiments to litigate their complaints or defend their actions. *Runaway Daughters* builds from family to neighborhood, to the larger community, and to the nation, in an attempt to illustrate how family members accepted, refashioned, or defied prescribed social norms in order to take control of and make sense of their own lives and worlds.[23]

Note on the Sources

Social historians favor criminal records for several reasons. Certainly, court depositions provide some of the most detailed documentation of plebeian lives, providing rich fodder for analysis. These records contain the voices, albeit filtered, of the popular classes, a group that left little independently produced documentation for historical study. Certainly, court officials prodded participants with leading and open-ended questions. Yet, both women's and men's testimonies reveal that gender ideologies were both understood and exploited in everyday lives. Moreover, rapto, although criminalized by the state, was a recognized courtship practice among working-class Mexicans.[24] In their testimonies, these "criminals" discussed courtship, family relationships, sex, love, and honor. It is one of the only sources where we can hear the voice of the historically silenced: minor girls, their poor suitors, and working-class parents and neighbors. Although judicial documents are contentious by nature, they are effective tools for recovering working-class voices.

The cases I reviewed are in the Archivo Histórico Municipal de la Ciudad de Oaxaca de Juárez (AHMCO), which houses criminal records for the capital city. Court officials organized case files individually by the defendant's name and the crime and the court where the proceedings ensued. An inquiry began when a parent or guardian, or occasionally, a girl acting on her own behalf, filed a complaint with the court. If the judge determined that the complaint had merit, depositions of the plaintiff, the victim, the defendant, and witnesses followed.

I primarily reviewed cases that were akin to elopement—where the couple had an acknowledged relationship—omitting those in which the girl did not acknowledge the defendant as her suitor. There was some inconsistency in the labeling of crimes, with some men who should have been charged with rapto being charged with *estupro* (deflowering) or both estupro and rapto. Thus, I included estupro cases if the girl had consented and the couple had eloped. *Violación* (rape) usually meant no romantic relationship had existed previously between the man and woman and the victim was forcibly violated, but some seduction cases were also erroneously prosecuted as rape cases. I read additional criminal cases, including those involving infanticide, adultery, attempted suicide, and slander, to better understand how the honor code operated and to analyze the structures and effects of community surveillance and gossip. The first rapto case was filed in 1841 and the last surviving case is from 1919, for a total of 212 case files. Most cases are from the Porfiriato.

From 1821 to 1920, Oaxaca City had twelve courts that primarily heard cases initiated by city residents, but residents of villages at the city's periphery also filed complaints, especially if the *alcalde* (village mayor) was unable to mediate the dispute. Because of the influence of Roman law on the Mexican legal system, juries did not decide these cases, judges did. If the male defendant was a minor, and he lacked a father or guardian, an advocate was appointed. Defense attorneys also participated in several cases.

Periodization

This study begins in 1841 and ends in 1919, which roughly corresponds to Mexico's half century of liberalism. The bulk of the cases (61 percent) are from the 1870s and 1880s; therefore, the Porfiriato receives extensive attention. Continuity and change characterized Mexico's transition from colony to republic.[25] At first glance, discussions of family honor, courtship, and marriage seemed to change little from 1850 to 1910. Further scrutiny reveals that the topics of discussion in court were the same, yet subtle shifts in meanings emerged, especially in the late nineteenth century, an era characterized by the consolidation of liberalism in society and politics. The study also contributes to the historiography of the Porfiriato and joins the fray that debates the validity of the notion of a *"paz porfiriana"* during this era. The epoch belied a mood of peace and stability, as lovers quarreled with each other, children disputed with their parents, and all actors in the rapto cases struggled with the state over notions of honor and citizenship, appropriate sexuality, and the rules of family formation. In particular, this political era witnessed intense intergenerational conflict, as children and parents battled in the courtroom over spousal choice. Even judges were affected by the emerging liberalism and its values of individuality, freedom, and liberty, as evidenced by the increasing tendency to side with working-class children in disputes with their parents.

Organization of the Book

The book is organized thematically rather than chronologically. Chapter 1 provides an overview of Oaxaca's political and ethnic history from the colonial era though the nineteenth century. As the birthplace of prominent liberals like Benito Juárez, Porfirio Díaz, the Flores Magón brothers, and Emilio Pimentel, this chapter argues that the state of Oaxaca was a crucible of nineteenth-century liberalism and that values of individuality and personal liberty emerged early in that society. Moreover, these values, a European import, were not at odds with more community-centered indigenous values found in the Zapotec and Mixtec cultures. The state's liberal history and unique set of gender relations shaped by its indigenous peoples undoubtedly played an important role in how families understood their rights and responsibilities in relation to each other and to the law.

Chapter 2 introduces the legislation and social norms that derived from and shaped family relations. It also charts the evolution of laws on seduction and sexual crimes and the social norms and ideologies that informed them in nineteenth-century Mexico. These laws are also placed in their international context, comparing them to the United States, France, Scotland, and Canada in order to delineate the underlying sex and gender systems at work in those countries. In addition, the official apparatus regulating rapto, or more accurately sexuality, is addressed, including the rise of a medical discourse on virginity. After all, many runaway daughters had their virtue validated or invalidated by a genital exam. In essence, this chapter lays out the structural context wherein the state and families mediated marriage, family formation, and appropriate sexual and courtship behavior.

Popular culture reinforced the symbols and practices of courtship. Literate Mexicans read chapbooks and penny-press publications that informally instructed them in the writing of love letters, the arts of seduction, and the foibles and pitfalls of romantic love. Illiterate Mexicans listened to these same tales recounted through oral culture. Abundant morality tales warned of the misfortune of the seduced and fallen woman or the perils of fraternizing with treacherous men. Illiterate Mexicans enjoyed caricature and ballads (*corridos*), both of which also disseminated social mores on mundane but crucial topics like courtship, sexual norms, and marriage. In chapter 3, these literary and visual sources of popular culture and the love letters written by the participants in the rapto cases are used to decipher how Mexicans constructed love. Those constructions were, after all, rife with the social values, especially the gendered norms, of that society.

Chapter 4 enters the dramatic arena of the neighborhood and examines the role of gossip and hearsay in controlling sexual behavior *and* in creating communities. Specifically, an examination of witness testimony in the elopement trials and other sources, such as slander complaints, shows how working-class individuals policed their peers' behavior and influenced court outcomes. In the rapto cases, witnesses not only testified to factual events but also to what they had seen or had heard about someone's past sexual history or reputation in the community. Parts of the body and articles of clothing figured, both literally and metaphorically, in the discussions of seduction, romance, and sexual possession. Girls described having their shawls or braids grabbed, a symbol of sexual danger or possession. In spatial terms, courtships were also carried out in the public spaces of working-class neighborhoods, and particular locales became symbolic of romantic and illicit relations.

Many scholars understand elopement as a way to weaken parental authority. Hence, chapter 5 introduces the families of the victim and the defendant in the rapto cases and scrutinizes generational conflicts over courtship and spousal selection. A review of the history of childhood and youth in Mexico focuses particularly on the civil codes that defined legal relationships between parents and children. Oddly, judges actually fostered rapto as a preliminary step to a civil union and the emancipation of minors, even as official rhetoric championed the overthrow of traditional and archaic customs. By siding with minors against parents, judges also promoted the liberal values of individualism and personal freedom. It is from criminal records of rapto that our stories unfold to highlight how civil and liberal legislation and its advocates negotiated with parents and their minor children over legal emancipation, family formation, and the boundaries of parental authority and filial obedience.

Chapter 6 zeros in on the girls and the conflicts they felt and the compromises they made as they struggled to form families or to fight their suitors or their own family members in court. The analysis concentrates on how the girls negotiated both official and popular gender norms in an attempt to determine their own destinies. It also penetrates the personal lives of the young couples. A few of the exemplary rapto dramas are discussed in uninterrupted detail to bring together the themes introduced in previous chapters. As they negotiate official gender ideology with both creativity and purpose, runaway daughters are front and center as the protagonists of these dramas.

In conclusion, this study is distinctive for its attention to an underrepresented social group—adolescent Mexicans—and also for its contribution to a mounting chorus of voices that seeks to understand how the working class negotiated the parameters of nation-building and citizenship. As the world rapidly transformed around them, young lovers made the decision to elope and, perhaps unwittingly, found themselves caught in a battle in which the definitions of honor and appropriate sexuality were contested in the public arena of the court. Their actions entangled them in larger forces that transformed not only families but also the relationship between subject and state.

CHAPTER ONE

The Physical
and Historical World
of Runaway Daughters
and Their Suitors

☙❧

Runaway daughters and their *raptores* (male defendants in rapto cases) negotiated a city with deep historical roots. The rapto dramas hail from the courts of Oaxaca City and outlying pueblos (villages), including El Marquesado, Trinidad de las Huertas, Jalatlaco, and Xochimilco. Wherever the young lovers of this study traversed, signs of their region's illustrious history surrounded them. Ruins of past civilizations sat on hilltops above the city, colonial churches cast imposing shadows on the paths below, and monuments to heroes past and present dotted the cityscape. Like most colonial towns in Spanish America, Antequera (Oaxaca de Juárez or, today, Oaxaca City) was built around a central *zócalo* (principal plaza) that was anchored by the cathedral and ecclesiastical offices to the north and secular government buildings and the palace to the south.

Under the eastern and western portals, business establishments sold clothing, food, and other products to residents and visitors. Two blocks southwest of the zócalo, an open-air market operated where vendors, both men and women, sold goods.[1] Runaway daughters worked with their mothers in these markets, and their suitors courted them in the gardens of churches and monasteries. Adjacent to the zócalo, an open park provided residents with shade, benches, and walkways to enjoy a respite from their workday, or, in the

MAP 1. Mexico and the State of Oaxaca. Courtesy of Kristian Underwood.

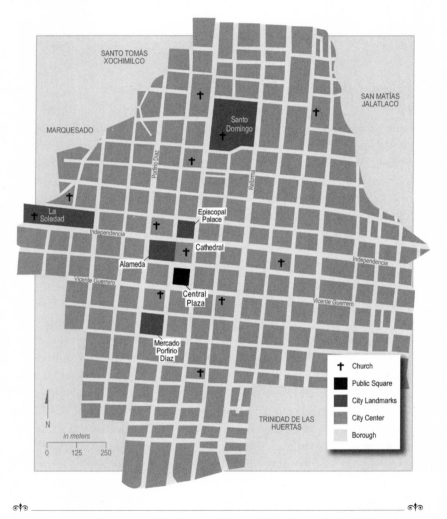

MAP 2. Oaxaca de Juárez. Courtesy of Kristian Underwood.

case of courting couples, a place to exchange notes or affectionate glances.[2] Oaxaca has a remarkable history, not so much for the political figures it has produced (the presidents Benito Juárez and Porfirio Díaz), but for the ethnic persistence of its many indigenous cultures. For example, the Zapotec and Mixtec cultures have persisted through centuries of social, political, and economic upheaval during Spanish domination of the area. Later, the Zapotec peoples endured many assimilation programs designed to homogenize Mexico's indigenous groups.

Conquest, Colonization, and Indigenous Land Tenure

The principal cathedral, one of the first colonial buildings constructed, was just one reminder of Oaxaca's colonial past. In contrast, the ruins that marked the landscape in all directions around the city represented the region's important pre-Columbian influences. While the young people in the city may not have pondered their state's history or their own indigenous heritage, both were imprinted in their historical memory and certainly shaped their perspectives on their lives and choices in nineteenth-century Mexico. Overall, the conquest and subsequent colonization of Oaxaca disrupted indigenous lives far less than in the Valley of Mexico. Unlike Tenochtitlán (the capital of the Aztec Empire and site of present day Mexico City), the Spaniards did not perceive Oaxaca as a hegemonic Indian center to be rapidly and thoroughly subjugated. Hernán Cortés (the conqueror of the Aztec Empire) would establish an extensive estate there, but relatively few Spaniards followed him to Oaxaca during the first centuries of the colonial period.[3] The Crown supported existing indigenous land holdings and legal rights in the region, which allowed those cultures to preserve a high level of autonomy, still a characteristic of village politics even today. Spain's fickle interest in Oaxaca resulted in the region's underdevelopment in relation to the Valley of Mexico. Oaxaca possessed some mineral wealth but lacked the abundant silver lodes of its northern neighbors, Guanajuato and Zacatecas. Cortés ruled early on as Marquis of the Valley, and by granting few *encomiendas* (land grants including tributary labor), he dissuaded other Spaniards from taking up residence.[4] To thwart Spanish settlement, he also encouraged Nahuas to live in Antequera.[5] Although Cortés demanded that the indigenous villages pay tribute, particularly through an exacting production of cochineal and cotton cloth, throughout the colonial period, Oaxaca's indigenous communities maintained possession of their lands and there was little change in land-tenure patterns. Land provided the indigenous people with the resource to meet subsistence and tribute demands, and few men migrated north to work in the mines. As a result, indigenous communities preserved their economic and cultural integrity relative to their northern counterparts.

The Spanish conquest of the Valley of Oaxaca, unlike earlier military defeats of the Zapotec by the Mixtec and Mexica (Aztecs), was largely religious and exploitative. The subjugation succeeded with thirty cavalry, eighty foot soldiers, and four thousand Indian allies in 1521. The war lasted one week, relatively little bloodshed occurred, and in some instances, Zapotecs collaborated with Spanish soldiers to battle their historical foes, the Mixtec and Mexica.[6] As an inducement to avoid indigenous resistance, Spaniards offered a peace agreement that recognized the rights of local *caciques* (Indian hereditary leaders). They also took advantage of existing political structures and simply placed themselves at the top of that hierarchy. Keeping local leaders in power in many ways protected village integrity, as caciques served as buffers and intermediaries between European and indigenous societies.[7] Dominican friars established parishes and set out to Christianize and Hispanicize Indians in the region, while just a handful of Spanish landowners, merchants, settlers, and administrators sought their fortunes. Unlike other areas of New Spain, power resided not with landowners but with the *alcaldes mayores* (mayors), Spanish peninsular merchants, and the Dominicans.

The indigenous land tenure presented the greatest obstacle for Spaniards who were seeking to gain an economic foothold in Oaxaca. In contrast to central Mexico, Europeans only indirectly controlled and reorganized native societies. Spanish colonists preferred to live in or near Mexico City, and the indigenous land tenure allowed them little access to the region's fertile agricultural land and pasture. Those who lived in Oaxaca City mostly acted as providers of services, including the transmission of goods produced in indigenous communities to other parts of the viceroyalty. The Zapotec center of Monte Alban, on the fringe of the city, had served the same role centuries before.[8] Spaniards consequently never amassed large agricultural landholdings as they did in other parts of New Spain. The Zapotecs and other indigenous groups also controlled a greater proportion of Oaxaca's pasturelands. In fact, indigenous communities received numerous awards for their cattle and sheep ranches, and Francisco de Burgoa noted in his *Relaciones geográficas* (1579–1581) that several families owned oxen, horses, sheep, and goats.[9] Suffering less economic and social disruption, the Zapotec and other Oaxacan ethnic groups preserved their traditional cultural norms and patterns. Remarkably, by the end of the colonial period, the indigenous population of Oaxaca retained two-thirds of the valley's agricultural land.[10]

Indigenous and Domestic Economies

On those lands, families produced goods for subsistence, tribute, and sale in the local markets. The daughters in this study who worked with their mothers in the various marketplaces or *tianguis* (itinerant markets) were continuing a tradition that dated before the Spanish conquest of the Valley of Oaxaca. They worked alongside other vendors, who traveled throughout the region selling the products and handicrafts of their regions. Indigenous women figured prominently in the marketplace, as they still do today. Commenting in the early twentieth century (though it could have been centuries earlier), French artist Manuel Touissant wrote "[T]he major interest of the market are the Indian women vendors" who traveled to Oaxaca de Juárez every Saturday for market day.[11] He described their presence in the city, where, if they had the funds, they remained until Sunday to enjoy music and visit the Church of the Soledad (the Virgin of the Soledad is the city's patroness). In the market, the vendors were "[S]eated with legs crossed in the manner of the Buddha, they seem to be monolithic sculptures."[12] Moreover, healers and herbalists were "old women that would horrify Baudelaire" with "beady little eyes sunken in two holes, mouths like a cave."[13] Historically, men planted subsistence crops that the women would process and sell in the Indian tianguis.[14] Zapotec pueblos in the Valley of Oaxaca traded with each other, but their products showed up in communities as far away as Mexico City and Guatemala. Each village within the regional marketing system specialized in different crafts and commodities. Some villages, such as San Bartolo de Coyotepec, concentrated on pottery; others were famous for their textiles, like the rug-making village of Teotitlán del Valle. One village crafted leather while another specialized in distilled beverages. The colonial administration reinforced the system of specialization through its tribute demands, in effect demanding a quota of these crafts from Oaxaca's pueblos that would then be sold to residents of Antequera.

Oaxaca's indigenous groups manufactured and distributed commodities in the trade routes across the viceroyalty. The Mixteca Alta raised cochineal insects, whose crushed bodies exuded a red pigment much coveted in the textile centers of Europe. The region also raised sheep and hogs and sent wheat and sugar to Antequera. The Zapotec Valley, south of the colonial capital, produced and exported maize, *pulque* (fermented cactus juice), and some silver to the major cities of New Spain. The Villa Alta district traded in cochineal, silver, but especially thousands of cotton *mantas* (bolts of cloth) sent to Mexico City and mining towns in northern New Spain. The coarse cotton fabric was used to clothe miners and other plebeians throughout the viceroyalty. Clearly, Oaxaca's indigenous villagers inserted themselves into a vibrant regional and international economy—mostly to meet tribute demands but also to trade in goods that their forefathers had exchanged from times immemorial. They also largely maintained autonomy over their economic pursuits, because some of these commodities (cochineal, maize, pulque, and mantas) were produced in economies that were owned by the indigenous people.[15]

Women's Roles in Indigenous Society

Many of the girls and their mothers discussed in this book were born in traditionally Zapotec or Mixtec pueblos. They have moved to the capital city for various reasons and most maintained some ties to their kin in their ancestral villages surrounding Antequera. Indeed some of the testimonies recount a trip to a village for a fiesta or to visit family members. The Zapotecs dominated indigenous life in Antequera and the Valley of Oaxaca. Already possessing well-developed concepts of private property and social stratification, the Zapotecs used the colonial courts regularly and effectively to defend their communal and individual rights.[16] Zapotec caciques served as intermediaries between villagers and Spanish colonial officials but individuals also litigated on their own. Spaniards recognized the noble status of the indigenous leaders and allowed them to retain some semblance of their privileged position. In order to be accorded the rank of hidalgo, they had to convert to Christianity and also be able to trace their lineage directly to a pre-Conquest lord. Caciques enjoyed prestige and some acquired impressive wealth. Gradually however, their position in indigenous communities declined as they assimilated to Hispanic society, which led to their increasingly alienation from their indigenous subjects or sometimes impoverishment as they became more entrenched in the colonial system. Caciques became either "non-Indians or common Indians."[17] In later centuries, ancestral ties to nobility mattered less in determining if a man could rise to the position of village leader.

As members of the popular class, runaway daughters and their families led lives that were closely circumscribed by ethnicity, gender, and class. Yet, the mothers and daughters stand out as individuals who understood the rules of seeking legal justice. Indeed, the women of the rapto dramas asserted themselves with remarkable sophistication as plaintiffs, defendants, and witnesses. Scholars have theorized that indigenous cultures, in general, and the southern Mesoamerican cultures, in particular, possessed a more egalitarian perspective on gender differences and roles. They have found that violent forms of male dominance—assumed to have prevailed in Hispanic-mestizo regions of central Mexico—were less evident in the indigenous regions of southern Mexico and Guatemala.[18] Certainly, indigenous women in Oaxaca have been recognized for their prominent participation in the village economy and in protests, actions that were both political and public. These women rejected the abuses of the Spanish authorities, even "brandishing spears and kitchen knives or cradling rocks in their skirts" to fight the better-armed Spanish militia.[19] In 1851, women of Zoogocho in the Sierra Norte terrorized a hated subprefect and "chased him from the plaza to the government offices, broke down the doors, threatened to kill him, threw rocks, sticks, and mud at him, spat on him, and stole his belongings."[20] The leading role of women in peasant rebellions in southern Mexico points to their greater participation in the social institutions and economic activities that maintained village unity. Although they did not lead pan-regional revolutions against Spanish authority, they protested assaults on the moral economy of their villages.

In Oaxaca, women took on formal and informal roles in village political life. Zapotec and Mixtec women inherited the position of *cacica* (female village leader).[21] In Zapotec society, descent proceeded ambilineally (from both father and mother) rather than patrilineally or matrilineally. Although males inherited the most important offices, the flexibility of the lineage system allowed women to hold key positions as well. References to cacicas occur regularly in the historical record. They usually owned land and wielded local political power based on a genealogy that connected them to past indigenous nobility and regardless of whether they had husbands or brothers.[22] The system of *cacicazgo* (leadership descent) in the Villa Alta of Oaxaca rested on family rights that included joint brother and sister rule.[23] Zapotec households were not divided spaces where men acted in the community and women operated in the home. Both participated in community life meeting their shared responsibilities and obligations.[24] Indeed, female identity revolved around community membership rather than their tie to a male authority figure, such as a father or husband. The emergence of indigenous women as cultural and political leaders, alongside men, suggests that gender power in Oaxaca differed from other regions in Mexico. In fact, the concept of cacica and female political power among the Zapotec and the Mixtec enjoyed "cultural normalcy despite the overall association of masculinity and political empowerment."[25] Of course, men held the majority of leadership positions in a complex structure that was also based on age. Nonetheless, the recognition of female power in indigenous Oaxaca undeniably influenced constructions of gender complementarity and contingent rights between man and woman and parent and child.[26] These values were transmitted from generation to generation and certainly influenced the mothers and daughters of the rapto dramas in nineteenth-century Oaxaca.

Daughters cited maltreatment at home as one of the chief reasons they eloped with their boyfriends. In rationalizing their actions, they alluded to a set of mutual obligations between parent and child and husband and wife. They referenced contemporary (nineteenth century) notions of reciprocal rights and guarantees but also social norms drawn from indigenous culture. Comparing gender relations in Morelos, Mexico City, and Oaxaca, Steve Stern found that men and women in indigenous Oaxaca negotiated a patriarchal contract on a more even cultural footing. The patriarchal contract signified a system of gender rights and obligations between men and women. Husband and wife (or *amasio* and *amasia* in consensual unions) each had different but equally valuable conjugal duties to perform. Men contributed economically to the household and eschewed extraordinary violence in their dealings with wife and children. Women cooked, cleaned, and cared for the children and behaved decorously and modestly in the presence of other men and in public venues.[27] However, traditional female tasks were not carried out in a private setting. Women left the confines of their home to wash clothes in the river or sell food in the market. Other women ran small businesses from their homes, selling pulque or renting out rooms, activities that, in effect, turned their homes into "public" spaces. Women also acted as midwives, healers, and long-distance traders, which required them to leave home altogether.[28] Although they only sometimes held political office, indigenous women of all classes regularly asserted their rights in the courts, provided witness testimony in legal cases, and lived "public" lives in their work as business owners. Most significantly, community members recognized a complementarity between women and men. When marital discord arose "[C]ommunities sometimes responded to gender conflicts and familial violence with a rhetoric of social peace that placed at least some of the onus on the man and proved close in spirit to female assertions of contingent rights."[29] Likewise, community members looked down on displays of confrontational masculinity, censuring men who behaved with violence and swagger. Their understandings of contingent rights propelled women into the courtroom to reproach husbands who were not holding up their "end of the bargain." These patterns of discourse and defenses continued after Mexico's independence from Spain. Twentieth-century ethnographers, Mexican and foreign alike, have mythologized Zapotec women, especially those of the Isthmus of Tehuantepec, as matriarchal figures who controlled public life and their men. Miguel Covarrubias, Diego Rivera, and Frida Kahlo all contributed to the myth of women from Tehuantepec. Kahlo regularly donned the region's native dress. Their tropical allure aside, Zapotec women "are powerful because of their important economic activities and because in Zapotec society women function in parallel, semiautonomous female domains through which they hold socially recognized roles of authority."[30] Matriarchy does not and never did exist, but in comparison with their Nahua and Maya sisters, Zapotec women fare better in terms of female power.

Rapto in the form of elopement was not a traditional practice in indigenous communities. Scholars have offered different theories about courtship practices. Some believe that parents customarily arranged marriages in the pueblo, although a degree of consent existed for the boy and girl. Either an elder of the pueblo approached the girl to ask if she wanted to marry a certain boy or the boy named the girl he desired to marry. If she agreed (assuming her parents did as well), her father would bring the boy to his house and the girl slept in her future in-laws house to not only seal the joining of two families but also to ensure that sexual relations did not occur before the ceremony.[31] Youngsters had some choice, of course, as parents would consult their children about prospective matches, and they would then meet with the other parents to arrange the wedding. In a small pueblo where everyone knew everyone else's business, elopement in defiance of parents' wishes must have been rather uncommon. When rapto did occur, it was less a secret elopement than a mock struggle between the families that would end when the girl's family finally relented and released her to live in the home of the boy and his parents.[32] Virginity was also prized in a potential wife, evidenced by the practice in some pueblos of gifting the blood-stained wedding night sheets to the parents of the groom to prove their new daughter-in-law's virtue.[33] During the colonial period, marriages occurred at high rates among indigenous Mexicans. In fact, the social groups with the highest marriage rates were the Spaniards and the Indians. The mixed race population of Mexico, most of whom resided in cities and large towns, married less frequently but lived in consensual unions.[34] The independence wars and reshaping of Mexican politics would have important effects on marriage and gender relations. The post-Independence secularization of marriage advanced, rather than eliminated, alternatives to formal marriage, such as consensual unions.[35]

Independence and Liberalism

The War of Independence would cause great suffering in Oaxaca. Although the region was subjected to fewer battles than occurred farther north in Mexico, Antequera was the first capital and only major city to fall into insurgent hands, when General José María Morelos and his army took the city in 1812.[36] Carlos María Bustamante, the conservative historian and statesman, presented a speech in 1813 chronicling Oaxaca's three hundred years of oppression and tyranny, and he called for the formation of a state congress and the drafting of a constitution.[37] The insurgents held Antequera until 1814 when royalists retook the city, but new political ideas had spread and some politicians sought to enfranchise the male workers in the city and to work to alleviate the suffering of the state's indigenous population. Independence from Spain in 1821 ushered in important changes in Oaxacan society. During Oaxaca's first fifteen years as an independent Mexican state, a bevy of politicians set about writing a constitution that would remake the state in their own vision. Their conflicting ideas resulted in incredible political conflict with partisan politics dividing the elite of Antequera. The working class suffered as the economic fortunes of the city waned, despite the entrance of foreign capital into the state.

Oaxaca's embracing of liberalism and especially notions of egalitarianism began years before the nation's independence. Peter Guardino surmised that the "years between 1808 and 1821 were pivotal in Oaxaca's transition from an Old Regime colonial political culture characterized by corporatism under the leadership of the Spanish monarchy to a more modern political culture of individual citizenship and popular sovereignty." He argued that Spanish liberals were more significant innovators than the insurgent leaders "even after the latter began to argue for independence." The legacy of this period was a notion of political equality among men and the increasing sentiment that all men had a stake in electoral politics.[38]

The state's first constitution made Catholicism the official religion, and its proponents viewed religious practice as the best vehicle to transmit social responsibility and civic duty to the populace. When Hidalgo hoisted the banner of the Virgin of Guadalupe as a sign of redemption and rebellion, it reinforced Mexicans' belief that Catholicism should be a key component of nationalism. Indeed, prayer preceded political speeches and ceremonies during this time. Religion united Mexicans of all classes and colors. By the 1820s, egalitarianism became a fundamental political value among Oaxaca's populace, elite and plebeian alike, and while a liberal precept, it did not connote the anticlericalism of later decades. The first constitution stressed equality, and lawyers, priests, and bureaucrats comprised membership of the early congresses. Legislators argued that Christianity provided them their sense of egalitarianism, and they acted to ameliorate the conditions of the state's majority, indigenous population. Accordingly, the new politicians exempted indigenous men from carrying firewood and supplies for the military and from the obligatory construction of the arches for the annual Corpus Christi feast in the capital.[39] This new spirit of egalitarianism did not focus on women even though women took on public roles in religious and charity functions. Their political presence was not very visible, yet a group of women in 1849 petitioned the national congress to ban Protestant denominations in the country. In response, a Oaxacan newspaper ridiculed their foray into politics, sarcastically musing that women wanted to "govern the universe."[40] Although women were encouraged to be "republican mothers," Oaxaca's liberals did not see a political role for the female gender.

In the years following the end of President Agustín Iturbide's reign in 1823, politics in Oaxaca revolved around a conflict between two political factions—the *aceites* (oils) and *vinagres* (vinegars). The aceites were the wealthy merchants of the state, many of them Spaniards, and they feared an egalitarianism that could bestow power on Oaxaca's mixed-race and indigenous inhabitants. The vinagres were men not only from the city's elite but also from the middling sectors of society. They feared the oligarchy and subscribed to a conspiracy theory that the aceites had aligned with Spaniards to retake Mexico. Both groups found common ground in promoting federalism, a national conflict pitting those desiring more centralized control in the national capital versus those that advocated for greater states' rights and autonomy. Vinagres supported full egalitarianism and reached out to indigenous communities on the outskirts of the capital, even publishing a letter in Zapotec, denouncing the actions of the aceite-led state government.[41] Virulent clashes, sometimes leading to bloodshed, characterized politics in Oaxaca from 1828–1835. Even after centralists won the presidency, a pattern of coups and civil wars plagued Mexico's fledgling states into the 1860s.

Oaxaca's most beloved president and a Liberal icon, the Zapotec Benito Juárez, got his early political training on Oaxaca's city council, in the national congress, and then as state governor. Juárez emigrated to Antequera from

Guelatao in the Sierra Norte in 1818 in order to pursue his education.[42] He first attended the seminary and then enrolled in the secular Instituto de Ciencias y Artes (Science and Arts Institute). Initially, Juárez was a moderate vinagre and federalist, and he worked constructively with aceite politicians and abhorred the partisan politics that had raged in Oaxaca since Independence had been won. The Zapotec politician became governor of the state in 1847, the same year Mexico fought for its northern territories against the United States. Juárez would soon be part of the movement that introduced anticlerical measures for the nation during La Reforma (the Reform, 1855–1876). However, earlier in his life, he had been a religious governor, "who in his own words looked to 'Divine Providence' to help him govern."[43] He, like many other liberals, saw religion as the vehicle to instill good morals and a sense of civic duty in Mexico's citizenry. In Oaxaca City, he presided over saint days feasts and the Holy Week and Corpus Christi celebrations. Juárez finished his term as governor in 1852, and not long after Santanistas made their final takeover of the government in Mexico City. Santa Anna issued an arrest warrant for Juárez, not forgetting that Oaxaca's former governor had once denied him asylum in the state after the disastrous Mexican-American War, 1846–1848. When his term ended in 1852, Juárez faced the end of Mexico's second republic after the Garrison of Guadalajara rebelled and the civil war between liberals and conservative factions escalated. The War of Reform (1858–1861) led to nationwide clashes and major changes in Mexican politics and society, as conservative and liberal armies faced each other in multiple theaters of battle. In his memoir, Juárez reflected on his political career in Oaxaca and refashioned his political tenure there as eminently liberal and anticlerical. In a sense, he attempted to reconcile his role as the chief architect of La Reforma with his earlier political career in his native state. However, although Oaxaca's vinagres shared the belief in federalism with the Liberals of the 1850s and 1860s, the vinagres also believed in political egalitarianism (for men), an ideology not shared by Liberals like Juárez, who desired to control who would have access to political power. Working-class men were never Liberal targets for enfranchisement on the national level.[44]

The effect of the La Reforma in Oaxaca, as in the rest of Mexico, was the divestment of Church property under the 1856 Ley Lerdo. The government confiscated 1,436 properties in the central district of Oaxaca City, the majority of Church holdings. Moreover, officials confiscated seven of eighteen haciendas in the central district, also Church-owned, and placed them on the auction block, although many of them would never have buyers.[45] The Ley

Lerdo also called for the privatization of communal lands, but unlike other states, in Oaxaca, the indigenous populations successfully resisted incursions by outside forces and maintained ownership of their ancestral lands. Elsewhere in Mexico, the Reform acted to concentrate land and wealth, but in Oaxaca, not only middle- and upper-income individuals but also indigenous individuals purchased real estate. Indians bought one-third of the properties around Oaxaca City.[46] La Reforma, seen from the eyes of the Zapotec community, resulted in the privatization of remaining communal lands, but private property was already the dominant land-tenure system for Indians in Valle de Oaxaca (the central valley of Oaxaca, where Oaxaca City is located).[47] Liberals believed that individual private property was a more secure and productive system of land tenure than communal holdings, which were vulnerable to usurpation.

The Porfiriato in Oaxaca

Porfirio Díaz, a Oaxacan native of Mixtec descent, ruled Mexico from 1876 to 1911, a period known as the Porfiriato. During this time, Mexico experienced unbridled but regionally uneven economic growth. Díaz strove to transform the nation into a modern state. The treasury, bankrupted by decades of strife, war, and corruption, could not support the vision, so Díaz turned to foreign capital. As a result, the railroad system expanded dramatically and major cities and ports were modernized.

In Oaxaca, the Porfiriato economic programs had less dramatic results. After a railroad line connected Oaxaca City to the national capital in 1892, foreigners invested in mining, breweries, and the manufacture of cigarettes and cigars, glassware, soap, and matches,[48] and the production of cash crops increased, with the state exporting beef, maize, and beans to other Mexican states. Coffee became the most important regional cash crop. Coffee growers invested in Oaxaca's coastal region, and coffee merchants shipped the beans from ports in Oaxaca's southern coastal region. Thus, those regions prospered during the Porfiriato more than the Valley of Oaxaca did.[49] Nevertheless, Oaxaca City, at the center of the Valley, saw its population double during Díaz's thirty-five-year reign.

A mining boom occurred between 1895 and 1911, fueling Oaxaca City's economy. This new exploitation of the region's mineral resources brought prosperity to the city and the surrounding areas. The Cananea Consolidated Copper Company in Nogales, Sonora, employed as many as six thousand workers; mining operations in Oaxaca generally employed one hundred or fewer workers per enterprise. Only the Natividad de la Sierra Juárez mine employed a substantial number of people, between 325 and 400 miners.[50] From 1902 to 1907, capitalists invested approximately US$10 million in Oaxaca's mines, with only the investment in the Guanajuato's mines surpassing this sum. More than 111 mining companies operated in the state, mostly financed by foreign and local investors. *The Oaxaca Herald*, an English language newspaper inaugurated in 1907, devoted its second section to mining news and statistics, owing to the importance of mining revenues to not only the many foreigners that resided in Oaxaca City but also the residents who benefited from the city's increased affluence. Oaxaca's mining boom increased the foreign population of the state. While only 844 foreigners lived in Oaxaca in 1900, 2,026 resided there by 1910.[51]

In addition to mining, other industries thrived during the Porfiriato. Three main textile factories operated in Oaxaca: La Fábrica de San José, La Fábrica de Vista Hermosa, and La Fábrica de Xía. The first two were Mexican-owned, the last was owned, in part, by English investors. The three employed approximately 570 employees in 1904 and 1905.[52] Other factories in the city manufactured cigars and cigarettes, matches, glass, soap, and beer. Nevertheless, textile manufacture in Oaxaca remained an artisan activity performed chiefly in indigenous villages, and many other products also continued to be produced as artisan activities and small-scale manufacture, outpacing factory production.

According to a statewide employment census of 1900, Oaxacan women worked in a variety of occupations. Most reported that they worked as *molenderas* or *tortilleras* (millers or tortilla makers), with domestic servants, seamstresses, and weavers ranking second, third, and fourth.[53] Women also found employment in Oaxaca City's cigar and cigarette factories as well as in some of its other factories. In the rapto cases, women reported that they earned income picking coffee beans and fruit, processing food for sale, cleaning houses and offices, providing childcare, and sewing dresses for the city's elite. Oaxaca City also registered hundreds of women who worked in the capital's legal brothels. Working-class men—artisans and laborers—in the state produced textiles, beer, and paper or worked for the mines, railroads, or ports. Living conditions varied widely. Workers earned more in mining than in agriculture, but "the possibility of returning to a parcel of land gave workers an excellent bargaining position and contributed to the continual increase in wages and frequent changes in occupation" among the state's working class.[54] While labor unions were scarce, many workers organized mutual aid societies. Some were multi-class, including both workers and managers in the society.

The first Society of Catholic Workers, founded in 1885, vied for the hearts and minds of Oaxaca's workers. Its mission was "the moralization of the working class through Christian education, the founding of Catholic schools which teach children the same lessons, and the formation of a common fund for associates to receive assistance in times of necessity and sorrow."[55] The Society, which was administered by an elite with a paternalistic orientation toward the working class, criticized the secular state government and the ideology of liberalism. The reorganization of the Society in 1905, under the indirect guidance of Archbishop Eulogio Gillow, was in part to fight the growing popularity of anarcho-syndicalism and socialism among Mexican workers. Operating out of a former convent, the Society provided entertainment—billiard tables and bowling—and organized a baseball team to promote unity and temperance among its working-class members. Membership swelled to at least 2,000 by 1907. Only artisans, farmers, and industrialists could become members; people practicing other professions were honorary members and protectors. The bylaws required that associates "fulfill their religious duties in general and . . . ensure that no member of their families read 'bad literature,' profaned the holy days, engaged in forbidden games, or frequented cantinas."[56]

Oaxaca was really two cities, one for the elite and one for the poor.[57] While electric lighting came to the state capital in the 1890s, a reporter lamented in 1904 that "few houses are truly inhabitable . . . there is no city with more shoe stores and shoe repair shops where the majority of people walk around barefoot."[58] Indeed, 689 lamps illuminated the zócalo and surrounding streets; peripheral, but unincorporated areas with workers' barrios, like El Marquesado, languished without electric light until the twentieth century.[59] While the elite enjoyed their carriage rides down the Calzada Porfirio Díaz, bicycles, and baseball, working-class Oaxaqueños enjoyed "uncivilized" activities like soccer, *fandangos* (working-class dances), and games of chance.[60] The elite may have attempted to control what occurred in public places but elite and plebeian alike navigated and enjoyed the city's marketplaces and parks. Leisure spaces for richer residents were work places for Oaxaca's workers, as vendors, shoe shiners, and candy sellers made their livings on the street. Churches anchored the urban landscape and seemingly dotted every other block in the city. Even with the increasing secularization and liberalization of Oaxaca during the nineteenth century, the Catholic

Church and religion would continue to play important roles in people's lives.[61] Many scholars have argued that Oaxacan liberal politicians colluded with Church officials in an effort to moralize citizens and further the modernizing mission of the state.[62] It is no wonder that some young couples chose to rendezvous on church grounds to take the first step of elopement, as visits to mass or nightly prayers were part of their daily lives. Marketplaces also provided lovers the space to plan their romantic and tactical trysts away from the scrutiny of parents or neighbors. Yet the marketplace could also pose dangers for women. More than a few criminal cases attested to the violent abduction of young women on errands to buy tortillas for their families. Leisure activities around the city provided young working Oaxacans with other opportunities to mingle and court. Although bullfights were outlawed except by special permit in 1826 and remained relatively infrequent, card games and dice, as well as cockfights and traveling circuses, entertained lower-class Oaxaqueños. Indeed, one foreign traveler remarked that men and women enjoyed games of chance on the zócalo.[63]

Civic and religious ceremonies occurred frequently in Oaxaca City. These events brought city residents and those from outlying villages together and provided opportunities for the youth to meet and not only court each other and also engage in rumor mongering and gossip. The state was also producing elaborate civil ceremonies to shape their version of history and governmental authority with an eye toward socializing these values into its citizenry.[64] New laws and regulations were even read aloud on the four corners of the plaza,[65] and political conversations undoubtedly occurred at cockfights, popular among male residents, as well as in the numerous theaters and places of leisure.[66] Religious pageants and saint's day fiestas also marked the calendar year, providing opportunities for young Oaxacans to meet and flirt or exchange notes to initiate or nurture a courtship. All these events allowed Oaxacans a chance to court, spend time with loved ones, gossip, and exchange information, whether commonplace or extraordinary.

Scholars have irrefutably shown that the state of Oaxaca was anything but a political and economic backwater of the larger nation and of the world economy.[67] Indeed, Oaxaca served as the crucible of the nation's project of liberalism. Oaxaca's congress enacted Mexico's first civil code in the 1820s (discussed in chapter 5), and the notable liberal politicians discussed here, Benito Juárez (1847–1852 and 1857–1858) and Porfirio Díaz (1881–1883), were governors of Oaxaca. Díaz fittingly called Oaxaca "eminently liberal" and when he rose to the presidency, he appointed many native Oaxacans to posts of national significance, including the Supreme Court and the governorships of other states.[68] Oaxaca's modernizing project gained momentum after the fall of the French-imposed Maximilian and Benito Juárez's return to central power. Indeed after an earthquake in 1870 destroyed much of the city, Oaxacan elites sought to rebuild, unleashing a campaign to redesign "spaces in the capital . . . to be hygienic, orderly, secularized, didactic, and, above all, rational . . . to rewrite the city as a readable text infused with the nationhood and modernity they so desired for their country."[69] This liberal reimagining and refashioning of the city both celebrated and denied its indigenous past. Civic celebrations linked modernity and Oaxaca's future to its pre-Hispanic glory, but city officials also remapped urban spaces to "confine nonwhite workers to the city's margins."[70] They increased expenditures for police forces in order to monitor and regulate the sections of the city perceived as being unruly, including the numerous brothels that dotted the urban fringe.[71]

Although Oaxaca's popular classes may have experienced increased scrutiny during the modernizing project, they traversed the city's streets every day. Indeed, their presence was crucial to the renovation of the capital's built environment. They constructed new buildings and renovated old structures, including a state-run pawnshop in 1882 and a city orphanage in 1896.

Ironically, their pattern of work contrasted dramatically with the increasing modernization of the city. While city officials strived for rationalism and modernity in urban spaces and administration, workers continued to toil in small enterprises that had more in common with their premodern antecedents than with their capitalist contemporaries. Only a small number of workers labored in the factories in the city and surrounding valley towns. At the beginning of the twentieth century, only 1,360 workers from the central valley toiled in textile, beer, cigarette, and shoe factories.[72] The overwhelming majority of people were employed in artisan-based workshops, staffed by just a few people, that more closely resembled a cottage industry than a factory floor. The defendants or raptores (abductors) featured in subsequent chapters worked in various occupations, including shoemaker, weaver, farmhand, carpenter, baker, and soldier. A few suitors were businessmen. Carpenters and or weavers were the most common occupations of those charge with rapto. Most of the runaway girls worked in their family home, or they assisted their mothers, who sold sweets or tortillas on the street or in the marketplace, but some cited domestic servant, laundress, or seamstress as their occupations.

Conclusion

Oaxaca is an exceptional Mexican state, having experienced periods of engagement and of disengagement with national politics and the international economy. Notably, in the face of colonialism and then rapid economic development during the Porfiriato, the indigenous villages maintained elements of their moral economy—land, village institutions, and cultural norms. This tenacious Oaxacan indigenous society revolved around relationships of harmony and peace and, at the same time, the social order culturally affirmed female power. Zapotec and Mixtec norms and values persisted whereas in other regions of Mexico, native folkways and culture broke down or blended into mestizo culture. Women played a significant role in the social, political, and economic life of the village, sometimes as cacicas but always as market sellers, handicraft artisans, pulque vendors, and agricultural laborers. Not confined to the private sphere of the home, Oaxaca's indigenous women forged identities based on community membership and their accepted roles in the social and economic life of the village.

Oaxaca was also exceptional for being a crucible of liberalism during the nineteenth century. Indeed, one politician referred to the state as the "soil of liberty."[73] Oaxaca had been one of the main theaters of war during the Liberal-Conservative conflict and the French intervention. Porfirio Díaz escaped from a French prison in 1865 and mobilized Mixtec peasants in his Liberal guerrilla army. Liberal clientelism and multiple liberalisms were a fact of life in nineteenth century Oaxaca.[74] Indian campesinos of Oaxaca did not renounce components of their moral economy, such as communalism and religion, but they did combine these indigenous values with secular liberalism. A major theme of this study highlights how individuals negotiated the parameters of hegemony. Certainly, "the indigenous peoples exercised their freedom of imagination and fashioned their own popular and hybrid versions of citizenship, liberalism, and the nation, rooted in what they believed to be their customs and traditions since time immemorial."[75] As we will see, family members wielded the semantics of liberalism and the prerogatives of citizenship to support their side in conflicts over marriage choice, filial obedience, and parental authority. The region's unique trajectory of historical development deeply influenced how they lived their lives and how they sought justice in the courtrooms of Oaxaca de Juárez.

CHAPTER TWO

The Legal and Normative World of Runaway Daughters and Their Suitors

∾

IN A LOVE LETTER WRITTEN IN 1892, TWENTY-THREE-YEAR-OLD CARPEN-ter Enrique Martínez professed his love for his girlfriend of three years, Carmen Llaguno. "Beloved and never forgotten Carmita, I am writing to greet you with the utmost love and affection I will ever declare until God decides to take my life," pronounced the young suitor. Alluding to their planned elopement, Enrique assured Carmen that he had "carefully thought of your departure" and that he would "support you and protect you from everything." He continued: "I don't want to overlook my obligations as a married man," and "Darling, you also ask me if I will use you like all men use women. My love, I will never betray you. You very well know how much I love you, and I would never use you." This letter and others comprised some of the evidence in a rapto case brought before the criminal court by Carmen's mother.

Enrique and Carmen, sweethearts who desired to marry, faced the oppo-sition of Carmen's single mother, who refused to give her permission for Carmen to marry because she was younger than twenty-one years of age. In another letter, Enrique warned Carmen, "We cannot get married here in Oaxaca because, remember, if you leave your home your respectable mother is going to make a big deal. . . . In your letter you tell me you are leaving on the seventh, I hope you keep your word and that you tell me the truth." Carmen fulfilled her promise and snuck out of her house under the veil of darkness to meet Enrique. Days later, the star-crossed lovers found themselves accounting for their elopement in court. Carmen testified that she ran away from home because Enrique had promised to marry her, and she wanted to escape physical abuse by her mother. Enrique alluded to her alleged maltreatment in another letter: "My Carmita, your situation at home worries me. You know well that I am a poor man, but I have my dignity, and I would fail as a man if I let you continue suffering under your mother's orders." Delivering an ultimatum couched in love and concern, Enrique persisted:

> Because of this you should either leave your home soon, or we need to break up our relationship for good. It is not possible for me to continue living in doubt. How can I remain calm knowing you are in danger? Do you think I will stand for this situation because I have always loved you so much? Do you think I will grin and bear it? My dear Carmita, I will not allow it. If you don't leave your mother, this will be my last letter to you, and you know it. This is all I have to say to you. Take it from somebody who has never been able to betray you because I have always loved you so much.[1]

These protestations of love and anxiety brought Enrique and Carmen to find themselves alone one night in June. They procured a room and had sex. Six days later the police apprehended them. The court trial ensued with all parties testifying to the events and the history of the relationship. Enrique faced possible imprisonment. Carmen confronted her mother and the public shame of her lost honor. All participants debated the limits of appropriate sexuality and parent-child authority and obedience, while judges mediated the discussion.

Elopement: Premodern Relic or Desperate Strategy?

Rapto, elopement, seduction, bride stealing—all are practices that in many minds signify male domination and female victimization.[2] At the very least, these concepts conjure up images of an archaic past, a tenacious relic of disappearing traditions that managed to survive into the ostensibly modern era of nineteenth-century Mexico. Indeed, who is not familiar with the seduction genre of world literature, which centers on the spectacle of a young maiden stolen from her father's home in order to forcibly "arrange" a marriage or satisfy the lustful intentions of the seducer? These narratives usually end in the undoing of the young woman—her spiral downward into prostitution or lunacy, her untimely and tragic death, or her forced marriage to her despicable seducer.[3]

In reality, many women were neither stolen nor unwillingly ravished by their "seducers." Many scholars agree that youngsters acted out a script of seduction or elopement in order to force their parents to consent to the couple's marriage.[4] Why? Across historical eras and well into the nineteenth century, marriage was connected to rapto in the eyes of most Mexicans. Spaniards, Indians, and persons of color associated sexual violence or trickery (including rapto, estupro, and violación) with marriage, although this connection probably did not exist in pre-Columbian indigenous societies.[5] Rape, elopement, or deflowering, all sexual scandals, could be ameliorated by marriage or a dowry paid by the perpetrator to make the dishonored girl marriageable again. Virginity determined honor for a girl and her family, and these reparations were intended to restore that honor. In legal terms, marriage nullified a criminal charge against the perpetrator of the sexual crime. Hence participants in a script of seduction or rapto could overturn parental objections, for parents often consented to a marriage over having their family honor sullied by a sexual scandal.

In nineteenth-century Oaxaca, when parents opposed a marriage, girls escaped with their suitors to form a union based on love, affection, and free will. For these working-class couples, rapto served as a dramatic step in a forbidden courtship, which sometimes led to marriage. In all of the 212 cases analyzed, only sixteen young women (8 percent) claimed that their boyfriends had sexually assaulted them, and all the couples admitted to an amorous relationship. The Oaxacan couples studied here swore that they had eloped with the goal of immediate or future marriage, a testament to the link between rapto and marriage.[6] The document constituting the initial complaint, and identifying the person who filed it, had survived in only 147 of the 212 cases. Mothers filed the complaint in 70 of the 147 cases (48 percent), and fathers filed in 50 cases (34 percent). It is likely that most of these 70 women were single mothers since female-headed households were not an anomaly in Oaxaca or in the rest of Mexico in the second half of the nineteenth century.[7] An overwhelming majority (96 percent) of the parents hailed from the popular classes.[8] Elite families most likely dealt with their children's rebellious actions outside the public, scandal-provoking realm of the court. A daughter of elite parents might be sent to a reformatory or a convent or to stay with relatives living outside the city, or the parents might negotiate a private arrangement with the suitor's family.[9] In seeking resolution through the judicial system, working-class parents hoped that the state would uphold their parental authority over their children and would act to control the sexual behavior of their minor daughters and their suitors. However, as virginity was the not the basis of male honor, judges almost never censured young men's sexual actions and unlike the young women, their sexual histories were seldom discussed in court.

Hispanic and Indian Sex and Gender Systems

Laws on sexual crimes were grounded in prevailing gender ideologies. Mexican mestizo gender imagery, a male-produced discourse, classified men along a continuum from hypermasculine (macho) to effeminate or homosexual (*maricón*).[10] Hence, masculinity could be continually contested as men vied for position with each other. Men remained men in a hierarchy of status that placed the macho above the maricón, who was on the receiving end of sexual relations.[11] The same discourse classified women in binary terms, discretely as honorable or dishonorable, decent or indecent. Unlike males, female archetypes lacked a hierarchy. Female honor was tied to virginity, in the case of a girl, and to chasteness, in the case of a wife. Moral character and an intact hymen defined femininity for unmarried women. For honorable wives, sexual relations could occur only within the marriage.

Two Mexican archetypes embody the honorable-dishonorable duality: the Virgin of Guadalupe and Malinche. Many Mexicans believe that the Virgin Mary appeared to Juan Diego, a converted Indian, on a hill in Tepeyac in 1531. The image of the Virgin of Guadalupe, as she is known, became a symbol of hope, and the War of Independence was fought under her banner. Year around, pilgrims and penitents flock to her shrine outside of Mexico City, and men and women alike invoke the Virgin daily in prayers. Malinche, or Malintzin, was an indigenous slave given to Hernán Cortés. She became his translator and mistress, and because she assisted the Spanish in bringing down the Aztec Empire, her name "Malinche" is synonymous with "traitor." Like Guadalupe, Malinche is an Indian mother, but she denotes shame whereas Guadalupe represents divinity. Malinche is symbolically considered the mother of the first mestizo, and her sexual violation tainted the race from the outset. In contrast, Guadalupe conceived without sex and gave birth to the son of God, and as the mother of Jesus, she is also the mother of all humanity.[12] A woman paralleled either Guadalupe (mother and virgin) or Malinche (whore and traitor).[13] These constructions of the feminine and the masculine were the foundation for the laws that determined the prosecution and punishment of sexual crimes. Only virgins analogous to Guadalupe deserved legal protection.

Rapto presented men with an opportunity to display their virile manhood in the traditional script of seduction.[14] Men sometimes employed rapto to initiate sexual relations and to determine if their girlfriends were virgins and, therefore, worthy of marriage. In effect, a man would coax a virgin into premarital sex to determine if she was pure, and he would then pledge to fulfill his promise of marriage. When a man spoiled a woman's honor by deflowering her, the act denigrated the honor of her father and her entire family, especially if it became public knowledge. While the seducer's honor and esteem climbed among male peers, the aggrieved father suffered a blow to his honor and reputation because he had failed to control and protect his female dependent. When a seducer "abducted" and deflowered another man's daughter, society expected the father to act swiftly and publicly to restore his own honor and the honor of his family. He could confront the perpetrator and demand that he marry or monetarily compensate his daughter. If that failed, he could enter the courtroom to challenge his foe. For instance, one father, Juan, threatened to shoot his daughter's seducer as he literally caught the boy with his pants around his ankles and his daughter on her bed. He testified that he thought of getting his gun to defend his honor, but that his daughter and her sisters wrapped their arms around his knees and pleaded with him to desist.[15] Rejecting violence, Juan entered the courtroom to defend his honor.

Likewise, a man who could boast about his sexual conquests of virgins would elevate his own masculine reputation among his peers. A man who despoiled a virgin but agreed to marry her also elevated his honor because he acted as chivalrous redeemer who saved the young woman and her family from disgrace. In general, when a man seduced, or eloped with, a young woman, he enhanced his own masculinity and, in turn, he emasculated her father. If no father was present in the household, the seducer simply proved his power over her single mother. In one case, a man named Francisco displayed swagger and power when, according to the aggrieved mother Sra. Montiel, after seducing Primitiva, he returned to her house and told her husband in vulgar terms that "he had enjoyed his daughter, and he took her because he was a man, and he would not return her." He then taunted him to contact the police.[16] In these abstract terms, it seemed that rapto simply perpetuated a patriarchal honor system that victimized women. But as subsequent chapters reveal, some women took on an assertive role in the drama of seduction and elopement, and men ran off with their girlfriends for love and passion rather than to assert their masculine prowess.[17]

Archetypes are inherently problematic but an analysis of the indigenous sex and gender system in Oaxaca can help to secure the norms to the actual events of rapto. Few scholars have studied indigenous sexuality in the state. However, anthropologist Lynn Stephen employed ethnography to examine how "different indigenous systems of gender interacted with shifting discourses of colonialism, nationalism, and popular culture to redefine gendered spaces and the sexual behavior within them."[18] The Spanish defined a two-gender system of man and woman, but scholars have suggested that a notion of a third gender existed in pre-Hispanic indigenous societies. The *muxe* or *biza'ah* (third gender, in Isthmus and Valley Zapotec respectively) illustrates that Zapotec culture, in particular, possessed a three-gender system. A *muxe* is predominantly male but identifies with and displays certain female characteristics, such as maintaining home altars, selling and arranging flowers, or doing embroidery.[19] Importantly, the *muxe* is not labeled "homosexual" or identified by his sexual practices, but by this personality, interests, and engagement in activities associated with women. He may engage in sexual relations with men, especially as the penetrated partner, but it is his manner of moving, socializing, and working, rather than his sexuality, that determines his gender.

Beside the presence of a three-gender system in Zapotec Oaxaca, the link between virginity and female honor suggests some modifications of the binary construction of virgin and whore in official norms. Again anthropologists may provide the most clues, although problems are inherent in applying present-day results to the past. Most scholars recognize a cleavage between a society's structure of norms and behaviors that occur in practice. Consider some of the girls of the rapto dramas. Josefa Calvo and others orchestrated their own "seductions" and arranged every step of the elopement. If these girls had adhered to Mexican mestizo societal norms, they would never have exhibited an active sexuality in designing their own flights from home. As chaste girls, society expected them to behave modestly and passively in romance and sexual relations. Boys chose them, not vice versa. Likewise, the link between virginity and marriage is not so simple for those involved in these rapto dramas. In the eyes of many men, and the girls as well, virginity was not the sole determinant of female honor and suitability as a conjugal partner. Undoubtedly for some runaway daughters, virginity was a form of capital that they brandished to defy parents and bargain with their suitors.[20] Thus, they lost their virginity to compel parents to allow them to marry and to seal a commitment from their suitors.

The elopement drama of Carmen and Enrique that introduced this chapter unfolds like any other timeless story of underage lovers running away together to satisfy their sexual and emotional longings, in spite of parental objections and their tender age. Elopement has occurred everywhere and at all times, because young people believed that they could freely choose their spouse in spite of familial opposition.[21] Couples generally eloped as an opportunistic strategy. Parents facing a daughter recently sullied often relented to allow the marriage. For instance Exiquio Morales defended his elopement with Beatriz Ramírez in 1888, testifying, "We were engaged, but (her) parents did not agree, and I wanted to marry right away."[22] Other couples merely ran off together to form a consensual union and found themselves dragged into the courts to defend and justify their crime.[23] In other words, young lovers in Mexico and other places, renegade in their flouting of parental opinion, followed the script of seduction to reorder power relations in families. The law supported them in that marriage of the aggrieved couple nullified the criminal proceeding. Sex may have been the goal for many, but the process of rapto could effectively serve as a means to an end—mainly to overcome parental objection to a union. For example, Carmen and Enrique, impeded by her mother's objection to their desired betrothal, adhered to traditional roles of seducee and seducer to attain their desires. Armed with cultural understandings of honor, virginity, and morality, they played out their scripted roles in order to achieve their aims. The seduction or rapto law created "legal weapons for weak" but also required that the female "victims" capitulate to traditional gender norms that undergird law and society by appearing as passive victims of their sexual disgrace.[24] Thus, the seduction drama of Enrique and Carmen and the rest of the actors under study here provide an excellent arena in which to evaluate plebeian moral codes about honor, marriage, sexuality, and gender relations and how they meshed with and diverged from prescriptive norms. The dramas also reveal important components of intrafamilial conflict and relations between the state and its citizens. A society's set of laws provides us some clues to this conflict on various levels.

Seduction Laws in Cross-Cultural Perspective

Seduction tort's historical roots "lie in the Roman law notion that some individuals may hold property interests in the bodies and sexuality of others."[25] This notion arose from master-servant laws that also applied to children, in that a father could sue his daughter's (or female servant's) seducer, especially when pregnancy resulted in loss of household labor. Loss of services translated into loss of family income, propelling many poor fathers into court in the late Middle Ages to press for monetary compensation. At that time, loss of honor or social status was not yet the issue. The property-law angle persisted in early seduction U.S. and Canadian laws, both based on English common law, until the nineteenth and twentieth centuries when officials reframed seduction within family and tort law. In the United States between 1846 and 1913, nineteen states enacted seduction statutes. All but one of these ceased to view sullied daughters or female servants as property and classified the crime as personal injury. Well into the twentieth century in the states that did not enact the new statutes, common law viewed seduced women as *in pari delicto* (in equal fault) and therefore unworthy plaintiffs. Iowa was an exception. As early as 1851 a woman could sue in civil court in her own name, a function that had been only available to her father or her master if she was a domestic servant. Over time the courts increasingly began to see seduction as a social injury because of the woman's decreased chances of working and marrying, and hence being a respectable and productive member of society.[26]

French courts interpreted *rapt* as a threat to property and family honor but, generally, sentences reflected the belief that men and women were both culpable in seduction cases. Sometimes death was meted out in situations of violent abduction (and rape), but increasingly judges viewed corporal punishment as counterproductive. Beginning in the middle 1700s, French courts drifted away from capital punishment toward compensation by placing a monetary value on the rehabilitation of a woman's and her family's honor.[27] This monetary value correlated with her social position and her marketability in marriage. Scholarship on seduction in *fin-de-siècle* France shows that judges investigating these cases had become more interested in paternity issues than breach of marriage promises. Order in society was linked to marriage and legitimacy but the issue became the future of the child born outside of marriage. If paternity could be established through letters, from witnesses, or by other evidence, a man would not have to marry the disgraced mother but he would have to pay child support until his child reached the age of eighteen.[28] Even conservative clergy influenced changes in French civil codes that allowed women to sue only single men who fathered their babies believing that "unpunished seduction was worse than acknowledged concubinage."[29] French women who took married lovers and found themselves pregnant and abandoned had little legal recourse or sympathy before the law.

Seduction laws from eighteenth- and nineteenth-century Scotland confound the complexity of issues further, although children born out of wedlock remained the critical issue. In England, Hardwicke's Marriage Act of 1753 defined a marriage as occurring after the reading of the banns and a ceremony in a parish church, whereas matrimony in Scotland could rest on simple consent between two adults. A man could promise marriage to a woman and have sex with her, and this was sufficient to found a lawful, if "irregular," marriage.[30] Women's ability to sue for seduction and breach of promise in Scotland predated the Reformation of the sixteenth century but was rarely exploited until later centuries with the rise in irregular marriages and conflicts over paternity. In fact in most Scottish seduction cases, the woman was either pregnant or already had a child and was seeking the court's help in making the father fulfill his obligation to her as husband and to the child as father. The seemingly insurmountable problem for the woman was that the court would simply ask the man if he had uttered a promise of marriage. If he responded negatively and no witnesses could be produced, the woman had no legal claim to marriage. However, the court could conclude that she had been deceived and defrauded and then reward her monetary damages (in essence, child support) for her fateful seduction.[31] Ostensibly, the law refused to grant her rights but concerned itself with the fate of her illegitimate offspring. As in other states that looked at seduction as personal injury, the virtuousness of the woman before the event mattered. Likewise, in every region, the onus of proof rested with the female victims.

In colonial Latin America, seduction or breach-of-marriage-promise cases fell in the jurisdiction of the ecclesiastical authorities until the eighteenth century. Parental consent for marriage for those under the age of twenty-five became a requirement with the codification of the Royal Pragmatic on Marriage enacted in Spanish America in 1778. Its ratification altered earlier concepts of marriage that had ensured an individual's freedom of choice in selecting a spouse. Previously, the church had protected free will in marriage, even secretly marrying young couples before recalcitrant parents had a chance to harm or exile them. Above all, the church denounced parents who attempted to thwart their children's marriages for economic reasons, such as when a parent did not want to provide an inheritance or felt that a suitor was not financially desirable as a son-in-law. The revised ruling sanctioned parental authority in determining whether a potential spouse was "fit" for their child—fitness meant racial equality but, in practice, economic inequality became an acceptable reason and could result in colonial officials supporting the parents. In essence, this change came about with increased concern over socially unequal marriages and racial miscegenation in Latin America.[32] By 1803, this edict applied to all marriages in Latin America, regardless of class or race. Subsequent civil codes lowered the age of majority for males and females to twenty-one.[33]

In post-Independence Mexico, jurists viewed seduction by deception (or abduction by seduction) as amoral behavior from which a woman and her family must be protected. It is telling that the 1871 Mexican penal code listed rapto among the "crimes against the order of families and public morality." "Order" was the salient word. Abduction was seen as a violation of family order—an order resting on the authority of a patriarch and by extension the state.[34] In nineteenth-century Mexico, as in most other nations striving for civilization and modernity under an ideology of liberalism, the elite believed marriage should be contracted through a civil ceremony. Consensual unions and concubinage, in their eyes, represented vestiges of a disorderly and traditional past characterized by perverse sexuality and depravity. Interestingly, the move toward promoting civil marriage and the individual rights it bestowed on Mexicans caused a good deal of confusion. In Oaxaca, officials of municipalities complained that some residents thought that church marriages were no longer valid, and several individuals, estranged from their first spouse, contracted marriage with someone else in a civil ceremony.[35]

Thus, Mexican jurists wrote laws on sexual crime, such as rapto and estupro, not only to protect family honor but also, importantly, to maintain the social order and to discipline the working class. Logically, the state had keen interests in promoting familial and social stability by protecting family integrity, which included the sexual purity of its female minors. Yet, the law blurred the line between seduction, rape, and marriage. The Mexican Penal Code of 1871 defined rapto as a man carrying off a woman against her will by means of physical violence, seduction, or deceit. If the woman was younger than sixteen, rapto occurred even if she voluntarily accompanied her "abductor," a situation akin to statutory rape in U.S. law. Indeed, the law presumed that abductors murmured affectionate words and false promises to convince young virgins to risk their honor and safety by leaving the sanctity and security of their parental homes. The Code recommended a maximum punishment of four years in prison and a fine of 50 to 500 pesos for the seducer.[36]

Victims under the Law: Passive versus Active Female Sexuality

What about the "victim" under seduction laws? In the United States, Canada, Scotland, France, and Mexico, nineteenth-century seduction laws rested on the premise that only men had an active sexuality and thus only men could commit sexual crimes. The intent of the laws was not only to prevent men from harming women but also to regulate the sexual behavior of both men and women.[37] Because only men were presumed to possess an active sexuality, it therefore became very important for women to portray themselves as helpless, passive victims of seduction. However, the notion of women's sexual passivity was confounded by the belief, held by the elite, that poor women past the age of puberty were sexually experienced.[38] One defense lawyer expounded on the sexuality of a poor, indigenous domestic servant who had been raped, noting that in the villages, girls lose their virginity at an early age.[39] Indeed, this dichotomy of male sexual assertiveness and female sexual passivity outlined the script in which court officials unraveled the tale of seduction. In the Mexican cases, judges questioned the young suitors on the sequence of events that led to the "crime." For example, did an amorous relationship exist before the "abduction"? Did the man promise marriage? Was there an exchange of prendas, such as love letters, photographs, or other personal mementos? Did the woman receive money or other *obsequios* (gifts)? How many times and where did the couple engage in carnal relations? Judges wanted to know the steps in the courtship process to determine whether a breach of promise had occurred, and if so, the court would "punish" the man by persuading him to fulfill his promise, but only if the young woman had been a virgin before the elopement.

In contrast, in late-nineteenth-century California seduction laws, the fault rested with the man. However, between 1900 and 1920, the California courts reoriented their previous model from female victimization to female delinquency. Society at that time openly acknowledged the sexual agency of women, placing blame not on the man but on familial and social environments that encouraged deviant sexual behavior in young women. In fact, working-class families filed seduction complaints in order to control their daughters' sexuality within the larger social arena where the conflict between urban youth culture and working-class ideals played out.[40] Thus, by the early twentieth century, judges increasingly viewed men as victims of scheming women. As a result, politicians enacted a series of "anti-heart-balm statutes" that portrayed women in these cases as perpetrators of sexual blackmail rather than victims of seduction. For the first time, judges in the United States considered the possibility that women lied about their situation in order to entrap men. This change in perspective from male aggression and female vulnerability to male victimization and female predation correlated with the growing autonomy and independence of women, especially in rapidly industrializing and urbanizing centers of the United States.[41]

Mexican popular culture (discussed in chapter 3) often portrayed women as seductresses or coquettes, but, generally, a minor girl was presumed to be without guile and easily seduced by words of love and promises of marriage.[42] For this reason, women consistently assumed the victim role, but the burden of proof also rested with them. The real-life example of a young woman's seduction beautifully illustrates this, and it also points to some interesting class differences. María Luisa Noecker, the fifteen-year-old daughter of a German businessman in Mexico City, committed suicide in 1909. The capital's newspapers had a heyday with the investigation and, much like the ideology of Mexican seduction laws, the reports considered the young virgin to be above reproach. Mexicans savored her tragedy, in particular, because she had been enamored with the famous *torero* (bullfighter), Rodolfo Gaona, and many speculated that he was the author of her disgrace. Noecker was so infatuated with Gaona that she wore his image in a locket around her neck, and she jumped at the chance to meet him in person. An egg vendor, who knew the torero and presumably had a crush on Noecker, invited María Luisa to a banquet that Gaona would attend. Noecker accompanied the vendor, Cirilo Pérez, to the dinner, but Gaona did not show up. However, she met his brother, Enrique, and she agreed to meet the partygoers later at a dance in hopes that Rodolfo would be present. According to many witnesses, she drank too much and left the party with Enrique. The brother swore that they walked around the Alameda until the wee hours of the morning. The sequence of events is not clear, however, since witnesses testified that the couple either went to a hotel or to Rodolfo's house. In the early morning, María Luisa returned home distressed. Unfortunately, her father was away on business in Germany and her stepmother was ill and in the hospital. Later that day, the girl shot herself. An autopsy proved that she died of gunshot wounds to the head and abdomen, and that she had recently been deflowered. Because María Luisa descended from wealthy Germans and her father worked for an American railroad company, a scandal ensued.

Some friends of the family mobilized in her defense, and they wrote to President Díaz, proclaiming the girl's innocence and unshakable honor and asking for swift justice. The press rushed to lay blame on the object of her infatuation—the famous bullfighter, Rodolfo Gaona. The judge sequestered several individuals including the egg vendor, María Luisa's maid, the hosts of the party, and the bullfighter and his brother, Enrique, who would confess to the crime. The press speculated that the loyal brother had confessed to the seduction in order to take the fall for his brother. And a ruse it apparently was, since doctors examined Enrique and determined that he could not be the author of the seduction as a certain ailment prevented him from deflowering the girl.[43] Surgeons had examined the cadaver of the dead girl much as they would evaluate a live victim of rapto or sexual assault. They determined that she had been recently deflowered but her body showed no signs of violence, implying that sexual assault was out of the question. They also asked chemists to determine her level of inebriation or incapacity at the time of her death. Results came back several days later with chemists deciding that she had not consumed enough alcohol to impair her mind or sense of rationality.

The story of the young girl's disgrace and suicide captured the attention of Mexico City residents and journalists. To see the daughter of the foreign, elite community disgraced by the famous bullfighter must have mesmerized readers, elite and poor alike. Rodolfo Gaona, a man of indigenous heritage and humble origins, had achieved remarkable fame in the bullring as a toreador known for his bravery and finesse. Several newspapers followed the story, chronicling the sequence of events leading to María Luisa Noecker's tragic death, and the three-month investigation, which would result in no convictions. Most newspapers condemned the famous bullfighter outright, charging him with rapto, finding no fault with the young girl who breached propriety and attended a dinner and dance with a man who was not kin. Witness stories conflicted and only circumstantial evidence placed the torero and the virgin in the same place. According to some reports, she accompanied Enrique to his house in order to pick up his coat. Journalists waxed eloquently on the young virgin's beauty, her "golden hair," and the friends who loved her. *El Diario* and *El Imparcial* broke the story first. Three days after María Luisa shot herself, *El Diario* stated, "Over the tablecloths stained with alcohol and between the harmonious chords of music, one toasts to the honor of the virgin queen presiding over a bacchanal of menacing men and lost women."[44] The writer went on to lament María Luisa's "profound affection" for bullfighters, noting that she had posters of them in her bedroom and Rodolfo Gaona's portrait in her locket. While not condemning her actions outright, the paper contrasted her increasing fascination with bullfighters with her many upright suitors and their futile visits to her balcony. *El Imparcial* and *El País*, two prominent newspapers in the capital, condemned Gaona as the perpetrator of the young virgin's disgrace. Two days after *El Diario*'s initial story, an article professed that "public opinion, which is rarely wrong, has decided that the perpetrator of the sinful crime is Rodolfo Gaona."[45] The paper especially delighted in the nullification of brother Enrique's confession, which turned the spotlight clearly on Rodolfo. The Catholic newspaper, *El País*, bemoaned that Gaona may have been the hero of former headlines but that now he was a "hero of the Tenorios [Don Juans] who deceives the maidens."[46] The articles continued, noting:

> Well known are the filthy exploits and scandalous orgies in which the majority of bullfight people [*gente de coleta*] live, hands full of money that they give out to their fans: but their repugnant parties were celebrated in circles of vice and idleness and mostly attended by persons of those hybrid and degenerate types that exist in all societies.[47]

Indeed, the gente de coleta or people associated with bullfighting received the most scathing treatment, being stereotyped as wild, predatory, and vile. Although elite residents attended bullfights, sitting in the more expensive covered sections of the stadium, elements of this group viewed the spectacle as barbaric, another Mexican pastime to be eradicated.[48] Many papers mocked Gaona's fame and pondered whether his status would provide him impunity from prosecution. *El País* warned, "when the Señor Inspector General de Policia Brigadier General don Felix Díaz knows the facts, we are sure that the necessary punishment will result."[49]

The English language newspaper, *The Mexican Herald*, reported almost daily on the case during the month of December. Like *El País*, *El Imparcial*, and *El Diario*, *The Mexican Herald* sanctified Noecker's upright life, noting that she was not a "wanton" person. Her solution to her disgrace, suicide, proved her good intentions, as she could not live with the shame of hurting her family. The newspaper highlighted her tender age, a "child, for she was nothing more, especially considering that she was of northern race."[50] The writer recounted her obsession with the bullfighter, who "tried to profit by the ignorance of the girl and dragged her into the horrid fate." The paper printed the letter of an "English-speaking lady" who asked the *Herald*'s readers, "Will the Saxons of the city remain silent while a crime against the honor of the womanhood of their own blood goes unpunished?"[51] As the investigation plodded on with multiple testimonies and twists and turns, it seemed that no one would be brought to justice. In response, almost two months after the suicide, a *Herald* article opined, "It will be seen whether to be a 'torero' constitutes a 'fuero' [special right of immunity] before the law."[52] In none of these reports is there a hint of the girl's impropriety in attending such a party unaccompanied by a family member or chaperone. All rushed to condemn the bullfighter and almost beatify the young Noecker. Interestingly, the popular press had a different perspective on the case (see chapter 3).

Even though the Rapto Law considered virgins vulnerable to seduction, plaintiffs and their victim daughters still had to prove that a crime had been committed. A parent usually initiated the case, but female minors also filed their own complaints. Néstora Cruz appeared before the court alone and accused Francisco Cruz (unrelated) of various crimes, including *rapto, calumnia, estupro, y separación de su virginidad* (abduction, slander, deflowering, and separation of her virginity). According to her testimony, Francisco, promising to marry her, had taken her from the home she served in. She remained "intact" (a virgin) for three days but when she prepared to leave, Francisco implored her to drink wine, prepared a *petate* (sleeping mat), put on his sleeping clothes, and took her virginity. She remained with him for five months, fulfilling her "wifely" duties by making tortillas in the morning, washing and ironing the clothes, preparing meals, and fulfilling other duties expected of a wife. Néstora appeared before the court in 1893 because Francisco had asked another woman to marry him. She testified that three of the new fiancée's family members visited her, called her a whore, and insisted that she sell the ring on her hand to Francisco's new betrothed for fifteen pesos. Francisco subsequently threw Néstora out. This forced her to appear before the court to ask that he return her clothing, bedding, and a black rebozo. She also asked for one hundred pesos for her lost virginity and seventy pesos for her lost honor.[53] She also testified that she did not know the year of her birth but thought that she was fifteen years old. Either she really did not know her birth year or she knew that the law protected girls under age sixteen who eloped with men. Unfortunately, her fate is unknown as the file contains only her initial testimony. Six years earlier, in 1887, another assertive minor, fourteen-year-old Juana González, filed a court complaint in which she claimed that she left home because her father mistreated her. She met her *novio* (sweetheart), Luciano Núñez, a twenty-one-year-old weaver, and they went to a house where he deflowered her and kept her for two nights. Now she pleaded with the court to make him marry her. Both these young women displayed assertive behavior in bringing their complaints to court on their own, but notably, in their testimony, they also emphasized that they were passive, deceived victims. Juana's case ended in her favor when Luciano agreed to marry her. Her father also granted his permission, but a marriage certificate was not included in the case file to verify the agreed upon resolution was fulfilled.[54] Although we have no way of knowing the outcome of Néstora's case, her actions attest to a notion of a "patriarchal pact" that outlines reciprocal conjugal obligations.[55] She felt justified in seeking justice and monetary compensation because she had fulfilled her part of the conjugal bargain but Francisco had not. By describing how she worked hard to perform her wifely duties and provide a home for Francisco, she succeeded in portraying her actions as honorable and rational.

Women like Néstora and Juana emerge as exceptional protagonists in these dramas, but whether female "victims" initiated the case or not, they still had to prove that marriage had been promised them and that they had been virgins before their seduction. A promise of marriage could be as simple as the exchange of love letters, mementos, or verbal expressions, if supported by witnesses. To establish that an amorous relationship existed, the judge listened to witnesses as they testified about having seen the young couple talking in the doorway of a home, in the street, at church, or in the marketplace.[56] Even when witnesses provided evidence that a man had had a relationship with a girl, he could still impugn her reputation and, if convinced, the judge would drop the case. In seduction cases, the law only protected chaste girls and women. Medical doctors and decreasingly midwives served as arbiters of sexual purity by examining the young woman for the presence of a hymen, or, in its absence, to determine the timing of her deflowering. If the doctor concluded that she had lost her virginity prior to the alleged seduction, the case terminated. Elite girls were spared the humiliating genital exam as judges only subjected poor girls to virginity tests.

Female Sexuality and Liberal Society

Laws had their basis in elite society's mores and norms. Although they did not precisely reflect reality, they did represent archetypes of how men and women ought to behave. The elite juxtaposed the vision of the moral, hardworking mother with the spectacle of the prostitute.[57] Proper women anchored their identity and worth to home, family, and nation, while prostitutes lacked fidelity to home or nation and lived a precarious existence in a seedy world of brothels, police stations, and disease. Women's periodicals of the time clearly substantiated this sentiment of home-based and family-centered self-identification for elite and middle-class women. Literate Mexicans, presumably upper and middle class, and some artisans read the print media. *La Mujer* (*The Woman*), inaugurated in 1881, announced its perspective by outlining women's roles in society by stating "[T]he social laws that exclude us from the grand scenes of political life give us sovereignty over the domestic and private. The family is our empire; we take care of it, maintain peace, and conserve it as the center of good customs. Thus, it is important that we teach our daughters to fulfill these attributes."[58] If women had to "sacrifice" to feed their families by working outside the home, they were considered "*pobre pero honrada*" (poor but honorable). Women workers, in the eyes of the elite, should possess the same code of conduct as their wealthier sisters—fidelity, sacrifice, and obedience—but also social submission as members of the underclass.

El Hijo del Trabajo, a periodical geared toward the literate working class, summed up the underlying social mission of women who had to work outside of the home as teachers, factory workers, domestics, or seamstresses:

> We are physically inferior to men . . . yet we possess some advantages that make us morally superior to men. We have a more generous and compassionate soul, a heart that is more passionate and without a doubt more chaste; we have the power to illuminate our country . . . and in the end, the prerogative to form the heart and spirit of future generations.[59]

Clearly, women of the upper and lower classes received contradictory messages, especially during the Porfiriato. On one hand, the message admonished them to conserve and promote the family and to derive their identity and happiness from their nurturing of loved ones in the family bond. On the other hand, working-class women had to leave the sanctity of their home to work to support their families but could be honorable workers. The budding industrial capitalism so coveted by Porfiristas required a cheap, docile labor force. The elite advised women to serve their nation in the home by caring for and nurturing their families but the economy also needed cheap workers to fuel the country's development. This illustrates an inherent tension in the elite's prescription for working-class Mexican women. Porfirian intellectuals would further elaborate on the proper roles for women as they increasingly looked to the sciences to analyze and manage Mexican society.

Científicos on the Natural Roles of Women

Positivism, the philosophy developed by Frenchman Auguste Comte and modified by Latin American politicians and ideologues, became the new "religion" of liberal politicians, which they used to steer their societies toward modernity and economic development. Positivism, the liberals hoped, would supplant Catholicism, and its perceived traditionalism and mysticism, as the spiritual foundation of Latin American societies. In their Latin American setting, Positivists championed "order and progress" as dual tenets to transform Latin American nations into economies and cultures on a par with Europe and the United States. They viewed the social order as the key means to reap the benefits of sustained economic development. Therefore, the Latin American elite looked to what they perceived to be the pathologically perverse in their societies, and they sought scientific solutions to cure this pathology. Viewing society as an organism was a key perspective of most Positivists interested in understanding Mexico's social pathologies. They saw society as a body with sick parts that needed to be healed systematically. The working poor, though necessary to Mexico's economic development, were the diseased hands and feet of the body politic. Women of all classes were a conundrum for the elite, but poor women, in particular, received dogged scrutiny. Where did women fit in a modern nation? Positivists were clearly ambivalent. On one hand, they wanted a compliant, hardworking labor force, and they also saw education as key to de-programming women from their traditional and mystical attachment to the Church. On the other hand, they argued that women's natural and ideal niche was the home.

It would be erroneous to label Mexico's Positivists as a pack of sexists since many championed the individual right of women to education. President Porfirio Díaz supported normal schools that trained women as teachers and women increasingly became teachers in public schools during the Porfiriato. In 1888, Oaxacan journalists applauded the federal edict that gave women the right to study for professional careers. One writer stated, "[T]he woman is authorized in this State to obtain, by means of the respective examinations, professional titles that until today were reserved only for men."[60] Furthermore, "[I]t is not strange that in the soil of Liberty, one has raised the throne of the woman and worked for her rehabilitation."[61] Nonetheless, Positivism and its complementary theories of Social Darwinism and natural law reinforced prevailing beliefs about the inequalities between men and women and between white and Indian. The elite clung to the belief that sexual as well as racial differences were a God-given fact, irrefutable and natural as the sun rising in the east and setting in the west. Natural law became the new morality, and it reinforced women's subjugation in an increasingly secular society that hoped to distance itself from its traditional and feudal past. The elite in Mexico also wielded science as a weapon of their new cultural power to combat Catholicism, which they feminized as anti-progressive, superstitious, and stubbornly traditional.[62] The same current surfaced among the Generation of 1880 in Argentina.[63] Positivists in Argentina feminized the Catholic past because of its perceived attributes of traditionalism and irrationality. It was hardly incidental that the vast majority of people who attended Mass were female.[64]

Gendered language flourished in the rhetoric of Mexican Positivists. Early on, masculinity and its attributes of initiative and action were linked to progress as tradition bogged down in the passivity and inertia of femininity. Society fell into three groups: the upper, middle, and lower classes. Lower-class individuals supposedly had inferior biological foundations that prevented their social mobility and moral redemption. The elite identified the lower class by its diet, sexual habits, and worldview. The media spread these notions to literate Mexicans, intensifying them as it did so. *La Mujer* proclaimed, "In spite of the supporters of absolute equality, there will always be differences and hierarchies in society. . . . These inequalities are necessary for the harmony of creation."[65] Women, whether they worked outside or inside the home, found their roles in society biologically determined (at least in theory). Andrés Molina Enríquez, a key científico (literally, scientist, a term used to refer to a group of Mexican officials, influenced by Positivism, who served during the late Porfiriato), attempted to delineate and understand Mexico's social problems. In *Los grandes problemas nacionales* published in 1909, Molina discussed at length the biological inferiority of women, and although he saw vestiges of complementarity between the genders, women did not receive equal worth in the equation. According to him, women's bodies ruled their minds and actions, and it was left to progressive politicians to figure out women's place in the project of modernization.

Although científicos like Molina, and their contemporary journalists, believed women to be biologically inferior and therefore socially unequal to men, they nonetheless recognized their crucial role in socializing new generations of Mexicans. Indeed, motherhood was a political activity, and Mexicans devoted much thought and ink to discussing how best to equip mothers to reproduce responsible, modern young Mexicans. For example, *El Correo de las Señoras* endowed mothers with special responsibilities, noting that "we harbor the intimate conviction that domestic life transcends the home, and we believe that a man properly educated since he was a boy is a peaceful citizen and will not disturb the social peace."[66] Under the notion that order in society derives from order in families, elite publications celebrated mothers who raised their children to be upstanding and loyal. Natural law dictated that men as fathers and husbands guided family life and maintained order in the home. Politicians promoted these ideals for working-class families as well. Who better to target than working-class mothers and fathers, the specific individuals in the best position to inculcate proper Positivist and modern values in future generations of Mexican workers?

However, not all Mexicans accepted the tenets of Positivism, especially as the glory of the Porfiriato waned and the eve of the Mexican Revolution neared. A Oaxaca weekly reprinted an editorial, which first appeared in Aguascalientes, that ridiculed Latin American nations for unconditionally embracing the ideas of Auguste Comte:

> A crazy Frenchman, Comte, looking in the trashcan for rubbish, found an absurd theory that has fallen by the wayside. It is called positivism, and wrapped in the clothes of French sensualism and pretentious writing, it was presented to the inexperienced Latin American nations . . . who adopted it with the same rashness that our virtuous women perfume themselves with the same scents Parisian prostitutes wear.[67]

This time the gendered language of Positivism was turned on its head, and its critics feminized its proponents, presumably the científicos, for subscribing to the foreign ideology. This article appeared in Oaxaca just three weeks before Francisco Madero's call to revolution, and after a contentious Oaxaca gubernatorial election that pitted the Porfirista and científico Emilio Pimentel against C. Benito Juárez Maza, the son of the great Liberal president and foe of Porfirio Díaz. Thus, although científicos published many tracts and influenced several laws, Mexico's citizens were not always pleased with the technocrats and their foreign theories.

Between Virgin and Prostitute: The Formation of a Sexual Science

The ideology of Positivism also manifested in a keen interest in the sociology of criminality and sexuality. Elite politicians and intellectuals alike sought to understand the roots of criminal behavior. They copied French models for identifying criminal types, which were based on a combination of nature and nurture theories, and they catalogued physical attributes and patterns of socialization that created the modern criminal. As subjects of this new sociology, they focused on prostitutes, who were easy targets since many were incarcerated in hospitals or asylums. During Maximilian's reign in the 1860s, the modern French methods of regulating prostitution, including the use of registers, photographs, and medical exams, were imported into Mexico. After the French expulsion, the Liberal elite continued registering prostitutes to limit their autonomy in an attempt to protect public health and morality. Later, Porfirian científicos, in trying to understand and explain the inferiority of the popular classes, intensified these measures of social control. They thought that by understanding inherent frailties of prostitutes, it might be possible to "fix" the problem through education, socialization, and tighter methods of surveillance and behavior modification. After all, the elite blamed the popular classes for Mexico's state of backwardness and inertia. Rarely did they look at themselves or question the nation's decades of political chaos, violence, and corruption. With missionary zeal, scientists (especially sociologists and physicians) endeavored to dissect society to examine and, hopefully, cure its diseased parts.

One energetic doctor, Luis Lara y Pardo, studied Mexico City's prostitutes in hopes of determining what inherent qualities in a woman led her to prostitution. A sociologist, Carlos Roumagnac, labeled prostitutes unhygienic and immoral viruses that would inevitably spread disease through Mexican society.[68] Without actually labeling them criminals, Lara y Pardo theorized that prostitutes suffered from social pathologies derived from their inferior genetic makeup and working-class socialization around poverty, alcoholism, and sexual promiscuity.[69] In that view, nature and nurture combined to create criminals. From studying prostitutes, Porfirian scientists pointed the magnifying glass at all women, and they emphasized the study of female sexuality because they believed that "the ovary and uterus are centers of actions that reflect in the women's brain."[70] These social critics and sociologists operated in tandem with other científicos who, alarmed with the increasing number of urban poor in Mexico City, initiated specific studies to examine the perceived social pathologies of the city's working class.[71] Medical strategies to treat insanity and venereal disease and spatial controls to prevent contagion were fundamental strategies of Porfirian sociology. To understand women and their pathologies, they studied their bodily functions. To answer the many questions surrounding the nature of the female body (sometime using prostitutes as test subjects), Porfirian scientists increasingly looked to the works on gynecology written by their European counterparts. Some citizens expressed outrage that prostitutes served as test subjects, but research on female sexuality continued to be steadily produced in the medical schools.[72] One thesis, completed in 1903 by Manuel Guillén, linked female physical anatomy with female pathology. He focused his study on:

> women's genital organs, for in them take place the capital phenomena of the female life, which in turn have great influence on their health. Female nervous predispositions are intimately linked to their genital life. In it, we can find satisfactory explanations for the numerous pathological, physical and psychological phenomena we observe in women.[73]

Guillén's conclusions coincided perfectly with prevailing Porfirian concerns about female sexuality. In order to understand why a woman became a prostitute or suffered from nervous conditions, a doctor only had to look to her genital characteristics. Hence, a flurry of medical studies surfaced in national and international arenas. Epitomizing the obsession with female genitalia, medical personnel presented a statistical analysis of hymens of Mexican women at the International Fair in Paris and wrote studies on the sexual "pollutions" of women.[74]

Porfirian científico Julio Guerrero studied the sexual histories of Mexicans in order to understand the norm and its deviancies in males and females. He was especially interested in delineating "dangerous types," and how their abnormal traits could be passed from one generation to the next.[75] He hoped to figure out how to prevent these traits from passing into the gene pool and contaminating future generations:

> [I]n Mexico, because of the low salaries, there is an abundance of people who are condemned temporarily or permanently not to form a family [because of the lack of means to adequately support one]. They constitute an enormous group that requires constant vigilance on the part of moralists in order to impede their reproduction, which would lead only to misery, crime, or death.[76]

He appears to be advocating for sterilization or sexual surveillance to prevent the indigent from procreating. Científicos delineated the sources and typologies of crime in Mexico City, hoping that by understanding its pathologies they could apply social engineering solutions to Mexico's lack of social, political, and economic evolution. If Mexico society was the body, its deviant parts or limbs needed to be healed to provide for its overall health.

Appropriate Gender Roles in the Modern Mexican Family

Normalcy and healthy families also inspired Mexican intellectuals. The liberal and conservative elite alike envisioned the hardworking family, headed by a just and firm patriarch, as the preferred model. Its existence as a norm, however, could not be farther from the truth as female-headed households were common in Mexico City.[77] Likewise, extended family and kin groups shared a variety of living arrangements. Working women rarely stayed within the private confines of the Porfirian ideal home. Indeed, they carried out economic activities in public—selling goods, washing clothes, or running small shops. Others entered the homes of the elite on a daily basis, working as domestic servants. Marriage may have been an ideal for elite and poor alike, but consensual unions were likely the norm for the urban popular classes. This propensity for domestic arrangements without state sanction confounded Guerrero and other elite members of Mexican society. In his view, the evolution of that society could be correlated to the sexual proclivities of its members. Guerrero included a chart in his study that delineated three stages of society, running from a rudimentary stage of promiscuity to the most developed stage, one of monogamy. The most destitute occupied the first stage; the urban working class, which shared many of the deviant characteristics of the destitute class but exhibited more self-restraint and promise for betterment, occupied the middle stage. The bourgeois elite family represented the most advanced stage, characterized by the nuclear, male-headed family and monogamy.[78] The *señora decente* (honorable lady) had a duty to be a good mother, a moral example to her family, and an object of elite male desire. Protecting her sexual virtue was key to maintaining and promoting the ideal social order—in the family unit and by extension, the modern nation. Guerrero and other Porfirian liberals distanced themselves from Church teachings that valued sexual abstinence over reproduction, recommending that women should embrace their sexual nature in the context of their marriage to bear future generations and for the "moral improvement of men."[79] They did not go as far as to advocate sex for pleasure, as procreation remained the goal of sexual relations.

Liberalism, National Paternalism, and Women's Rights

Liberalism promoted several values, which changed over time and region. In general, its proponents sought to modernize and secularize society, and they upheld individual guarantees. They targeted the Church during the Reform and divested it of its wealth. They also attempted to privatize communal landholdings. Generally, the privatization of land and the secularization of society diminished women's historical rights to property and reinforced their subordination to patriarchal authority. Yet, at the same time, governments passed laws that protected women from male violence. In the second half of the nineteenth century after the Reform ended, leaders turned their attention to enacting new codes and laws that governed private property, inheritance rights, and parental authority. In Mexico, civil codes released unmarried adults from parental authority and reduced the age of majority. However, wives were excluded from this general expansion of individual rights.[80] Inheritance laws also harmed women in Mexico. Parents' legal obligation to divide property equally among their legitimate children was abolished in Mexico under the Mexican Civil Code of 1884. Hence, women lost their inherent right to a portion of their parents' estate and the economic security that this gave them, no matter how grand or humble they might have been. Interestingly enough, mandatory partible inheritance remained in effect in Uruguay, Argentina, and Brazil until the middle of the twentieth century. Dowries also disappeared, and Mexican jurists passed laws that allowed men and women to exclude their spouses from sharing ownership in their assets.[81] How these laws affected women varied by their race, ethnicity, and class. Additionally, state policies did not always match social practice. In some cases, partible inheritance continued even after the passage of new property regulations, when parents believed in providing for all their children.

Beside reforming laws to promote private property, the Latin American elite attempted to secularize society, wresting it from the control of the Church. The new national elite usurped powers previously wielded by the Church over marriage, annulment, sexuality, and legitimacy of birth. It has often been argued that the Catholic Church has historically undermined gender equality and conversely that secularization has modernized the gender order.[82] In reality, neither assumption is true for Latin

America. The relative benefits for gender equality depended upon nation, class, ethnicity, and race as well as personal experience. Many scholars argue that the secularization of marriage and the promulgation of the civil codes increased the wife's subordination to her husband. The example of adultery best illustrates this conclusion. Before the ecclesiastical courts, adultery by husbands or wives was equally sinful and warranted censure and punishment.[83] In nineteenth-century Latin America, "civil codes virtually legalized adultery for males and made it a capital offence for females."[84] In Mexico and Argentina, a husband's adulterous actions were neither criminalized nor considered grounds for divorce unless sex with the other woman occurred in the marriage bed or created a public scandal. If a man could prove that his wife committed an infidelity, he enjoyed the impunity within the law to kill her, although angry husbands rarely turned to murder as a retribution.[85] Many of these laws that made adultery legal for men and criminalized it for women endured into the twentieth century. Oaxaca's Penal Code of 1887 held adulterous women culpable if they had sexual relations with a single man wherever it occurred. Conversely, only married men who slept with another woman in the conjugal home faced censure before law. This clearly recognized that many men supported mistresses in other abodes, a double standard that still exists today.[86] Indeed, during the nineteenth century, the secularization of society and the privatization of land crystallized patriarchal authority in many areas, especially familial and sexual life, and in particular, for elite families. As will become evident in subsequent chapters, the state acted as the patriarch in working-class family conflicts, illustrating that liberalism and modernization—and its fortunes for gender equality—depended on region, race, ethnicity, and class.

Especially in an era of "scientific" racism in the form of Social Darwinism, Mexico's nineteenth-century elite had a schizophrenic attitude toward the nation's indigenous population. Charles Darwin may have turned over in his grave, but científicos bastardized his theory of natural evolution and accepted an ideology of inferior races, going to great lengths to rationalize their superiority as white Mexicans and the inferiority of the masses of dark-skinned Mexicans. Generally, científicos, expecting indigenous Mexicans to assimilate into the nation as hardworking citizens, undertook systematic attempts to weaken ties to traditional practices. Education was just one tool. Many viewed indigenous women, in particular, as fanatically religious and superstitious and bemoaned their backwards thinking and customs. More benign liberal politicians, committed to bettering the lives of their indigenous brethren, offered them education and moral guidance. Oaxaca's indigenous population had been negatively caricatured and stereotyped through the nineteenth century. This racist rhetoric was disseminated at the everyday level—in school textbooks, poetry, and cartoons. For instance, in a book destined for Oaxaca's primary schools, the author described the anthropology of the state's indigenous population:

> Even though it is difficult to delineate the dominant anthropological constitution and character of the Indians . . . in general terms . . . [they are] sober, but not with alcoholic drinks that they abuse lamentably, suspicious, distrustful, superstitious and fanatical, egotistical and tenaciously attached to the land that sustains them.[87]

Foreign travelers also disparaged Oaxaca's indigenous residents describing them as "tattered," "swarthy," or "dirty." This particular traveler believed that Indian women accompanied their men to market in Oaxaca City "for she fears desertion if he once goes away alone."[88] Journalists also lamented the fate of young indigenous working-class women. The worker's daughter, "ignorant," "tired from poverty," "lacking moral principles," abandoned her father to "sell caresses at whatever price and fall into a prolonged state of orgy."[89] Oaxacan writer and politician Andrés Portillo published a book of poetry in 1899 organized around different types of women (mother, spinster, girl, wife). In his chapter titled "La Obrera" (The Female Worker), he wrote:

> The daughter of the worker is a pale flower,
> Open to pain, in this daily battle,
> Of work and of pay . . .
> Today she is young and graceful, with beautiful black eyes,
> Maid of rich and powerful masters; but tomorrow,
> She will be an impure courtesan, voluptuous and disloyal . . .
> Alone in the street? Poor virgin!
> What do you see in your path? Misery today, prostitution tomorrow.[90]

These diatribes and educational material perpetuated popular myths of immoral and superstitious Indians. If a young woman worked and walked the streets, her inevitable future was prostitution, according to the elite. This was just one reason that the law only protected virgins in trials of sexual crimes.

Era Niña o No Era Niña: Judging Virginity in Porfirian Culture

The existence of sexual crimes and social deviance presented grave threats not only to the woman and her family but to society as well. In a nation determined to be civilized, the elite attempted to control the presumed rapacious desires and actions of commoners. Although the penal code laid out a series of sexual crimes, its definitions of specific violations appeared superficial at best. Thus, court officials had wide latitude to decipher and enforce these laws. The judges and lawyers had to interpret the law and gauge the honesty of the plaintiffs and defendants in the cases. First, the judge had to decide whether the young woman had been a virgin before the crime. Definitions of "virgin" proved to be problematic because the young women's honesty could also be challenged by witnesses and the defendant. They could cast doubt on her virtue by slandering her reputation as an honest and chaste woman. Ultimately, the young woman had to make the case that she was worth defending and protecting by asserting her reputation as a virgin.

Once a case began, judging a woman's virginity presented numerous contradictions and interpretations. Besides possessing a hymen, moral behavior also determined a woman's virginity or honor. Did she go out with more than one man? Did she walk alone in the streets at night? How did she spend her days? For these Oaxacan cases, there was little discussion of whether women walked in the streets without a chaperone since feminine physical seclusion was not an option for working-class women, who had to work outside the family home. These women also had frequent contact with men, through their work as domestics, in shops, on market trips, in their neighborhoods, and at church. When a defendant or witness attempted to sully a woman's reputation, he or she would recount rumors that the victim went out with other men or that she had sex with a particular man. The victim usually testified that she was a virgin before eloping and that she succumbed to her lover's sexual passions because he had promised marriage. Employing the classic language of the elite, the women swore to their honor (virginity), and initially, they denied having previous boyfriends. In some cases, a woman would recant her testimony and again, using mutually comprehensible language, would tell the judge that she had been deceived when she was young and therefore was not a virgin when she was *raptada* (abducted/seduced).[91] Conscious of the dominant discourse governing honor and shame, women argued that men had "deceived" them, thus reinforcing the elite-defined notion of feminine vulnerability and passivity. By portraying themselves to judges as victims of their boyfriends' deception, the young women manipulated prevailing stereotypes by claiming their passive sexuality led to their defloration. Even those who engineered their own rapto, and hence obviously possessed an active sexuality, could switch roles if their interests demanded it. Clearly, sexual identity took on several faces depending upon the audience, situation, and ultimately, the strategy of the young women.

If a judge found substantial merit and evidence to continue a rapto case, medical doctors sometimes performed a gynecological exam to determine the woman's virginity. In the rapto cases from Oaxaca, midwives conducted virginity inspections before 1870, and surgeons affiliated with the General Hospital performed them after that. Prior to 1870, when midwives performed the exam, the presence of a man during it could provoke a scandal. During the Porfiriato, however, medical doctors, who were almost always men, were in charge of the examination.[92] In Porfirian Mexico, an era that emphasized science and rationality, it is not surprising that trained medical personnel took over this function. Doctors looked for two things: signs of violence and evidence of deflowering. They inspected the victim's body, looking for bruises or abrasions that signaled force. They also inspected her clothing, especially noting bloodstains on her underclothes, and they believed that they could determine the difference between old menstrual bloodstains and the stains resulting from a ruptured hymen. An analysis of her genitalia occurred next, with medical personnel noting the existence of swelling, lacerations, signs of infections or venereal disease, and most importantly, the condition of the hymen, in order to determine if it had been ruptured only recently or at an earlier date. Thus, doctors held enormous power in determining the fate of some girls.[93]

Although experts argued over the hymen as a reliable proof of virginity, that symbolically charged membrane figured prominently in elite discourses of sexual honor especially for poor women, whom they more routinely subjected to humiliating physical inspection. This interest in virginity defined by the condition of the hymen inspired many medical students' theses. In Brazil, the new science of "hymenology" provoked debates that centered on how imprecise a hymen examination could be in determining virginity. Indeed, the phenomenon of the "complacent" or "elastic" hymen defied guidelines for determining deflowering.[94] Mexican medical student Francisco A. Flores published his thesis *El hímen en México* in 1885. Complete with illustrations of different types of hymens found in Mexican women, Flores sought to establish medical proof of virginity that could be employed in sexual-crime cases. Guilt in sexual crimes could only be attributed if the victim had been a virgin. Flores waxed eloquent about his subject, linking virginity to a woman's physical and spiritual beauty and purity of heart. Flores wrote, "[T]oday virginity is one of the jewels that a man looks for the hardest."[95] His study endeavored to reveal the variants of hymen forms in order for judges and doctors to be able to more accurately determine whether a victim had been violated or not. After examining several female virgins of varying ages (presumably poor and maybe orphaned girls), Flores devised a typology of four hymen structures in Mexican girls, including one type that he argued was unique to Mexicans, the horseshoe-shaped form. Besides having an artist render sketches of the hymen forms, he subjected his subjects to an experiment of how much resistance their hymen presented to force. Resistance to penetration fit closely to some doctors' investigations in the rapto cases, as they commented on the ability of a girl's vagina to accept something the size of a finger or penis. Flores advised judges that the hymen took its definite form after age ten, the age at which the crimes of deflowering and rape could also be realized.[96] Before that age, sexual violation was usually labeled *estupro inmaturo*, and in one Oaxacan case, a defense lawyer attempted to exonerate the child rapist by arguing that sexual penetration was impossible in such a young girl.[97]

Conclusion

In all regions discussed, seduction laws placed the burden of proof on the woman. It was up to her or her father (under early common law that viewed daughters as property of their fathers) to prove that seduction by deception had occurred and that they were worthy of protection (virginal). Yet, the intent and ideology informing the different seduction laws differed significantly. In Mexico and other parts of Latin America, the law viewed women as vulnerable victims of male sexual aggression and trickery. This was also true for early nineteenth-century law in the United States and Canada. However, by the early twentieth century, the ideological underpinnings of those nations' seduction laws accepted the possibility of female sexual agency and hence duplicity in attempting to ensnare men in a dishonest marriage or, at least, to extort money from them.

As the subsequent chapters attest, the girls in the Oaxaca court cases had a keen understanding of the gender norms that underlay seduction or rapto laws. It is also possible that many residents of Oaxaca de Juárez also had a basic knowledge of the criminal structure because in 1879 an enterprising lawyer published a inexpensive basic guide to portions of the 1871 penal code.[98] Although runaway daughters asserted an active sexuality by planning their own "abductions," under questioning by court officials, members of the elite, these girls could easily slip into the role of passive victim that was expected of minor virgins. By switching roles according to the situation and their audience, they could manipulate legal constructions of gender and sexuality to good effect. After all, playing out the script of seduction often achieved their aims—namely, the autonomy to choose their lovers in the face of parental opposition. The runaway daughters, mostly poor and working-class, emerge as the protagonists in these dramas. Seemingly the most disenfranchised group of nineteenth-century Mexican society, they nevertheless displayed a remarkable ability to play the system against their parents and, sometimes, against their lovers. The next chapter revisits gender norms in oral and popular culture, which informed how individuals understood honor codes, appropriate gender relations, and models of good citizenship. Indeed, laws and social mores were sometimes reinterpreted in the culture of the street.

CHAPTER THREE

Making Love in Mexico

The Cultural Context of Courtship and Gender Relations

༒

FOUR LOVE LETTERS SERVED AS EVIDENCE IN THE 1875 CASE AGAINST nineteen-year-old Arcadio Ortega for rapto of his girlfriend, Anastacia Delgado. He stood accused of scaling the wall of her house, breaking a locked window, throwing the girl on a bed, and ravishing her. In his testimony, Anastacia's father said he burst into the room and caught Arcadio red-handed, standing at the foot of the bed with his pants around his ankles. The angry patriarch filed a complaint the following day. For his part, Arcadio acknowledged the liaison but denied ever having had sexual intercourse with his girlfriend. He never mentioned the alleged whereabouts of his pants to the judge.

Anastacia mobilized her resources and gathered the love letters she had left with her neighbor, Carmen, submitting them to the court as evidence of her amorous relationship with Arcadio. When he picked up a pen to express his sentiments to Anastacia, he surely had no idea they would be read by other eyes. But his letters and others like them found their way into criminal dossiers and became central pieces of evidence in elopement trials.[1] Mexican society viewed love letters as prendas, or love tokens, that signified a serious relationship between sweethearts and that they intended to marry. Indeed, when a relationship ended, the estranged paramours often demanded their letters back.[2] Parents confiscated love notes and turned them over to authorities in order to prove that the man had promised marriage to their now dishonored daughter. Girls also relinquished their letters when they wanted to prove that they had consented to sexual relations in exchange for a promise of marriage. Just finding a love letter hidden in a daughter's belongings put parents on the offensive to thwart any illicit amorous activities that might imperil her or jeopardize family honor. Clearly, love letters were powerful artifacts that not only communicated the most tender emotions but could also be wielded as weapons. To the liberal judges and lawyers, love letters embodied the individuality of their authors, something that liberalism held dear and sought to promote in modern Mexico. They were missives that expressed modern sentiments of love and reason, twin attitudes also condoned and promoted in late nineteenth-century society.

Lovers penned words and phrases to express their passions, fears of betrayal, or practical plans to elope with the objects of their desires. Lovers who could not write would have visited the marketplace and paid a few centavos to hire a scribe, such as Jesús Sosa, to pen their romantic words.[3] Undeniably, some individuals crafted their love letters with great skill. Striving to evoke a certain response in the reader, authors employed strategies derived from society's formulas for expressing love and other emotions in written form.[4] They could be both very personal and also formulaic, as they drew on manners of expressing emotions in popular culture. These written communications sprang from the oral culture of song, theater, poetry, and fables. The exchange of love letters proved that couples and families possessed affective lives and this chapter examines romantic correspondence to determine its cultural meanings and influences.[5] The content of love letters reflected gender expectations, rituals of courtship, and the social conditions that determined their form and style. Thus, it would be foolhardy to believe that they embodied exact manifestations of the inner lives of nineteenth-century Mexican lovers. Indeed, the "content and structure [of these letters] were no less crafted than . . . [were] court depositions."[6]

Popular culture could both shape and reflect social norms, morals, and behaviors.[7] Although the legal structures of runaway daughters' lives imposed a particular gender ideology on the young couples involved in the rapto cases, norms born out of popular culture sometimes differed from those propagated in law. Several extralegal vehicles disseminated codes of honor and morality to minor children. Parents recounted legends and fables and sang songs to their children. Throughout Mexico, sellers hawked chapbooks and broadsides designed to teach lessons based on real-life events.

On the streets, in markets, in plazas, and at fairs, ambulatory vendors sang *corridos* (ballads) to advertise this immensely popular literature.[8] Many nineteenth-century Mexicans could not read, so much of this popular prose was transmitted orally. In working-class barrios, people may have stood in markets or on street corners reading a chapbook aloud to passersby, adults and children alike.[9]

In this world dominated by oral tradition, friends, coworkers, and family members exchanged stories and songs that reflected themes of love, passion, betrayal, and other emotions pertinent to the rapto cases. Humor and sarcasm lightened these messages, but lessons of love and morality were still conveyed. A lively and instructive visual culture also surrounded urban Mexicans, as they looked at the illustrations in broadsheets and gazed on photographs pasted to walls, enjoyed street theater, and laughed at the humorous dialogues and antics of puppet shows.[10] An analysis of popular culture ultimately suggests how the young lovers of the rapto dramas may have been socialized on issues like romantic love, morality, the rules of courtship, and sexuality. Romantic and sexual norms expressed in popular culture certainly reflected a society's attitudes or worldview, but in the end, each individual interpreted the norms on their own in order to make sense of their daily lives.

The Penny Press and Popular Sentiments

The broadsheets, also called broadsides, and the chapbooks were some of the most widely circulated journalism at the turn of the twentieth century in Latin America. Significant numbers of Mexicans purchased this literature. One- or two-page broadsheets set their buyers back 1 or 2 centavos. The chapbooks cost from 3 centavos for a songbook or letter-writing manual to 12 centavos for a nativity play.[11] Titles ranged from *Discursos patrióticos* (*Patriotic Speeches*) to *El secretario de los amantes* (*The Secretary of Lovers*), from *La cocina en el bolsillo* (*Pocket Kitchen*) to *Juan soldado* (*Soldier Juan*).

Although scholars have not been able to estimate reliable circulation figures, the satiric workers' weekly *La Guacamaya* boasted a distribution of 29,000 copies.[12] Lighthearted chapbooks and broadsheets probably had a larger distribution, since they would have appealed to a wider cross-section of society. Farther south, broadsheets "were perhaps the most widely circulated reading material in Chile during the period of rapid economic growth and urbanization at the turn of the century."[13] In both Mexico and Chile, broadsheets reflected on the woes and downsides to modernization during the late-nineteenth century. Inexpensive to purchase, embedded in oral tradition, composed by poets, song writers, and journalists, printed in small artisan shops, hawked on city streets, and purchased by urban residents, chapbooks and broadsides displayed attributes of "folk, mass, and working-class cultures while not falling readily within one category."[14]

Broadsides and chapbooks were the literature of the street. This ephemeral journalism, produced in Mexico from the late nineteenth century through the Revolution, commented on gender relations, politics, sensational crime stories, natural disasters, as well as religious observances. The broadsheets particularly illuminate the mentalities of the popular classes, a group that has left few written documents. In terms of understanding rapto cases, the sheets reflect average attitudes about real events in the lives of Mexicans, as well as popular notions about childrearing, romance, courtship, sexuality, and honor. These publications reflect the worldview of their mostly working-class, urban readers.[15]

Posada's Broadsheets

The printing house of Antonio Vanegas Arroyo, established around 1880 and operating until the second decade of the twentieth century, dominated the production of broadsheets in Mexico. Sales agents plied the sheets in Oaxaca, Coahuila, Veracruz, Sonora, and other Mexican states.[16] Vanegas Arroyo is also noted for having employed the now-famous illustrator, José Guadalupe Posada.[17] Posada illustrated a large number of sheets that communicated human-interest stories.[18] His work covered "murders, suicides, natural disasters, bullfight gorings, folk heroes: all were eagerly bought up by the capital's urban peasantry, and taken together, they form a 'people's history' of life in Mexico during the years bracketing the turn of the century."[19] More than half of Posada's broadsheet illustrations were related to crime stories, and murders got the most attention, probably reflecting the keen interest of the populace in gruesome or sensational homicide dramas.

Mostly widely known for his depictions of *calaveras* (caricatures of skeletons), Posada's illustrations were always fantastical. The stories they depict varied in their level of drama but a "number of them were plainly sensational and meant to elicit moral condemnation, like the story of the woman who tortured children with burning matches, or the man who murdered his parents and ate his baby son."[20] Sensation, gore, and deviancy enthralled readers, especially when the extreme scenarios involved intra-familial crime. Crimes committed by women figured prominently and outpaced their actual levels in the criminal record. Curiously, upper-class criminals were rarely depicted in broadsheets.

Mexicans read broadsheets, considered their graphic illustrations, judged their protagonists and victims, and reflected on their messages. Crime was certainly on the mind of Mexicans, especially those that lived in Mexico City during the Porfiriato. Many Positivists, such as Julio Guerrero, theorized that the preponderance of violence in Mexican society had its roots in the recessive genes of its Aztec heritage. Guerrero argued that "the ferocious tendencies of the Aztecs have reappeared. After ten generations, there has returned to beat within the breasts of some of our compatriots the barbarous heart of the followers of Huitzilopochtli."[21] The Oaxacan press complained that the Indian impeded the progress of the nation because of his apathy, laziness, and propensity for immorality.[22] Not surprisingly considering his working-class and mixed-race audience, Posada's take on sensational crimes diverged from this official view. Indians and lower-class Mexicans were not criticized for having a genetic propensity for deviancy. Instead, in the works of Vanegas Arroyo and Posada, faulty upbringing or weak character usually propelled people into crime.

No matter how sensational the crime and unusual the perpetrator, these stories projected a moral lesson to their readers. The lesson was not related to race or even necessarily to class but to how the antagonist had been brought up. Readers of the broadsheets may have been repulsed by the criminals, but they also learned something from their stories. People related to the plight of the victim or the madness of the criminal, and parents could retell the story to their children to reinforce lessons, such as obedience to parents, behaving honorably, not letting passion rule the mind, and avoiding malevolent people.

Sensational Crimes: Lessons for Parents and Children
Murderous Sons and Daughters

The broadsheets had plenty to say about love, betrayal, marriage, and relations between parents and children. In addition to graphic illustrations of the horrific crimes, the broadsheets narrated the events and offered a poem that relayed a moral lesson. Causes of crimes sprang from personal morality and family relations gone awry rather than from "national trends, ancestral tendencies, or climatic conditions."[23] Readers especially devoured tales of parricide.[24]

The madness and homicidal rampage of Norberta Reyes illustrates this (fig. 1). The only child of Anselmo Reyes and Pascuala Rosas, Norberta was the antithesis of the good daughter. The broadsheet informed the reader that her parents doted on her every whim and loved her unconditionally, and as a result, she grew to be a demanding and irrational child. The narrative continued: "Because she was not bad looking, it did not take long for a rascal to fall in love with her, and because she was used to getting her way," at age sixteen, she impulsively eloped with the man, not respecting her parents enough to ask for their blessing. One-and-a-half years passed and the suffering parents received no word from their wayward daughter. One day, alone, "half naked, shockingly dirty, and with scars all over her body," she returned, and her parents rejoiced and forgave her trespasses. The man she had run off with had beaten and abandoned Norberta, leaving her angry, damaged, and capricious. She lived amiably with her parents for a short time, but then her violent quarrels with them upset the community peace. The broadsheet tells the readers that she "did not stop thinking of her infamous seducer." Her parents decided to move out of town rather than confront a community scandal. At first, Norberta refused to go with them because she hoped for the return of her estranged lover. Finally, relenting on the day of the move, Norberta stashed a large carving knife in her skirts and set out with her blindly devoted parents.

After a day's journey, the family stopped to camp for the night. When her parents had fallen asleep, the treacherous daughter brandished the knife, and in one blow, she nearly severed her father's head from its neck. Then, she turned on her loving mother, repeatedly stabbing the poor woman until "nearly all of her insides came out." Norberta fled the carnage and began wandering back to their village. Eventually, she got lost, and so she stopped to rest. As in many of the Vanegas Arroyo broadsheets, retribution materialized in the form of a pack of wild dogs that attacked the treacherous daughter, biting her all over her body before tossing her over the side of a cliff. She died at the bottom, and her corpse went unburied because the authorities could not reach the spot to recover her remains. The moral lesson closes the text: "This singular example should teach parents their duty to not give in to their children too much, and to control their bad tendencies, even from the earliest infancy."[25] Importantly, however, "their bad tendencies" did not derive from genetic defects but from upbringing. As Norberta's tale implies, her parents indulged her until she became a psychopathic killer. The parents' first mistake was pandering to her every whim; their second was taking her back and not standing up to her disrespectful behavior. The broadsheet ends with the customary verse, which in part warned:

Terrible y verdadera Noticia

*del espantoso ejemplar ocurrido con Norberta Reyes,
que cerca de la ciudad de Zamora asesinó a sus padres el día 2
del mes pasado del presente año.*

En una pequeña población a inmediaciones de la ciudad de Zamora, Estado de Michoacán vivía Anselmo Reyes y Pascuala Rosas, que solo habían tenido en su matrimonio una hija, Norberta, a la cual querían ambos con un cariño ciego y entrañable tanto por ser mujer como por ser la única prenda de su amor.

Desde muy pequeña demostró Norberta tener un genio caprichoso e indomable; y fomentado esto por el consentimiento de los autores de su vida, acabó por ser una criatura insoportable para todas las gentes excepto para sus padres, que en su ciego cariño todo lo tomaban como gracias de su hija. Así creció y llegada a la edad de 16 años y como no era de mala cara, no tardó mucho en hallar un pillo que la enamoró y como ella estaba acostumbrada a hacer su voluntad, a pesar de los consejos de sus padres correspondió a sus exigencias y cuando menos se pensaba, desapareció con su amante.

Había pasado año y medio sin que los padres de Norberta hubiesen vuelto a saber de su hija a pesar de cuantos esfuerzos hicieron para averiguar su paradero; cuando una tarde la vieron entrar en su casa en un estado verdaderamente triste, casi desnuda, piojosa llena de mugre y con multitud de cicatrices en todas las partes de su cuerpo.

Al verla en tan lamentable estado sus infelices padres olvidaron su ingratitud y con mil caricias procuraron consolar su triste situación; pero esta ingrata lejos de agradecer la bondad de sus padres cada día se portaba peor para con ellos, y como Norberta no dejara de pensar en el paradero de su infame seductor, y esto la tenía cada vez mas endemoniada todos los días armaba grandes escándalos en su casa hasta el punto de alarmar a los vecinos por lo cual los ancianos padres de Norberta decidieron abandonar el pueblo para ir a otro donde no fueran conocidos. Aquella perver-

---

FIGURE 1. *Terrible y verdadera noticia del espantoso ejemplar ocurrido con Norberta Reyes, y que cerca de la ciudad de Zamora asesinó á sus padres el día 2 del mes pasado del presente año* (Mexico City: A. Vanegas Arroyo, 1910). Courtesy of Caroline and Erwin Swann Caricature and Cartoon Collection, Library of Congress.

Because of my parents' blind affection
They spoiled me
Causing me a disgrace
So very late they realized
Two victims they were
Of my bad upbringing
Sowing my perdition
A love badly entertained
And because there was no control
My perverse inclination.

Another undated Vanegas Arroyo broadsheet by Posada continued the moral lessons for children and their parents. In "Horrible and Shocking Event," the story of Ramón, a rich, pampered son came to light.[26] The parents' indulgence caused him to acquire "all of the worst vices in the world." He even stole 10,000 pesos from his father. At the breaking point, the father threatened to throw his son out if he did not mend his ways. Ramón spurned his parents, and agreeing to move out, he demanded his share of the inheritance. When his father refused, the son poisoned his parents, stashed their bodies in the basement, and fled with all the money he could find. The stench emanating from the house brought the authorities eight days later. Meanwhile, the son was plagued with nightmares, in which his parents haunted him, promising God's wrath for his parricidal deeds. As fate would have it, on the road to Colima, a hurricane blew in, and lightning struck Ramón dead on the spot, but not before he was "dragged by a thousand demons."[27] Again, like Norberta, his body could not be buried because no one could recover its parts. Lacking a body for a proper burial further damned both these ingrates. The broadsheet ends with an admonishment to children and parents alike: "Look, oh parents, what happened to the evil Ramón. Read these pages to your young children so that they will learn to fear God, obey their parents, and always take the path of good."[28]

Vanegas Arroyo published more than eight reports of parricide at the turn of the century (figs. 2–5),[29] all illustrated by Posada. Especially in urban areas where children had more recreational outlets and parents felt the pains of modernization, this may have reflected readers' anxieties about their relationships with their minor children. Parents expected their children to obey and respect them and to express gratitude for the love and care they had received, but in the broadsheets, rude and ungrateful youth became the murderers of the very individuals who had nurtured them. The warning to

FIGURE 2. *Horrible Crimen. Cometido por Juan Riesca, que asesinó á su padre el dia 1 de enero del presente año, en la Ciudad de Monterrey* (Mexico City: A. Vanegas Arroyo, n.d.). Courtesy of Mexican Popular Prints Collection, Center for Southwest Research, University of New Mexico Libraries.

FIGURE 3. *Ejemplo: Infame hija que da muerte á sus queridos padres* (Mexico City: A. Vanegas Arroyo, n.d.). Mexican Popular Prints Collection, Center for Southwest Research, University of New Mexico Libraries.

FIGURE 4. *Ejemplo: Espantoso parricidio. Sensacional acontecimiento espantoso parricidio y verdadero ejemplo en el Saltillo, el día primero del mes pasado* (Mexico City: A. Vanegas Arroyo, n.d.). Mexican Popular Prints Collection, Center for Southwest Research, University of New Mexico Libraries.

FIGURE 5. *Ejemplo: El hijo desobediente* (Mexico City:
A. Vanegas Arroyo, n.d.). Mexican Popular Prints Collection,
Center for Southwest Research, University of New Mexico Libraries.

parents was clear: Do not spoil your children. Demand their respect. It was
no coincidence that this sentiment played out constantly in the testimonies
from the rapto cases. For instance, one mother lamented her daughter's
defilement and asked for the defendant's punishment to serve as an example
to the youth of the village, who behaved in libertine and rebellious ways. Her
plea indicated that the young people, acting with caprice and little attention
to the good customs of the pueblo, respected their elders less and less.[30]

Murderous Parents and Guardians

The sensationalistic tales in the broadsheets also portrayed parents who
became deranged and killed or tortured innocent children. Again, race or
class was not the cause. Instead, alcohol or greed could propel the antagonist
to kill his loved ones. Like Ramón, Antonio Sánchez murdered his parents
over his inheritance, but he also turned on his own child. The broadsheet
relates that his parents always treated him with the utmost affection, yet
he responded with fury and odium. When the police arrived, they found
the murderous father surrounded by the victims swimming in a pool of
blood, and the homicidal maniac "tranquilly devouring the body of his own

son."[31] Another killer of children, Guadalupe Bejarano, fascinated readers, and Posada created several illustrations about her case. Known as the "*mujer verdugo*" or "the female torturer," Bejarano tormented and killed children in her charge, including burning their flesh with lit matches (fig. 6).[32] Another character, Aunt Tomasa, terrorized her six-year-old niece María Consuelo (see fig. 7). The broadsheet noted that the child's suffering was apparent at first sight, her skin tone likened to the color of a cadaver. One day she fainted and the root of her long-term agony came to light. As her rescuers lifted her off the floor, she exhaled a pitiful yelp and uttered that her underskirt and stockings had been seared to her skin by her aunt. The broadsheet lamented "The torture of a girl of such a young age! This infamous wickedness is impossible to understand. People of this kind are even worse than savages. Worse than soulless fiends that feed on blood."[33]

Again the spectacle of an adult, especially kin, abusing an innocent and helpless child provoked outrage but also keen interest on the part of the consumers of the broadsheets. In one of Vanegas Arroyo's publications, the *Gaceta Callejera*, the public learned of a Bejarano-imitator who also tortured young children (fig. 8). The broadsheet relates the story of another six-year-old girl tied to a wooden cross. The police rescued the girl and took her godmother into custody. As it turned out, she regularly subjected her goddaughter to "inquisitorial punishments." The tale unfolds, telling readers that the victim and her younger brother lived with their abusive godmother because their mother was ill and hospitalized. The little girl also testified that her godmother punished her relentlessly, not letting her play or otherwise distract herself, let alone leave the house. The broadsheet ends with a call of justice: "It is necessary to punish these brutes who pitilessly torment the innocent." Posada graphically depicted murderers and abusers of children as stark raving mad monsters more perilous than fiends and controlled by devilish forces. Sons and daughters who murdered their parents appeared monstrous as well, but they had, for the most part, been corrupted by bad parenting. Hence, the popular literature warned parents to raise their children with a firm hand and not to give in to their every whim. Through the extreme cases and real-life examples of the murder and torture of innocent children, the broadsheets lamented the existence of child abuse in families. Children received special attention during the Porfiriato, as most Mexicans were recognizing the need to protect those of a tender and innocent age. As we will see in the rapto cases, when a runaway daughter charged one of her parents or stepparents with abuse, the judges often ended by ruling in her favor.

FIGURE 6. *Guadalupe Bejarano en las bartolinas de Belén. Careo entre la mujer verdugo y su hijo* (Mexico City: A. Vanegas Arroyo, n.d.). Mexican Popular Prints Collection, Center for Southwest Research, University of New Mexico Libraries.

FIGURE 7. *¡Espantoso crimen nunca visto! Mujer peor que las fieras!! Una niña con la ropa cosida al cuerpo* (Mexico City: A. Vanegas Arroyo, n.d.). Mexican Popular Prints Collection, Center for Southwest Research, University of New Mexico Libraries.

FIGURE 8. "Martirio de una niña," *Gaceta Callejera*, no. 13, October 3, 1893 (Mexico City: A. Vanegas Arroyo, n.d.). Mexican Popular Prints Collection, Center for Southwest Research, University of New Mexico Libraries.

The Corrupting Influence of Acquaintances

As children became adolescents and went out into the world, the advice continued. Peers could be particularly corrupting influences and undo a person's careful upbringing. For example, a Posada broadsheet recounted the moral lesson of the brothers Tomás and Cleofás Urrutía. The sheet began with the admonition: "You will be good with the good and bad with the bad." The two brothers had supportive parents, and the sons loved them deeply in return. Their troubles surfaced when they moved to Mexico City to pursue their studies. After parting from their parents with abundant tears and affectionate embraces, the mother reminded them not to forget their moral upbringing. They moved in with a good friend of their father, and in the first year, they diligently applied themselves to their studies. During vacation, lamenting that their horses could not bring them home fast enough, they went to visit their beloved parents. Then, after returning to Mexico City, they befriended a fellow student. The "bad friend" convinced them to take a break from their studies one weekend and join him at a friend's country home. The brothers' intuition sparked their trepidation, but they reluctantly agreed in the face of the acquaintance's persistent chiding. The broadsheet goes on to tell the reader that the nefarious friend tricked the innocent boys, who found themselves waylaid at an infamous brothel instead of a country retreat. Calling the brothers "pichoncitos" (baby birds or novices) their new friend asked the madam for "teachers" for the boys "who don't know how to live." For three days, they wallowed in the brothel, "engulfed in the orgy . . . drunk with the impure love of lost women and wine and liquor." At daybreak on the fourth day, the devil arrived to purloin their souls. Like most broadsheets, a lament in verse summarized the story and moral. It admonished parents "to be careful with your children and watch over their actions." It warned children "to be alert because the most fun times can be our downfall."[34]

Consider the case of María Luisa Noecker (see chapter 2). A virginal daughter of an elite foreign resident of Mexico City, she shot herself after she lost her virginity. The day before, in the hope of meeting the object of her intense infatuation, the brave bullfighter, Rodolfo Gaona, she had gone to a banquet, and then, a dance. The mainstream press immediately faulted Gaona, a man of humble background and mixed-race heritage, who fraternized with the wild and unseemly bullfight aficionados. In the eyes of the press, Noecker was beyond reproach. Posada's broadsheets offered a more objective rendering. They outlined the bare facts of the case but stopped

short of indicting suspects. However, in the requisite lament of this literature, Gaona mourned his ruined reputation and loss of honor.[35] In a subsequent broadsheet, Vanegas Arroyo and Posada placed the blame for the
crime firmly on the disgraced girl, María Luisa Noecker. This sheet does
not even mention Gaona but rather blames the woman for putting herself
in harm's way. The lament follows:

> I killed myself for my honor
> Which I lost in a single night.
> Because I was with some toreros
> Who would not treat me right.
> Together we drank liquor
> And I let myself go too far.
> Cirilio brought me to a party
> Which was more than I bargained for.[36]

The broadside goes on to attribute María Luisa's poor judgment to her
young age, only fifteen, and it urged girls to avoid parties when they did
not know the other invitees. Finally, Noecker, reflecting from the other
side, advised parents "to exercise vigilance over their children and to teach
them right from wrong."[37] Neither the newspapers that covered the case
(see chapter 2) nor Posada's broadsheets faulted her parents: the stepmother, who was hospitalized, and the German father, in Europe on business. Mr. Noecker could not file charges until three weeks after María
Luisa's death because he had to return to Mexico and then go to St. Louis,
Missouri, to get his daughter's birth certificate. It is interesting that elite
society wanted to condemn the indigenous bullfighter who had allegedly
disgraced one of the capital's elite daughters, whereas popular culture
placed the blame on the young girl's lack of judgment. It may have been
a question of audience and popular norms, as the urban workers hun-
grily consumed broadsheets that depicted crime stories. Gaona was an
immensely popular hero, evidenced by the crowd that rallied to his defense
outside of the Belén prison, shouting, "Let him out!" "Let him go free!"[38]
In addition, María Luisa Noeker had failed to conform to popular literature's norms of female behavior. Specifically, she professed an unrequited
love, did not wait to be chosen by the man, and went to Gaona's house
voluntarily and without a proper escort.[39] Her love for the bullfighter and
her risky behavior in attending a party with strange men were certainly
not condoned in the penny literature (fig. 9).

FIGURE 9. *La libertad caucional del famoso diestro Rodolfo Gaona* (Mexico City: A. Vanegas Arroyo, 1909). Mexican Popular Prints Collection, Center for Southwest Research, University of New Mexico Libraries.

Legends and Stories from Childhood

Sensational crime stories were not the only vehicles parents used to warn their children. Stories and legends provided moral lessons as well. Mexicans all know the legend of La Llorona (The Weeping Woman), who haunts the streets at night crying for her lost children whom she murdered. The tale of infanticide takes on different forms depending upon the time and place, but in general, the mother has killed her children in revenge after being betrayed by a man.[40] Other legends, similar to La Llorona, taught particular lessons to children of Zapotec origin in Oaxaca. Parents told the tale of Matlacihua, a phantasm in the beautiful and svelte form of a woman dressed in white. Sometimes called the White Lady or the Bride, she would appear at night and with her seductive songs and irresistible beauty, lure men of bad conduct into the forest, scaring them half to death. She also sought out illicit lovers in clandestine rendezvous.[41] If they fell into her embrace, they would suffer an immense fright so that they would return home repenting their lasciviousness. A similar ghost, but in male form, also scared those looking for illicit amorous liaisons. Parents recounted the legend of (The Ghost), or Huechaa Nayotete in Zapotec, a giant phantom that could be dressed in black or white. He roamed the dark streets searching for lovers seeking the privacy of a dark night to engage in prohibited relations.[42] The moral was clear: the bogeyman or bogeywoman awaited you if you behaved immorally and roamed the streets seeking sexual gratification or committed behaviors that transgressed community norms. These legends reinforced popular norms of appropriate sexual behavior and applied to both men and women. They differed little from legal norms, except that men seeking illicit sexual gratification were also condemned, something less prevalent in the double standard of the Mexican courts. This slight difference may be due to the indigenous roots of these legends, which reflect the greater gender equity existing in native cultures in Mexico (see chapter 1).

Children also received moral lessons that were far less frightful. In a Vanegas Arroyo eight-page chapbook for children, titled "The Brave Cricket," there are three illustrations by Posada—a family of crickets, a cricket and a beetle dueling, and two crickets greeting each other. The chapbook dramatizes the story of two enamored young crickets. The female cricket, whom the writer describes as a beautiful *doncella* (virgin) with an unsurpassed countenance, has several "machos" contending for her affection, including crickets, cockroaches, and beetles. One day, a rich beetle, Don Escarabajo, sees her and becomes hopelessly smitten with the cricket-virgin. He gives her "the most exquisite honey that bees make" and delicious fruits. The cricket suitor gives her gifts as well, although more humble, and the cricket-virgin loves him with all her soul, even though her parents want her to marry the rich beetle. The beetle orders his beetle henchmen to kill the cricket suitor. They attack and injure the unfortunate cricket. He valiantly fights back, and his attackers flee, but the next day while wooing his beloved, an army of various insects surround him. He defeats the regiments of ants and beetles, one by one, and in the end, he must face Don Escarabajo. After a harrowing fight, the cricket succeeds in killing the beetle and maintaining the love and devotion of his sweetheart. The message is familiar—love triumphs over evil. Yet, in addition to the final moral, the tale reinforces certain norms related to courtship. Girls deserving of devotion and marriage were virginal and demure, beautiful, and loyal. Suitors destined to win the objects of their desires were valiant, steadfast, passionate, and not necessarily rich. Passion and love tempered by reason and calculation were winning combinations in stories of romance and love, both in the literature and rapto dramas of the era.[43]

Sensational real-life murders and suicides, stories and fables read or recounted by parents, and legends about phantasms and malevolent spirits that roamed the night seeking sinners all combined to reinforce moral lessons for Mexican minors. Children, spoiled by their parents, could become murderers. Girls who showed poor judgment and did not protect their honor would not escape shame and even death. This was the stuff of nightmares, but it also provided not-so-subtle messages about appropriate behavior for girls and boys.

Lessons for Lovers and Spouses

Incest and Consanguinity

Popular culture also had plenty of lessons for lovers. Star-crossed paramours appeared regularly in popular renditions of sensational crime stories and humorous chapbooks. Indeed, deviant women served as literary devices in Vanegas Arroyo's and Posada's creations. Besides Norberta, the murderous and ungrateful daughter, and María Luisa Noeker, the foolish victim of an irrational love, other female protagonists in popular culture reflected attitudes towards women's capacity for violence, deceit, and betrayal—themes that also appear in the love letters of the rapto cases. In 1910, Posada illustrated a broadsheet entitled "Horrible Assassination" with the image of a crazed and vengeful woman murdering one Agustín Lara (fig. 10). In the illustration that draws the reader in, two demons egg her on. In the tale below the

¡HORRIBLE ASESINATO!

Acaecido en la ciudad de Túxpan el 10 del presente mes y año, por María Antonia Rodriguez, que mató á su compadre por no condescender á las relaciones —de ilícita amistad.—

Esta desgraciada jóven fué de familia honrada y de regular educación, hija de Rafael Rodriguez y María Juana García, fué convidada por Agustin Lara y Paula Romero para el bautizo de un niño de dichas personas. Dicha jóven tenía en su corazón un amor profundo reservado para su compadre, pero éste no la quería por lo mala, sino la respetaba antes y despues de ser invitada, deseosa, pués, la desgraciada comadre de hablar con su compadre, manda á un criado y le dice: "Anda á ver á Don Agustin Lara y dile que Doña Antonia Rodriguez lo espera en su casa á las 8 de la mañana" El criado corrió inmediatamente á lo mandado. Al dia siguiente, Agustin Lara se levantó de su cama y fué á misa, después regresó á saludar á su comadre y á saber que era lo que quería.

Llegó, pués, á la casa de su comadre y tocó la puerta al tiempo de que esta añalaba un puñal y le dijo al criado: "Anda á ver quien es; y si es Don Agustin, dile que espere un poco que ya voy á abrirle" El compadre la esperó. Esta como ya tenía el corazón dañado, se metió el puñal en la cintura; entró con el compadre y le sal udó diciéndole: "Compadre, años hacía que soñaba en las relaciones amorosas é ilícitas para con usted; pero no había habido oportunidad hasta ahora, le he mandado llamar para saber si usted me ha de cumplir mi deseo ó no porque me he propuesto hoy mismo á hacer un hecho de cualquier especie, pues yo, la verdad, compadre, lo he querido, y siempre lo querré hasta que me muera" El compadre le dijo: "¿Cómo quiere usted faltar al respeto sabiendo que es usted comadre de sacramento? no quiero ofender á Dios que nos ve y que nos escucha yo no consiento, comadrita, dándome la licencia me retiro." La desgraciada se llenó de soberbia, le tomó el brazo y le dijo: "Es decir que usted se burla de mí por no condescender á mis des os?" Y sacando el puñal le dió á su compadre diez puñaladas mortales dejándolo tendido á sus piés. Entonces su infeliz compadre lleno de dolor y con lágrimas en los ojos, le dice que

FIGURE 10. *¡Horrible asesinato! Acaecido en la ciudad de Túxpan el 10 del presente mes y año, por María Antonia Rodríguez, que mató á su compadre por no condescender á las relaciones de ilícita amistad* (Mexico City: A. Vanegas Arroyo, 1910). Mexican Popular Prints Collection, Center for Southwest Research, University of New Mexico Libraries.

sketch, the reader learns that Antonia Rodríguez is the godmother of Lara's baby boy. It begins "This disgraceful young woman was from an honorable family and good upbringing." Antonia had a deep love for her *compadre* (kin by godparenthood), and she devised an intrigue so that she could meet him and reveal her feelings. Being honorable, Lara responded that he did not want to offend God and asked for license to leave her company, whereupon she wielded a dagger and stabbed him ten times. From his knees, the victim swore that because Antonia was an ingrate, he would not die. Furious, she delivers the final and fatal blow to his heart. Like many other fables that end in holy retribution, in this one, God lets the whole house be consumed by flames. The ashes of the innocent compadre remain whereas there are no signs of the ungrateful *comadre*. The narrative ends by suggesting that roaring monsters carry off infamous women, who disappear like dust in the wind.[44] Parallel to the tales of the murderous Norberta and Ramón, nothing remains of Antonia for a proper religious burial. In Mexican society, amorous relations between individuals linked by godparenthood were akin to incest. In fact, one of the only defendants to receive a prison sentence in the rapto dramas committed "incest," in that he deflowered his goddaughter. It did not matter that he had fallen in love with her. They were considered kin, and sex between the two was likened to sex between father and daughter.[45] Antonia may have had an honorable upbringing, as the broadsheet narrated, but an irrational passion consumed her and propelled her to sin, first, by falling in love with Agustín, and then, by killing him. Again, like all the murderous antagonists of the broadsheets, religious retribution was the final outcome.

Jealousy, Honor, and Deception

Crimes of passion also figured prominently in the penny press and as subjects of several corridos (ballads). The depictions of these crimes reflected prevailing honor codes among the popular classes in nineteenth-century Mexico. Society believed that a man ought to react forcefully, and sometimes violently, when he was wronged by a woman. Thus, jealousy often led to murder, an act that readers might feel was justified. However, the broadsheets also presented the women's side of the story. Sometimes the woman provoked violence by her coquetry; other times she was a victim of outrageous slander. One broadsheet, "The Tragedy of Belén Galindo," chronicled the lamentable tale of a young wife falsely accused of infidelity by her mother-in-law (fig. 11). Indeed, mothers-in-law cross-culturally seem to be meddlers and sources of anxiety for married couples. Another broadsheet,

FIGURE 11. *El crimen de la tragedia de Belén Galindo* (Mexico City:
A. Vanegas Arroyo, 1910). Mexican Popular Prints Collection, Center
for Southwest Research, University of New Mexico Libraries.

"Carlotita," bemoans the homicide of an innocent woman killed by her jealous suitor.[46]

When the woman provoked her killer's wrath, he became the victim. Even brothers could fall prey to bad women. In the corrido "The Two Brothers," the singer bewails the discord created by a woman who comes between him and his brother. In the corridos "La Güera Chabela" and "Micaila," other coquettes met their just fates. In the first, the perpetrator found his woman dancing in the arms of another man and shot her with his pistol. In the second, the jealous killer exacted revenge on both his woman and his rival. Finally, in "Rosita Alvírez," a mother advises her daughter that her flirting would only lead to disaster, but Rosita fails to listen and a jealous suitor shoots her. From the grave, Rosita counseled her friends, "Don't forget my name; when you go to the dances, don't snub the men."[47] Jealousy provoked passions, and in the popular press, an adulterous or coquettish woman deserved her fate. In law, as well, adulterous women were more strongly censured than were straying husbands, and men could be exonerated if they killed their wives when they found them in the marital bed with another man.

Although legal and elite norms criticized common-law marriages, "the penny press presented *el amasiato* (consensual union) as an accepted fact" and was also tolerant of adultery.[48] This certainly reflected the acceptance of consensual unions and serial monogamy among the urban working class. Moreover, the broadsheet dedicated to the crime of Arnulfo Villegas against Carlota Mauri reveals that in popular literature, "marriage was not a sacred institution." The elite may have lauded the harmony and love that existed in the conjugal and nuclear family, but the broadsheets were often more cynical. The married couple, Villegas and Mauri, had one daughter, but the writer opined that "almost always marriages without true affection and only for the interest of social propriety" could result in such a tragedy.[49] Mauri receives nothing from her husband but *la mala vida* (the tough life), since he drinks too much and spends his wages on his mistress. However, their tale reinforced certain norms. It was acceptable for a husband to take a mistress, but he could not overlook his economic obligations to his family. The sheet breaks into verse to condemn fathers who waste their wages on alcohol:

Malnourished children are born
of those dissolute fathers,
syphilitic and blind,
with other faults or craziness.

In vice he squanders
All that he has earned,
his children, wife, and he,
always poorly nourished.[50]

Notably, alcohol abuse and the failure to provide for the family economically, not extramarital sex, constituted the father's sins against the family.

SUICIDIO

Causado por envenenamiento y celos de dos seño ritas en el Bosque de Chapultepec á inmediaciones del Castillo.

Una carta. Un abrazo estrecho. Un tóxico violentísimo, la convulsión y la muerte.

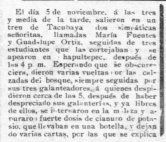

El día 5 de noviembre, á las tres y media de la tarde, salieron en un tren de Tacubaya dos simpáticas señoritas, llamadas María Fuentes y Guadalupe Ortiz, seguidas de tres estudiantes que las cortejaban y se apearon en Chapultepec, después de las 4 p. m. Esperando que se obscureciera, dieron varias vueltas por las calzadas del bosque, siempre seguidas por sus tres galanteadores, á quienes despidieron cerca de las 5, después de haber despreciado sus galanterías, y ya libres de ellos, se internaron en la maleza y apuraron fuerte dosis de cianuro de potasio, que llevaban en una botella, y dejando varias cartas, por las que se explica que se privaron de la vida por decepcio cio es amorosas. Se dice que un susodicho individuo llamado D. Elías Rojas se hizo amar por ambas y que, descubierta tan repugnante traición, decidieron arran carse la vida, por lo que se les halló abrazadas en decúbito supino y muertas.

Las dos eran íntimas amigas y vivían en la 2a Calle de los Aztecas No. 19, de donde salieron para el Baño del Carmen, donde se asearon y vistieron de riguoroso luto.

Los tres jóvenes que las cortejaban al ver que no parecían, las buscaron y encontraron sin vida, por lo que dieron aviso á la policía, y fueron detenidos para las averiguaciones respectivas.

Despedida de las Sritas. María Fuentes y Guadalupe Ortíz.

Qué hermosa, qué bella sería la existeucia
Si todas las almas pensaran así,
Amar cual las flores, su cáliz, su esencia
Amar con el alma, con gran frenesí.

Dejar q e los ojos penetren al pecho
Y vean si allí existe pureza y amor,
Obrar con limpieza en palabra y en hecho
Jamás ser la causa de amargo dolor.

Amamos con toda el alma
Al mismo varón las dos,
Por él perdimos la calma
Por él la gloria de Dios.

Del dolor en la violencia
No podemos más sufrir........
¿Es buena así la existencia?
¡Mil veces mejor morir!

FIGURE 12. *Suicidio. Causado por envenenamiento y celos de dos señoritas en el Bosque de Chapultepec á inmediaciones del Castillo* (Mexico City: A. Vanegas Arroyo, n.d.). Courtesy of Caroline and Erwin Swann Caricature and Cartoon Collection. Library of Congress.

Suicide appeared as a theme in another Posada broadsheet. Published sometime between 1890 and 1909, "Suicide poisoning of two young women due to jealousy, in Chapultepec Park, near the area surrounding the castle" chronicles the tragedy of María Fuentes and Guadalupe Ortiz. Discovering that the same man had been courting both of them, the best friends sealed a suicide pact to escape their unbearable grief and mutual jealousy. The best friends took the train from Tacubaya to Chapultepec Park, followed by three suitors who had unsuccessfully tried to court the beautiful girls. Once free of their pursuers, they drank the deadly liquid and were found shortly afterward by their shocked suitors. Skull and crossbones figure prominently on the back page of the broadside, filling half of a page and denoting death by poisoning. As was common in Posada broadsides, a verse followed the narration of the events: "We loved the same man with all our soul. Because of him we lost calm. By him the glory of God. The violent pain we can no longer endure. Is this life good? It is a thousand times better to die!"[51] In a similar vein, another broadside portrays a man with a tiny glass in hand accompanied by a maudlin verse that laments a hopeless love. The reader wonders if the tiny glass held poison as the man also braces himself on the table that holds a love letter and suicide note. On the second sheet, the broadside offers two additional songs, "The Angel of My Loves" and "The Little Virgin."[52] Suicide was certainly not condoned as an outlet to escape an unrequited love. Those who killed themselves over an impossible love or because of lost honor were criticized for their lack of reason and good behavior.

Lessons in Humor

The popular literature of the street was not all death, destruction, and doom. Moral lessons were derived from fiction as well as from stories of real crimes. Penny presses printed humorous chapbooks that recounted the stories of bickering spouses, star-crossed lovers, dandies, and flirtations in the street. In a dialogue between two friends, one chapbook recounted the story of a lover imprisoned because of a woman. Don Catarino likened his betrayal to Adam's temptation by Eve in Paradise. The woman, a flirt without shame, provoked Don Catarino, so he cut off one of her braids. Cutting a woman's hair marked her as a dishonored woman and was taken very seriously in Latin American society, and so Don Catarino found himself in prison.[53] His friend empathized, noting that women will deceive anyone in the interest of getting money.[54] In another dialogue, a husband and wife exchange insults and taunts (fig. 13). The husband complains, "I am bored,

FIGURE 13. *Pleito de casados que siempre están enojados* (Mexico City: A. Vanegas Arroyo, n.d.). Mexican Popular Prints Collection, Center for Southwest Research, University of New Mexico Libraries.

disgusting and fat woman. Don't tell me that you are my wife or that I am your husband . . ." The wife responds, "Do you think I am afraid of you? . . . drunk, dirty moocher . . ."[55]

Another quarrel between spouses related a familiar story of suspicion and mutual recrimination. One night a man comes home late, exhausted from job hunting, and his angry wife confronts him. She accuses him of spending their money on prostitutes and alcohol. He responds sweetly at first: "Look, my dear, that is wrong, because I have spent three days walking the streets looking for work in all the tailor shops." Her anger rises: "I know the *porquerías* (filth) that you deceive me with . . ." The husband's tone becomes less entreating: "You already know how tired I am, and you should calm yourself because if you don't, I will hit you." The dialogue continues with the wife threatening to hit him with the pots, dishes, and jars. He warns he will smack her with the iron. She swears that she will take all her possessions and leave him. Finally, a police officer arrives and escorts the husband to the station. The broadsheet ends with words from the police officer: "I have always observed that they fight day and night . . . off to the police station once again."[56] Readers delighted in couples' arguments and hurling of insults.

The broadsheets also depicted relations between couples in stereotypical and humorous terms. Flirting and courtship figured prominently. In an illustration and accompanying poem, a young suitor convinces his friend to stand with him under the balcony of his love interest. Portraying a high-class fop, the sheet ridicules his exploits, which undoubtedly appealed to lower-order readers. The prospective suitor recites sonnets to the young lady, but she has no time for him because her dinner is waiting. In the end, his overtures are spurned for a warm meal! In another dialogue, a water carrier attempts to flirt with a cook (fig. 14). He invites her for a drink, and she retorts, "I am not that kind of woman." In the end, the cook states that she must attend to her lady, but not before they join a procession honoring the Madonna.[57] In another short dramatic poem or *loa*, a *catrín* (dandy) flirts with a *tortillera* (tortilla maker). In a discourse rife with double entendre, she offers him warm tortillas and he comments on her brilliant and luminous eyes (fig. 15). He states that he would like to buy them all but for the pain he feels in his heart. She thinks him prosperous as he is dressed to the nines and she asks how such a young, rich man could feel depressed. The catrín responds that he cannot be happy because he has never succeeded in love. The tortillera counters, "Is that right? That isn't true, you of such handsome face and so rich and well dressed . . . that would be

LOA DICHA
POR UNA COCINERA Y UN AGUADOR,
—EN HONOR—
De Nuestra Señora del Rosario.

MUSICA.

¡Oh, María, que sois de Dios
Su más rico relicario,
Míranos con compación
Pues rezamos el rosario.

(*Sale la cocinera y dice:*)

¿Qué se hará el maestro aguador
Que no lo puedo encontrar,
Si quebraría el chochocol
O se habrá ido á emborrachar?
Ya no es posible aguantar
A este diablo de tortugo,
Pues por más que le suplico,
No lleva el agua el tarugo
No le he de dar un mendrugo
Aunque la escamocha sobre,
Por informal y borracho
Mejor se la doy á un pobre.
Ya mi ama estará gruñendo
La vieja de Satanas,
Y el aguador no parece
¡Qué diablo de Barrabás!

[*Sale el aguador cargando su chochocol
y sin ver á la cocinera, dice*]

Vamos en nombre de Dios
A la fuente á trabajar,
Pero primero en la esquina
Me la tengo de encachar.
Para poder aguantar
Regaños de garbanceras,
Media lana me echaré
Pues son pior que chimoleras,
¡Con que el tragito, muchacho,
Y luego á contentarlas á ellas!

(*Al dar la vuelta ve á la cocinera.*)

¡Qué dije! Aquí está una, sí
Que me hace ver las estrellas.
C —Buenos días, Don Pascualito,
¿Qué sucede con usté?
¿Qué me echa la agua de balde,
O no se le paga á usté?
A —No se enoje, señorita,
Ya se la voy á llevar,
Pero vamos á la esquina
¿No se la quiere encachar?

FIGURE 14. *Loa dicha por un cocinera y un aguador, en honor de Nuestra Señora de Rosario* (Mexico City: A. Vanegas Arroyo, n.d.). Mexican Popular Prints Collection, Center for Southwest Research, University of New Mexico Libraries.

FIGURE 15. *Loa de un catrín y la tortillera* (Mexico City:
A. Vanegas Arroyo, n.d.). Mexican Popular Prints Collection,
Center for Southwest Research, University of New Mexico Libraries.

impossible." The dandy warms to her compliments and flatters the tortilla vendor, who in turn spurns his advances. During the dialogue, she becomes increasingly friendly. She leaves him with the tortillas in order to buy some ingredients to make him some tasty tacos. She returns and lovingly prepares tacos with marinated pork, cilantro, avocado, and good cheese. The irony is not lost on readers as the catrín succeeds in having a warm meal for free. She asks his name. "Ricardo Platas," he responds. "Then you are very rich because of [your names] Platas y Ricardo . . ." she retorts.[58] He asks her name, and she responds "Juventina Rabos." Not comprehending, the dandy flatters her, "How beautiful your name is . . . Jedentinita (Little Foul Odor), I love you."[59] She corrects him instantly, and he dismisses it to an error of language. Her anger rises, and he tries to calm her with sweet words. He asks her to forget his folly and give him a kiss, and she calls him a *"catrín sinvergüenza"* (shameful dandy). At that moment, she is about to hit him, but a religious procession in honor of Mexico City's patron saint, San Felipe de Jesús, nears, and the tortillera prays, recites incantations, and asks for the saint's benevolence and forgiveness. She tells the dandy to get down on his knees and ask for the saint's absolution for mistreating her. The dandy repents to the saint and asks San Felipe to pardon his bad words because he wants to marry the pretty tortilla maker. They clasp each other's hands and kneel, uttering their vows to marry and liberate themselves from evil and wickedness.[60]

Clearly, the short dialogue was intended to be humorous, but in jokes reside subtle messages. The Mexican dandy was a frequent subject of nineteenth-century popular literature. For Posada, the figure of El Catrín, who wore the clothes of the elite but lacked their deep pockets, mocked pretentious elegance. Dressed in top hat and waistcoat, the dandy represented the excesses and pompous complacency of the Porfirian elite. The dandy falling for the lowly tortillera must have incited laughter and derision in the dialogue's readers. Yet San Felipe de Jesús was the maker of miracles, and he bestowed his blessing on the unlikely couple.

Emotions and Popular Culture

In addition to the dialogues of flirtations and arguments between couples, chapbooks provided advice for lovers, including the proper formulas for writing love letters. Advice for courting men and women also figured prominently and included warnings that physical beauty and wealth were less important than honesty and good work habits. The first value insured happiness; the second, the economic survival of the couple. The manuals advised women not to obsess about a suitor's physical appearance and suitors to awaken a woman's passion but also convince her of his sincerity and good habits.[61] The series *Colección de cartas amorosas* (*Love-Letters Collection*) offered sample letters of love, reconciliation, and indignation, as well as useful advice for people in love (fig. 16). The back cover of one of the volumes in the series included a series of couplets, "Women's Caprices." One insightful verse read: "A woman chooses for her husband a man, even though he is plagued with vices, but rich. She doesn't appreciate a working-class suitor, honorable and of good standing, only because he is poor." Another read: "The woman with the most suitors always chooses the worst one."[62] The manuals admonished girls not to fall for a handsome

FIGURE 16. *Colección de cartas amorosas*, no. 1 (Mexico City: A. Vanegas Arroyo,
illustrated by José Guadalupe Posada). Mexican Broadsides Collection,
Center for Southwest Research, University of New Mexico Libraries.

face but consider the habits of the man, as economic security ensured marital bliss. Also confounding official norms that believed women to be passive in romance and sexual relations, the popular literature advised girls to be covertly active in courtship, guiding them in behaviors to make boys fall in love with them.[63] In popular versions of courtship, young men and women played active roles. The chapbooks poked fun at youthful love but also provided practical advice when girls desired to keep their courtships hidden. Hence, folding certain corners of a love letter could communicate rejection, interest, or a potential meeting. Girls could wear different colored ribbons to express their emotions. For example, a lilac ribbon signified that the girl's heart belonged to another, and through that sign, she could repudiate a potential suitor.[64] Handkerchiefs were another vehicle for communication. Advice manuals instructed that if a girl passed it by her mouth, she signaled her desire to meet the man. If she rolled the handkerchief around her index finger, it communicated that she was promised to someone else.[65]

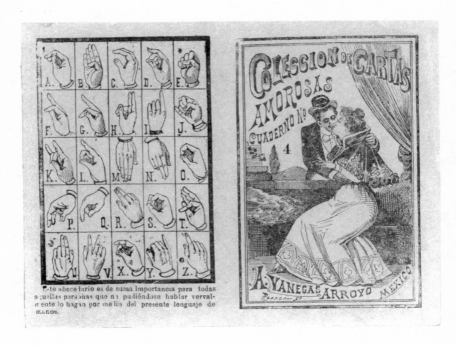

FIGURE 17. *Colección de cartas amorosas*, no. 4 (Mexico City: A. Vanegas Arroyo, illustrated by José Guadalupe Posada). Mexican Broadsides Collection, Center for Southwest Research, University of New Mexico Libraries.

The chapbooks also included illustrations of the international sign language so lovers could communicate in a code that could not be deciphered by parents or chaperones (fig. 17).

Some of the couples of the elopement dramas also employed rhetorical structures from popular culture to express their sentiments in the missives written for their loved ones. The letters of the rapto cases resemble those found in the *Colección de Cartas Amorosas* series.[66] Writers used familiar tropes in popular song and the dialogues between men and women discussed above. The love letters from the Oaxacan court cases have three main themes: fear of betrayal, exalted love, or practical elopement plans. Several male suitors also expressed concern about the sweetheart's welfare, primarily apprehension about the abuse the girl suffered at home. For example, in his first letter to Anastacia Delgado in 1875, Arcadio Ortega wrote:

Tell me why you don't do what you say [you will] and [instead] always deceive me. Several times you have told me that you love me, and I will never be capable of forgetting you. I received these tender words with so much pleasure, and I believe they were dictated from the center of your heart. . . . Tell me why you didn't keep our date that I set with my desperate letters. Why didn't you do what you said you would? I surely doubt already that you have love for me. But if this is not true I will wait for you all day on Sunday in the designated place because I want to talk to you.[67]

Angst, deception, love, and desperation were among the emotions voiced by Arcadio in the letter above penned after Anastacia failed to meet him at the appointed time and place. Letter-writing manuals, fables, and poetry followed similar rhetorical structures and provided rhetorical cues for lovers to express their most intimate thoughts.[68] Arcadio's first letter dispensed with the customary salutations of affection and went straight to the point, expressing not only his fear of betrayal but also his undying love for Anastacia, even to the point of swearing that he would wait all day Sunday for her to come to meet him.

The printing house of Vanegas Arroyo published the *Colección de Cartas Amorosas*. One sample letter provided men with an example of how to write to a girlfriend whom he feared no longer returned his affection:

Idolized Chonita: I write you this, overpowered by a deep sadness, fearing the reality that could be my eternal misfortune. Today an individual presented himself to me . . . assuring me that he had the rights to your affection . . . offering to bring me indisputable proof, like your letters, hair, and other prendas [love tokens]. . . . I want to implore your frankness. . . . I don't want to see in his hands the proof of my misfortune because it would be very painful to show my defeat to this triumphant rival. Trembling, I await your decision, and I will always love you. Pablo.[69]

Like Arcadio's letter, which expressed his dismay and fear that Anastacia had lied about her true feelings, the letter written by the fictional Pablo expressed the anguish of a man faced with a romantic rival and potential heartbreak. Indeed, the fictional lover in the manual reinforced the importance of prendas as signifiers of a serious relationship. If another man could produce a lock of Chonita's hair or letters penned in her hand, not only would her amorous suitor face heartbreak but a public shaming or "misfortune." Professions of love and fear of heartbreak appeared regularly in the letters in the case files, and writers expressed these feelings with a most profound passion and desperation. Real individuals like the lovers of the rapto dramas found rhetorical structures in popular literature and song (fig. 18).

In a subsequent letter, Arcadio seemed less desperate for Anastacia to prove her love to him:

> Señorita: My gentlemanliness and the desire in my heart directs my sad and bitter suffering . . . I told N. of the extreme passion that locked in my chest . . . it is impossible to keep this secret because I remember the tender and loving words that left your red lips for the consolation of my soul in those seductive days full of pleasure that we had together. . . .[70]

> My illusion: What I would offer you on this splendid and luminous day is a new life when the angel of glory comes with garlands for your *morena* and attractive face. I cannot offer you more than the honey of contentment of my poor heart and the sea of happiness that runs through my veins when I see you smile. . . . You know well that I have loved you with all the sentiment of a man that loves honestly. . . .[71]

The language of the manuals was less passionate, as none of the sample letters mentioned "seductive days full of pleasure" between lovers. However, popular song and poetry often reflected the ardor and passion of lovers like Arcadio. A popular Oaxacan song expressed it succinctly: "I remember promises, I remember love affairs, and my suffering, and they come closer, come with passion, and break this loneliness." Another song likened love to the heavens: "Only an angel of God, up there in the heavens, will love you like my soul adores you . . ."[72] Other songs expressed the longing and desperation that love wrought: "Listen and forgive my sad song that I raise up to you. Poor me. Sad is my life, dark without you. You I remember, darling of my life. I feel like dying, don't deny me your sweet love . . ."[73]

Aside from their tender phrases of love and painful passion, the love letters conveyed a palpable fear of betrayal or infidelity. A song published in 1896, "La Cubanita," lamented a woman's false promises to a heartbroken man:

FIGURE 18. *Nuevos versos de apasionado* (Mexico City: A. Vanegas Arroyo, n.d.). Mexican Popular Prints Collection, Center for Southwest Research, University of New Mexico Libraries.

I don't love you anymore, nor do I love anyone, with love comes sentiment. Crying, crying, tears of emotion for a woman who doesn't know how to love me. She swore that she loved me until death. Blinded by passion, I loved her constantly; what is more, I couldn't believe she had another lover. What cruel betrayal she gave me![74]

Emotions such as deceit, betrayal, and love unto death were sentiments common to the suitors' love letters to their sweethearts. One suitor expressed this emotion of betrayal well. In 1889, he wrote:

Tomasita: I have this terrible uncertainty that the matter we are dealing with has not been resolved. You can guess what I am referring to. You appear to be insensitive and indifferent because you have deceived me several times . . . I'm sorry to have to communicate to you using this sad piece of paper. I feel like tearing it apart and throwing it away, but I can't. I worship you.[75]

The writer, Juan González, had promised to marry fifteen-year-old Tomasa Rivera, but her mother refused to give her permission. Perhaps this desperate and passionate letter persuaded Tomasa to slip out of the house one night to meet Juan. The lovers spent two nights together before Tomasa returned home. The mother filed a lawsuit to ensure that Juan repaired Tomasa's honor by marrying her.

Sample letters from a letter-writing manual expressed similar concern about being betrayed:

Adored Maria: It has been many days since you wrote me, and since then, I have received nothing from you, and I know from your conduct that you are neither sick nor suffering from serious concerns. . . . You should understand how much I suffer from your silence. I don't want to think about why you haven't written me . . . I hope you will do me the favor of sending me tidings about yourself. . . . As always, with an immense love for your purity. Miguel.[76]

Suitors also penned letters that expressed an exalted love for their girlfriends. In 1885, soldier José María Palacios extolled his love for María Quiróz: "Beautiful and enchanting Mariqueta, sweet is my infinite love that makes my poor heart impatient. . . . Mariqueta, my life, I don't have much time to wait for you to be at my side. . . . This man suffers so much for your love . . . my intention is for you to marry me and I await an answer from your beautiful lips. . . ."[77] Another lover from the rapto dramas, Roque Cabrera, expressed similar passions to María Rafaela Carrasco in 1905:

> From the first time I saw you, my thoughts have been in the end to marry you. My heart suffers a passion that devours my soul, and it is not possible to cope with it because of a young woman as beautiful as a celestial angel. For me, you will be my constant companion . . . [78]

Other letters combined expressions of passion and undying love with practical plans to engineer the elopement. Let us revisit the letter that introduced chapter 2. In 1892, Enrique Martínez wrote Carmen Llaguno:

> I take the pen to greet you with the utmost love and affection I will ever express until God decides to end my life . . . I have thought of your departure [the elopement] and I will support and protect you from everything. . . . I don't want to overlook my obligations as a married man . . . and darling, you also ask me if I will use you like all men use women. My love, I will never betray you, you very well know how much I love you and I would never use you. Because of this you should either leave your home soon, or we need to break up our relationship for good. It is not possible for me to continue living in doubt. How can I remain calm knowing you are in danger? Do you think I will stand for this situation because I have always loved you so much? Do you think I will grin and bear it? My dear Carmita, I will not allow it. If you don't leave your mother, this will be my last letter to you, and you know it. This is all I have to say to you. Take it from somebody who has never been able to betray you because I have always loved you so much.[79]

Enrique stressed his honesty and faithfulness but also threatened Carmen that if she did not leave her mother, he would leave her. Such threats often persuaded girls to elope. Also note that as the love manuals advised, Enrique labored to persuade Carmen of his honorable intentions, noting he would not "overlook his obligations as a married man" or use her "like all men use women." His professions convinced Carmen to take that dramatic step and run off with Enrique.

Manuel Canseco was also direct in his letters to his sweetheart, Teresita Valle. His letters dispensed with the poetic declarations and seemed businesslike in their form. In the court case, he actually claimed that the aggrieved Teresita and her mother forged the letters to trick him into marrying her. Nonetheless, no matter who penned them, they stress the importance of secrecy in a courtship when parental consent for marriage is not forthcoming:

> Teresita, my life: I thank you for your kindness. My father is better, thank you. Perhaps we can meet on Thursday if my brother is not there [at the store], but it has to be as late as possible, so that nobody can see what's happening. You know I love you, Manuelito.

> Teresita: It is not true what they told you. I am not crazy, and I don't have any loose screws. Tomorrow I will explain to you where we went. If you still want me to give you back your letters I will. Manuel.

> Beloved Teresita: Tell me how everything went because I haven't had any news. Don't forget to let me know if it is possible [to see you] on Monday since my brother leaves that day. Remember, I love you. Manuel. If you think it's dangerous don't do it. Tear up this piece of paper after reading it.

> Teresita, my life: In my letter I told you to come over, and I waited for you. If you can come tomorrow, I will wait for you. Thursday would be better because there is nobody here in the afternoon. I love you. Manuel.

> Teresita, my life: Forgive me that I didn't wish you a happy birthday. You know the ignorant are just like the blind. You will say I am being rude, and you are right, but you know I wish you many years of happiness. Now I remember a conversation I had with your mother, when she told me the day of . . . was the day of your birthday, but I couldn't remember; what else can you expect from me, my life? Tell me how you are doing . . . and I will fix it later. Lots of love, Manuel.[80]

Let us assume that Manuel did indeed write the letters. Although Teresita's letters to Manuel have been lost, we can surmise her thoughts and demands. Manuel thought it best that she meet him when no one was around the store, which signifies that their love affair had not been sanctioned by her parents. He also seems to answer to her feelings of jealousy, assuring her that he will explain where he had been. Although he may not be as passionate as Arcadio (he apparently forgot her birthday and does not bother to compare her to the angels in heaven), his letters reveal much about the need to keep courtships hidden from prying eyes. Likewise, they attest to the ability of lovers to steal time together while unchaperoned. In Teresita's case, instead of walking to her piano lessons, she went to Manuel's store in a very public place, the principal plaza of the city.

Most of the letters included in the case files were written by the male defendants, because a girl's parents, or the daughter herself, submitted them as evidence of a committed and contractual relationship, but there are a few letters written by women. Josefa Calvo's letters to Manuel Vivas were similar in form and content to the examples above. An assertive young woman, Josefa engineered her own rapto, even threatening Manuel that if he did not accede to her plan, she would find a man who would! Her letters also display a remarkable rationalism combined with affection, two attributes championed by the popular press and by liberal society:

Manuel: You will understand the affection I have for you even though I have avoided showing it. Out of necessity, I have always acted with my head. I haven't left home to talk to you because they haven't let me go anywhere. You know my mother's temperament. Thursday I wanted to talk to you but I couldn't talk because of the blowout we had. Talk to me through letters because I can't talk like I would like to. . . .

Manuel: I told this girl about the money but she caused me many difficulties and I don't believe she wants to lend me money but she told me that she would resolve the matter for me. I have wanted to let you know. . . .

Manuel: If I didn't have affection for you, I would have already gone, but as I have love for you and for this, I didn't go nor am I going, as I have told you that my friend wanted to take me. I want you to tell me with total honesty if you want me to go with you. I am going to take my friend [when we elope] because she has already gotten the money for us to go. Don't think you have to pay for her. She is going to pay. . . . If I go with you, it is because I love you but your mother has a very horrible character.

Josefa's communications to her suitor expressed affection and impatience.

In them, she assured Manuel that her affections were steadfast and proven because she had not run away with another man. She also insisted that her friend, Teresa, accompany them on their elopement in part because she had the money to rent a room but perhaps also to have a female ally to protect her. Her letters also relate her conflict with her mother who worked hard to thwart their love affair, even though, in the end, she fled with Manuel and Teresa. Writing these letters allowed Josefa to express her affection, reveal her insecurities, and talk about her home life. She also expressed concern about her future mother-in-law, a genuine fear that played out in the penny literature and in the cases of family strife. Significantly, she stressed that reason and love ruled her heart, another important theme of "appropriate love" in the popular press of Vanegas Arroyo.[81] Indeed, the press exalted love and passion but only as long as it was tempered by reason. María Luisa Noecker's type of passion—rash, impulsive, and unrequited—found few fans among the editors, and probably among the readers, of this literature. As will become evident, judges in the rapto cases also valued rational arguments combined with expressions of sincere love in the youngsters' testimonies.

Popular culture provided Mexican youth an education intended to guide their lives and actions. From early childhood on, family members regaled their offspring with legends and stories that imparted moral lessons for life. Likewise, songs listened to at home or heard at fandangos (dances) certainly transmitted popular notions of love, betrayal, and courtship to old and young alike. Moreover, the telling and retelling of real stories—whether sensational crimes or honor killings—undoubtedly communicated lessons and warnings about deviancy and its causes in society. All of the mediums contributed to a process of socialization so that popular culture both reflected and shaped a community's norms and values. Of course, through give and take, individuals adopted these norms, but the social cues were unmistakable. In the elopement dramas, the young couples, armed with a set of cultural norms, could accept them, reject them, or tweak them for their own purposes. In penning love letters, these individuals mimicked community sensibilities about the proper way to express love, the fear of betrayal, and jealousies. Young women and men like Josefa and Arcadio possessed emotional lives, and they expressed this dynamically through their written and spoken professions of love. Unfortunately, because of their love lives, they would be dragged into the courtroom to defend their actions and misbehavior as minor children. As the next chapter reveals, the working-class community served as the setting for these forbidden romances, but it also provided witnesses who acted as arbiters of honor and shame in these criminal cases.

CHAPTER FOUR

Bearing Witness
Courtship and
Working-Class Neighborhoods

☙❧

EIGHT WITNESSES TESTIFIED TO THE ALLEGED ABDUCTION AND DEFLOW-
ering of Carmen Falledos in Cuilapam, a village outside the capital. Walking
home from school one afternoon in 1888 with three friends, Carmen met
Inocente Zárate on the road. According to her, he dragged her to a *milpa*
(cornfield) nearby and raped her. Several witnesses challenged her claim
and offered contradictory depositions. All agreed that Carmen never made
it home from school that day and that she spent eight days alone with
Inocente. The distraught mother searched the pueblo for her daughter and
urged the municipal president to do something. On the ninth day, the official, Lucas Santos, apprehended Inocente and sent Carmen home. A community scandal ensued, as neighbors argued over the facts of the couple's
relationship and the girl's loss of honor. Santos claimed that the couple
came to him and swore they eloped with the intention to marry, but he
jailed Inocente for three days. Meanwhile, Carmen's father returned from
the coast and learned that he and his family had been dishonored. Not satisfied with Santos's cursory punishment of his daughter's seducer, the father
traveled to the capital and filed a charge of rapto against Inocente.

The young couple testified first. For her part, fifteen-year-old Carmen
swore that Inocente leaped from a ravine and grabbed her by the braids

as she walked home from school. She also avowed that she screamed and fought her attacker. This is significant since had she remained passive, it would have implied her consent.[1] Instead of rallying to her defense during the alleged assault, her school chums ran away. Continuing her testimony, Carmen stated that Inocente raped her, and then, pulling her by the braids again, he led her to the house of fifty-year-old Marcelo Martínez, where he kept her against her will for eight days. She also denied that she had had any relations with him previously.

Inocente, a twenty-five-year-old musician in the village band, countered that Carmen had staged the entire episode because she preferred to live with him rather than her parents. He expressed surprise that she could be so "ungrateful" and deceitful. Furthermore, he no longer desired to marry her because he had discovered that she was not a virgin when they had sex.

Witnesses further confounded the drama. The owner of the house, Marcelo, told the judge that he had provided *posada* (lodging) to the couple because Inocente has said they were engaged. He also noted that Carmen seemed amicable with Inocente, which undermined her claim that she was abducted and ravished unwillingly by a man she barely knew. On the other hand, if Carmen had spent eight nights with Inocente against her will, Marcelo could never admit it or he would be an accessory to a crime. Convoluting the narrative further, Carmen's friends agreed that Inocente met them on the road, and as they ran for cover during a heavy afternoon rainstorm, they saw him pull her by the braids. As the girls ran to escape the deluge, they could hear their friend's screams from the direction of the cornfield. One school friend, Mariña Santos, swore that she could not tell if Carmen had been forced to go with Inocente or not. Her testimony, contradicting Carmen's allegation of rape, placed doubt in the judge's mind.[2] Expert witnesses also had their turn. Surgeons from the General Hospital inspected Carmen's body and decided that she had been recently deflowered without force. They commented that her vulva appeared normal and her hymen had irregular borders but could admit an index finger. Basically, their medical diagnosis hypothesized that sexual intercourse tore her hymen, but she bore no bruises or swelling as a result of sexual assault. They further concluded that she had not engaged in coitus more than once or twice because remnants of her hymen remained visible. With these preliminary and contradictory testimonies, the judge remitted Inocente to jail and assigned him a defense attorney. Carmen remained in her parental home while the proceedings continued.

Judges relied on witnesses to help fill in the "facts" in the rapto cases. They could attest to the events they saw, provide hearsay about a couple's relationship, and share prevailing gossip in the community. They also served as character witnesses by vouching for the reputation of the victim and the defendant. In some cases, witness testimony seemed damning for the victim, but the judge still punished the abductor. Consider the case of Inocente. While he waited in jail, a couple of male community members provided their version of the story. His friend, Pablo Martínez, told the judge that Inocente and Carmen had a long-standing, public romance in their pueblo. Another friend recalled seeing them talking, and he was able to give the judge the exact date and time. Both claimed that it was public knowledge in the village that Carmen had wanted to run away with Inocente. The two friends also provided details about an event that had occurred a few days before the incident on the road: Carmen had arranged a meeting with Inocente in the church cemetery. When she arrived, she launched into a tirade, first ridiculing Inocente for wanting to ask her parents' permission to marry and then calling him a "coward." Even though Inocente pleaded with her to be patient, Carmen threatened him that "if he did not meet her after school, she would go away with the first man who presented himself." His friends lamented that Inocente, against his better judgment, agreed to meet Carmen after school on that fateful day. One of the friends ended his testimony by noting, "In Cuilapam, it is well known that Inocente did not compromise and seduce Carmen; rather she compromised and seduced him."[3]

Regardless of the motivations for these testimonies, their prevalence and the weight they were given point to the important function of gossip, insult, and slander in public life.[4] Judges listened attentively to hearsay, in part to establish whether the girl deserved legal protection. The defendant's conduct received attention as well. Judges primarily wanted to determine if the young man had a criminal record or an unsavory reputation among his peers. No doubt gossip supported a structure of norms and mores in communities. Yet, each social group and gender displayed its own rules for the diffusion and exchange of gossip. Gossip—talk about other people—worked at the community level in that its disseminators had to know each other and the person who was the subject of rumor. Gossip could also escalate to outright insult and slander. Discussing the most personal details of people's lives in the streets or other public arenas contributed to the shaping of social values.[5] In fact the act of gossiping created communities with shared values and expectations.[6] Besides its formative role, gossip acted as a tool of community surveillance to police an individual's behavior, especially the sexual behavior of women. Additionally, it possessed a disciplinary arm as it could result in serious social, political, and economic sanctions.[7] Gossip most impacted individuals who vied with one another for social precedence. For example, many cases survive in the municipal archive that pit market woman against market woman. Insults slung before customers could certainly have a deleterious impact on a vendor's sales. Working-class individuals also lacked the privacy of their upper-class counterparts. It must have been impossible to hide a pregnancy or love affair in lower-order barrios where more than one family shared living space.[8] Thus, although working women may have had more freedom to walk public streets and spaces as they traveled to work, their peers could observe their every action, including with whom they fraternized.

Viewing social relations through the prism of gossip and insult reveals important characteristics of community building. Participants in the rapto dramas repeated gossip and insulted each other to make their case more believable and defensible before the judge.[9] Their calculated utterances drew an animated portrait of how power relations operated in working-class communities but also how communities endeavored to influence behavior through these processes of hearsay and mudslinging. The cases capture the structure and content of gossip in the corner stores, *pulquerías* (establishment that sold the fermented cactus juice, pulque), markets, and other public spaces of working-class neighborhoods. An analysis of witness testimonies and the young couples' depositions reveals that courtship and family relations were not private but community affairs. When neighbors discussed a man's reputation or came to the defense of a young victim, their actions and words reflected popular standards that did not always coincide with elite norms. Likewise, individuals who used the court to attest to the honorable or dishonorable conduct of a peer, or to charge another with insult and slander, "helped distinguish themselves as members of a group of honorable people."[10] In other words, it was important to defend your honor publicly both in the community and through the courts when necessary.[11] An analysis of witness testimony from rapto and other criminal cases provides a better understanding of the rules and honor codes of popular culture and sheds light on how these norms influenced the lives of parents, their children, and the larger community.

Working-Class Communities and Families

Working-class neighborhoods were anything but cohesive entities. The "working class experience was, in fact, a mosaic of different identities shaped by the street, corner shop, family and relatives, pub or club, and by paid work outside the home."[12] The corner or neighborhood store, many run by women, played an important role as a clearinghouse for local gossip and information because of the presence of regular customers who lived close by and shopped daily or who would stop by just to chat or catch up on neighborhood news. Indeed, female storeowners often appeared as witnesses in rapto cases, attesting to having seen a couple together or exchanging letters. The pulquería also provided an intimate social space for men and women. Female purveyors of pulque suffered as targets of malicious gossip.[13] If they allowed scandalous drunkenness in their establishments, their own honor or reputation became suspect, and the community took measures to censure them.[14] The church also provided individuals with the space and society for the exchange of news and hearsay, whether in visits to mass or the numerous religious observances that filled the calendar. The marketplace could be a particularly contentious arena for gossip and insult. Daily banter in these venues corroborated the oral traditions of the community. Through conversation and gossip, the values of community life were shaped and dispersed, and behavior was censured and regulated. Malicious words destroyed honor, and victims scrambled to defend it, sometimes going to court to do so. Importantly, these locally shared values and beliefs suggest an alternative culture dissimilar from the dominant one. Although the elite may have attempted to impose its values throughout society, an alternative working-class culture persisted and represented local conditions and values. It allowed ample space for maneuver and mutual accommodation, especially in indigenous Oaxaca.[15] At times though, underage couples felt hard pressed to forge plans, as their lives were neither private nor independent of activities of the neighborhood or workplace.

Privacy may not have meant much to a working-class family living in cramped rooms that ringed a patio shared with several other households. In the home, family members often all slept in one room, but daughters still managed to slip out while their parents were dozing. In these crowded conditions, what happened in the domiciles of neighbors could easily become public knowledge. The patio served as a communal space, an environment where neighbors shared and disseminated information while they washed clothes, sharpened tools, or cared for their children. In these circumstances, young couples found creative ways to seize a moment for affectionate words or an embrace. Courtships could be carried out by letter and arranged meetings that took place in stores, the street, or at church. As the letters attest, set meetings did not always happen, as parents and peers watched the couple's every move.[16] Indeed, neighbors often informed the parents that their daughter had run off with a certain boy or man. Other people would report seeing the sweethearts talking, implying that the girl and family were in danger of losing honor. These mechanisms of peer surveillance acted to manage behavior and provide some sort of stability in community life. Neighbors' meddling could either protect or impugn the honor of a young girl. Indeed, many planned elopements must have been foiled by vigilant neighbors. For parents who worked outside the home, community gossip and surveillance allowed them to police their children's behavior.

Surveillance operated on many levels. In an 1889 infanticide case, fourteen-year-old Herlinda Hernández testified that while she washed dishes in her kitchen, she heard a woman yell, "Hurry! Micaela has just given birth to little twins." Next, she saw Micaela's mother drop a wrapped bundle into the patio's dry well. Some weeks later, she testified in court: "I don't have any hate for the family, but today, . . . I noticed many worms and fetidness" in the well. Apparently, Micaela's mother had dumped the placenta and soiled, bloody clothing in the well. Unbeknownst to Herlinda, the family had also clandestinely buried two fetuses in the cemetery. For her part, eighteen-year-old Micaela Velasco, who lived with her single mother, testified that she had consumed only a peach before the onset of early labor, an attempt to convince the judge that she had not eaten herbs to induce an abortion. Micaela further testified that the midwife came and applied a pomade and wet tortilla to her genitalia in order to forestall labor. Her aunt, Francisca Pérez, swore that the babies died soon after their birth, and she placed them in a cigar box for their burial. The judge had the dead twins exhumed, and doctors determined that they had not been viable when born since they were apparently four months premature. He thus dropped the charges against Micaela, her mother, and the aunt.[17] Nevertheless, the charge of infanticide had arisen from a neighbor's suspicions that a crime had been committed, a crime against the state but also against community values. The young witness, Herlinda, felt it was her moral duty to report a potential assault on community norms—namely the murder of an infant.

In a less fatal case, Tomás Bazán brought an assault and lack-of-respect charge in 1850 against his wife, Eligia Escobar, and his daughter, María Bazán. Apparently, the wife and daughter accosted him on the street as he walked by with his mistress. The father wrote to the court that "the act of a wife and daughter attacking a husband sets a bad example for society and [causes] a grave scandal." Remarkably, while the wife and daughter pummeled the husband and mistress, other women joined in to strike the man.

In this raucous case, the women of the community acted together to censure the unseemly behavior of the man and, probably more importantly, of the woman who had stolen another's husband and dared promenade with him in public.[18] Although a wife might tolerate her husband's more discreet infidelity, when his actions became flagrant and public, it upset the community's sensibilities. In this case the community of women rallied together to shame him, just as his public flouting of his adultery shamed them.

Indiscreet sexual behavior was just one cause for neighbors to meddle in seemingly private affairs, and troublesome marriages were another. Especially when it found itself divided over a couple's misfortunes in marriage, the community intervened in marital discord, siding with husband or wife.[19] For instance, Isabel Pérez in 1853 pleaded for relief from the court. She stated that her husband, Benito Martínez, repeatedly beat her, accused her of being a prostitute, and did not provide her *alimentos* (food and clothing). When she had asked the subprefect to intervene, he had ordered her to go back home, where she had to endure the blows of her drunken husband. One male witness and fellow village member had observed them fighting on numerous occasions, and he even witnessed Benito threatening Isabel with a machete. Neighbors testified that Benito gave Isabel *la mala vida* (the tough life) but could not swear that he didn't feed and clothe her. Another community member came to the wife's defense, recounting the common knowledge in the village that Benito abused Isabel and the embarrassing fact that her father actually supported her. Other witnesses testified to her good conduct and perpetual suffering in her marriage. Benito, a twenty-three-year-old charcoal maker, swore that he never threatened his wife and that he gave her food and clothing, for which he received in return her insolence and disobedience. He stated that he loved her very much and that she fled from his home because her meddling parents had "filled her with crazy ideas." When asked about the witness testimony that condemned him, Benito claimed that his wife was carrying on an affair with one of the witnesses. The mayor provided the final witness testimony and supported the husband, noting that he was a hard worker, an orphan with no family, and that Isabel was one of the most troublesome women in the village. Indeed, the mayor testified that her family conducted themselves badly and that Isabel had no sense of fidelity to her husband or to the rules of the community.[20]

Witnesses for Isabel and Benito presented testimony within the parameters congruent with popular values and expectations. The community (and the law) tolerated spousal abuse, but if the husband failed to provide alimentos, or used excessive force, then he was breaking the conjugal bargain that dictated that patriarchs must provide food, protection, and shelter to their dependents. Wives, in turn, had to fulfill their duties by cooking, keeping house, and behaving modestly. When the conjugal pact was torn asunder by mutual recriminations and officious neighbors, the goal of the community was to reconcile the couple. If an informal resolution could not be reached, the courts were the last resort, and usually the goal of that process was also resolution.

In an 1888 case, the judge admonished Manuel to be nicer to his amasia, Juana Hernández. She had swallowed fourteen matches (in a suicide attempt) because he had called her a "public woman" (prostitute) and had beaten her. After finding her convulsing on the floor with severe stomach pain, Manuel fed her salt to induce vomiting, gave her boiled coffee without sugar, and took her to the hospital. The court charged her with trying to commit suicide, but the judge released her to Manuel, advising them to resolve their differences.[21] The judge did not investigate the charges of spousal abuse but chose instead to champion reconciliation as the best solution.

Another case highlights the significant role of in-laws in couple's lives. In-laws played an important role in married life—as both meddlers and protectors—depending on their affinity for the spouse. Abused wives frequently sought sanctuary with their parents to escape their violent husbands. Shortly before Christmas in 1852, Agapita Pérez took her husband and father-in-law to court for mistreatment and other abuses. The court had mediated their reconciliation four years earlier, compelling Agapita to return to her husband's side after promises that he would treat her better. The judge also required that his parents not meddle in the couple's life anymore. Now, Agapita testified that almost daily, her husband and father-in-law beat her. She had complained to the pueblo's mayor and shown him her bruises, but he sent her home and warned her to hide her injuries. Clearly, by silencing her, he desired to avert a public scandal that would upset community harmony, since the residents would ally themselves with one side or the other. Agapita told the judge in Oaxaca City that her father-in-law was a leader of the pueblo, and she could not get any justice because of the "bad customs of the natives." She also charged her mother-in-law with forcing her to get drunk in another village. According to the aggrieved woman, her mother-in-law escorted her to a fandango (dance) in a neighboring community and encouraged her to drink heavily in order to conspire with her husband to assault her. As they were returning to San Agustín, thoroughly inebriated, her husband and father-in-law met them on the road, and they beat her, kicked her in the stomach, and strangled her. When her father-in-law threatened to kill her, she packed a few belongings, fled the pueblo, and sought shelter with her brother and sister-in-law in Oaxaca City. There, she took her complaint to the courts of the capital city, since it was clear she would not receive justice from the officials in her village.[22] Her initiation of the case restored her honor and publicly shamed her husband, the village elders, and her in-laws. Unfortunately, the case file does not include the outcome. She may have reconciled with her husband or decided not to pursue the case in court.

Mothers-in-law were not always devious meddlers and home wreckers. In a particularly unfortunate case of infanticide in 1869, María Josefa Felix found herself in court charged with murdering her infant girl. A thirty-year-old tortilla maker from Xoxocotlán, María Josefa was widowed with four surviving children. An investigation established that her infant girl had died of traumatic head injuries. The accused stated that she had hoped to marry the baby girl's father but his family objected, so she continued to live with her deceased husband's mother and sister. She claimed that the baby girl had been sickly since birth, and she had a difficult time caring for her. Each day, María Josefa rose early to prepare tortillas for sale in the capital city a few miles north of her village. Beside the burden of hauling tortillas and her infant girl, she had to carry her four-year-old son with her as well. These troubles, she hoped, would explain her duress. Her mother-in-law vouched for her widowed daughter-in-law, noting that she worked hard and had sought a cure for the infant from a local midwife that very morning. Her sister-in-law recounted María Josefa's tragic history as a young widow and confirmed that she had been abandoned by the infant's father. A neighbor also swore that he saw María Josefa make tortillas every day and carry them to the city, in effect attesting to her diligent work habits to support her young children. Another community member rallied to her defense by noting that he saw her enter the home of the midwife that morning, presumably to seek a cure for the ailing infant. The key motive was to establish that she was a good mother, hard worker, but also a poor widow suffering from a recent abandonment. Not one person questioned the young mother's integrity or honor. Doctors concluded that the type of head injuries the baby suffered could not have occurred naturally, but nevertheless, the judge released María Josefa from jail and placed her with a temporary guardian.[23] Although we do not know the ultimate outcome, it seems from the judge's action that he was lenient largely because the community, including her in-laws, vouched for her hardworking and honest character.

Gossip and Reputation

In addition to a surveillance function, gossip linked men and women in the community into a broad information network. Group values were shaped and maintained through talking about peers, and the street acted as a venue for shame and ridicule to censure behavior that transgressed community norms. In fact, gossip and the lack of privacy could protect women from excessive domestic violence, as neighbors could intervene when necessary, and women could flee to the relative safety of nearby kin or friends. Community members of Trinidad de las Huertas, a village southeast of Oaxaca City, assisted one of their own. News spread quickly that a young woman, Juana Martínez, was captive in a local home. People had seen one of the village locals, Demetrio de Jesús, entering and leaving the home through the window. After he left one day, several community members approached the house, called to Juana, and pried open the window. They had been concerned about the young woman's welfare and were ready to rescue her, if necessary, but she said she had voluntarily run away with her captor. Community members, satisfied that a crime had not occurred, returned to their own affairs, leaving Juana to stay or flee. In fact, the situation played out a typical script of elopement. In 1869, Demetrio, a married laborer, met fourteen-year-old Juana in the marketplace in Oaxaca City. He brought her back to Trinidad and kept her in the house for five days, at which point she climbed out a window and returned home. During the court case, Juana swore she was a virgin, but the doctors determined otherwise. Juana also confessed that Demetrio had given her three pesos, which did not sit well with the judge. In the end, the judge dismissed the case against Demetrio, reasoning that Juana had gone voluntarily with him.[24] Her acceptance of money had undoubtedly weakened her case, making it possible for the judge to view Juana as a prostitute or since Demetrio was already married, as his amasia.

Sexual behavior was a fountainhead of gossip. Its discussion could impact a person's social status and reputation among peers. Clearly, the community and the law held women to higher standards of sexual morality than men. Men were judged by a different set of rules; however, indigenous communities did not condone excessive sexual activity by either men or women. For instance, in 1857, sixteen-year-old Brígida, the daughter of Valentín Osorio of Atzompa, was four months pregnant. Valentín pleaded with the court to force Pablo de la Cruz, also sixteen years of age, to fulfill his promise to marry Brígida. The father protested that the author of his daughter's disgrace had "offended the community," emphasizing to the judge that it was public knowledge in the village that his daughter had been seduced and impregnated by Pablo. Indeed, witnesses from Atzompa acknowledged the amorous relationship and provided additional details of the courtship. Neighbors had seen Pablo enter their house on several occasions when Valentín worked out of town. Strangely, Pablo contradicted the community's testimony, swearing he knew neither Valentín nor his now-pregnant daughter. Brígida vowed that Pablo impregnated her, noting that they had sexual relations on six separate occasions. Witnesses again testified that Pablo lived a half block from the father and daughter and repeated that while they had been working in a nearby cornfield, they had seen the culprit come and go from Valentín's house.[25] Unfortunately, we do not know whether Pablo married Brígida, but the case illustrates the parameters of community surveillance and gossip. A courtship and pregnancy quickly became public knowledge and community members willingly stepped in to ensure that the young seducer account for his actions and fulfill his obligations. In their testimony, witnesses did not question or criticize Brígida for allowing Pablo to enter her home while her father was away. However, they expected Pablo to fulfill his responsibility to the young woman. In the eyes of the community, Brígida had done nothing wrong. She was simply pregnant. But the community expected a resolution: the young couple must marry. The year of this case, 1857, is also important as the case predates the 1871 penal code, the nation had just created a civil registry for births, deaths, and marriages, and Valentín must have been desperate to defend his honor in the courts of Oaxaca City. Clearly, the community and the aggrieved father viewed marriage as the only way to restore the family's honor and community harmony.

Community gossip about a man's sexual behavior and exploits did not have the similar effect on judges. Men were never described as worldly.[26] Although a judge would listen to testimony that impugned a man's sexual reputation, those cases rarely ended in a judgment against the male defendant. For instance, in 1888, Macaria Calderón contracted a scribe to write a complaint to the criminal court. She claimed that the day before, Jesús García had appeared at her house on horseback, stating that he had taken her daughter, Juana Alcazar, because Macaria mistreated her. The mother had sought justice in her village, but local officials only briefly incarcerated the seducer. In her statement, she emphasized that Jesús was a man of bad conduct, who had committed these types of crimes on more than one occasion. A witness for the plaintiff, twenty-eight-year-old widower Refugio Hernández, testified to Jesús's unsavory reputation, labeling him a serial womanizer who had cut Refugio's niece's face in Mexico City. Notably, in this instance, a male community member censured the womanizing and treachery of another man. The judge listened to various community members. Macaría's star witness, Manuela, swore she had seen Jesús talking with Juana several times in the doorway of her home, a sight akin to elite couples conversing from balcony to street, which implied a romantic liaison, but Manuela failed to sway the judge, who cast doubt on the testimony because Manuela was married to her own stepfather. Strangely, Juana never testified, but Jesús, a twenty-four-year-old button maker, expressed outrage at the false slander spread in his absence. He swore that he had left town on October 20 to attend a fiesta in Xoxotepec, a village several days away, and he did not return until November. The plaintiff alleged that the seduction and abduction had occurred on October 25, five days after he allegedly left town. He spent one day under arrest and then the judge released him, citing a lack of evidence.[27] In this case, the judge accepted witness testimony. However, he determined that the plaintiff lacked sufficient evidence, primarily because Macaria could not prove her daughter's age, and rapto laws were designed to protect virgins under sixteen years of age. Marcaria had originally said that Juana was sixteen or seventeen years old, but later, she recanted her statement, when she calculated that her daughter was eighteen months old when the earthquake of May 11, 1870, wracked the city, which would mean she was nineteen or twenty. Macaria was not the only parent to have trouble documenting a daughter's age. Many parents scrambled to obtain, if not civil birth certificates, at least baptismal records, but these held less weight with judges than did civil documents, because a baptism could occur months or even years after birth.

Reputation can be viewed as a form of capital for these working-class individuals. Their publicly affirmed character connoted their status and honor in the community. A young woman's reputation rested firmly on her sexual behavior and public comportment. In testifying, young women first assured the judge that they had "no kind of relations" previously with any man, in effect laying claim to respectability and their worthiness for protection by the law. Yet female honor did not rest solely on an intact hymen (virginity), especially among their peers. Indeed virginity and legal marriage may have been ideals, but not absolute realities for nineteenth-century Mexicans. Nonetheless, girls had to convince the judge that running off with men to have sex was not their usual pattern. They could do it once for love, a promise of marriage, and/or to escape abuse at home and expect to be protected by the court. Young women also emphasized their modest behavior in the street. For example, Josefa Calvo wrote to Manuel Vivas that even though she had to go out in public as a poor working girl she did not talk to strange men, thus staking her claim to honor and respectability.[28]

Slander and Honor

Gossip and hearsay uttered to denounce an individual's reputation could become slander, a crime that many working-class Oaxacans addressed in public and in court. For the most part, words of slander or insult even in rapto cases stressed a moral code that was sharply different for men and women. Women's honesty was delineated by their sexual behavior; men's, by the sexual purity of the women connected to them, as well as character traits like hard work and the ability to control their female family members. Yet sexual purity was not the only wellspring of honor for lower class women. Other attributes such as hard work, modesty, and good mothering served as additional foundations of working class honor. Adultery cases are particularly useful for unpacking the process of slander and the social harm it wrought in communities.

Francisca Soto accused her husband, José María Serna, of cohabiting with Carmen Velasco. Since Francisca denied him all the services of a wife, José María had sought the first opportunity to find an amasia. The couple settled for legal separation. The agreement required José to pay Francisca three reales per day for alimentos and to relinquish his custody of their three children.[29] Other women were not as lucky as Francisca when it came to being awarded alimony from their adulterous husbands.

Micaela Quiróz, a washerwoman, initiated adultery proceedings three times—in 1894, 1897, and 1899. In the first case, she supplied a marriage certificate and complained that her husband had abandoned her after sixteen years of marriage. The "other woman" testified that she entered into a relationship with Sebastián Robles because she thought he was single.[30] The public record does not show that Micaela received any compensation or Sebastián any punishment. Yet the act of initiating the complaint in court at the very least publicized her plight as an abandoned but honorable woman. Indeed, she emphasized her status as worker, businesswoman, and married citizen worthy of legal protection. Moreover, Micaela exacted a double whammy by pursuing the criminal case three times against her estranged husband and his amasia. The exposure of a court case not only harmed Sebastián's reputation, but the amasia's reputation probably suffered even more than that of the adulterous husband. Micaela must have seen her esteem rise by taking the step to protest her husband's adultery.

Doubtless, it was necessary for her to fight for her reputation as a washer-woman turned businesswoman.

The specter of sexual dishonor made slander an effective tool in the community and in court. It was so effective that defamed individuals were quick to prosecute their verbal tormentors. *Puta* (whore) was the most common slanderous insult against women but *ladrona* (thief) was another common charge that propelled working-class Oaxacans to seek legal redress. Ladrona could connote a thief of another woman's man or a woman who cheated customers. Ladrona and puta used in combination represented the summit of slanderous insults leveled at women by other women. Studies of sexual honor have undeniably shown that women stood on an uneven footing with men. Defamation of a woman's sexual honor could create irreparable injury to her status in the community. Yet when women wielded slanderous language, they employed a concept of honor that could empower them.[31] Ironically, it can also be argued that when women wielded words like "whore" against each other, they also perpetuated the uneven honor system. The community was not a community of sisters. It seems that women faced steep competition with other women over men, clients, and status in the community.[32] In fact, women pursued slander and insult cases in Oaxaca more than men did. They felt they needed to persistently defend their honor against the smallest slight, especially as working-class women, since they suffered the damage of dishonor more seriously than their elite counterparts, who were protected by privacy, concealment, and wealth.

Gossip and insult acted to police behavior and perpetuate community norms but also comprised more complex roots and motivations. The morals expressed in slander and insult certainly paralleled those of contemporary culture whether elite or plebeian, but they could also be creative manifestations of familiar moral teachings. The spectacle of the whore in popular culture and literature proved to be a potent symbol for slanderers. Most of these insults were leveled at women but sometimes their men were charged with being *padrotes* (pimps) through association.

In 1910, Petrona García complained to the court that Higinia Cruz had insulted and defamed her on the street in the presence of other women and a police officer. She testified that Higinia called her a disgraceful whore, a *soldadera* (camp follower), and Petrona's amasio a pimp who maintained her whoring.[33] The soldadera, while now regaled and promoted in Mexico's historical memory, had been a much maligned figure, a woman who followed the troops trading sex and food for the soldier's *diario* (daily wage). Women usually defended themselves in court, but sometimes husbands entered the courtroom as well to defend their wives. In one example, Encarnación Jiménez called Antonio Sánchez's wife a whore because she sold sweets in the streets. He produced the marriage certificate to prove their honor as a legally married couple to the court.[34] Again, by defending his wife's honor, he also defended his own. A man married to a "whore" had much to lose in public esteem because it implied he was a cuckold. Proving to the court that they were legally and civilly married also elevated their esteem in relation to other working-class couples, especially during the Porfiriato, which promoted civil marriage.

The marketplace was apparently a hotbed of gossip and a venue for slander, since market vendors initiated several complaints in court. In 1907, Manuela Ruiz complained that another vendor called her a whore and her husband a pimp in front of the other sellers and customers. Witnesses vouched for her testimony and the offender received a twenty-five-day sentence.[35] In the same market, a couple of years later, Carmen Castillo purchased cheese and visited her daughter, a bread seller, at her stall. She complained to the court that Isaura Chávez publicly insulted her in a very aggressive manner, finally telling her *"chingar a mi madre"* (to fuck my mother).[36] Another vendor from the same market, María Sánchez, initiated a slander case against two other vendors, Constantino Flores and Ysable Pacheco. She told the judge that she simply minded her own business and sold her peppers, but the offenders yelled at her, "Disgraceful whore, stepmother, thief, infertile, and no man in Etla would touch you."[37] Market vendors felt compelled to seek justice in court, since to acquiesce to the slander would diminish their reputation and harm their business. After all, who in the community would buy meat or fruit from a whore or thief? Slurs targeting women were almost always related to their sexuality and gender roles as wives or mothers. They were whores, infertile, or witches and stepmothers. The structure of insults against men and women played out in the courtroom testimonies of witnesses in the rapto dramas especially when participants attempted to dishonor or undermine another.

Witness Narratives

By asking leading questions, court officials certainly played a hand in shaping the narratives of witnesses and litigants. Yet participants also strategically crafted their personal testimonies. It is undeniable that several people can observe the same event and recount it with different facts and interpretations. However, witnesses and litigants provided testimony, communicated hearsay, and offered their own opinions about the facts and actors in the rapto dramas from a shared perspective of community mores.[38] For the most part, witnesses called in for the plaintiff or defendant provided testimonies that meshed with community norms. Moreover, with some important variations, witness narratives for both the plaintiff and the defendant matched contemporary societal expectations about morality, honor, and gender relations.

Logically, the authority of witness and litigant testimony depended on the ability to recount the dramatic facts of the courtship and elopement as well as the skill to appeal to common social expectations. In other words, these narratives had to make sense to the people in the courtroom and in the larger society. Plaintiffs had to link their daughter's seduction to the general plotline of the innocent girl deceived by a predatory seducer. On the other hand, the defendant and his witnesses had to portray the girl as sexually experienced, and hence, as a young woman unworthy of legal protection. This was the basic script of seduction as played out in the courtroom theater and, abstractly, in the consciousness of society. An alternate script was simply the "abduction" of the girl as a prelude to marriage and as a strategy to overcome parental objection. Playing to either script ensured that judges listened to both sides, because this script was also linked to legal formulas that advocated the reparation of the innocent girl's honor through marriage or financial compensation.

Courtship in Private and Public

Many of the witnesses who presented testimony in court were close friends or neighbors of one of the sweethearts. Courtship played out in the public arena of the community and often took place outside the young woman's home. These were not elite homes where parents invited suitors for refreshments and light conversation. Friends passed love letters or verbal messages from one of the lovers to the other. Neighbors noticed the pair chatting in the street. Others were confidantes and understood the couple's wish to marry or elope. Friends hid letters and gifts so parents would not find them. Some community members witnessed the flight of the young couple and knew their whereabouts and could keep it secret . . . or make it public. All in all, it was extremely difficult to carry on a serious relationship in strict privacy, and the community could easily enable or thwart the couple's dramatic plans to elope.

For example, José Inés Caballero's fifteen-year-old niece, Marcelina Robles, assisted him in his scheme to elope with one Candelaria. The niece found Candelaria in the plaza, and told her, "Come with me! My uncle is waiting for you with the burros."[39] She would later be charged as an accomplice to rapto. José Inés promised to take Candelaria to Tehuantepec and marry her. José Inés justified his actions, telling the judge that Candelaria felt bored at home and afraid of her stepfather, who constantly made sexual advances. He wanted to marry her before she was deflowered by him. Candelaria corroborated most of his testimony stating that she agreed to run off with José. The fugitives did not get far, as witnesses intervened and notified authorities. These individuals later became important witnesses in the trial, but the couple got their wish, as the judge closed the case when José swore he wanted to marry Candelaria.

A serious amorous relationship between two people could be solidified by the exchange of love tokens and a written or verbal promise of marriage. Public knowledge of the engagement remained a key component as well. The transition from private to public courtship and engagement was extremely important in the eyes of judges and the community. Court officials did not require evidence of a written contract of betrothal, but family members and peers had to publicly recognize an engagement for it to have validity.[40] Indeed, what may have begun as a private courtship quickly became public, especially as parents, neighbors, and servants scrutinized the behavior of virginal girls. For example, the maid of Señora Ramírez testified that even though she did not know "the type of relationship" that Melquiadez Barzalobre and Juana Silva had, she did notice that they talked frequently and that Juana voluntarily ran off with Melquiadez one afternoon. To the judge, this meant that the girl acquiesced to her seduction. Likewise, the presents she received from Melquiadez figured prominently in the court case, as Juana recounted that he had given her clothing, a rebozo, and candles. These artifacts constituted a serious relationship, although Juana testified that they had agreed only to an *amasiato* (consensual union).[41] Many of the witnesses attested to the exchange of prendas between the lovers, as this connoted a relationship that would lead to marriage, even if only far in the future.

As courtship moved toward plans for marriage, friends and family became crucial to its success or failure. If parents sanctioned the union, the marriage could occur without any problems. If parental objections existed, friends and family could assist the couple in achieving their aims.

The love affair of Josefa Calvo and Manuel Vivas illustrates this point. Her orphaned friend, Teresa, actually accompanied the lovers on their elopement and paid for their room. The three posed as siblings looking for posada, an act that otherwise might have been difficult for a solitary young couple. While Teresa slept in one room, Josefa and Manuel consummated their relationship in another. In this case, Teresa accompanied Josefa as they walked through the streets of the city to meet Manuel at the Church of the Soledad. Then the three walked north to the barrio of Xochimilco to rent a room for the night. Teresa also testified that she passed letters between Josefa and Manuel.[42]

In another case, Faustina Medina, a mother of one suitor, faced a charge of rapto in 1896 for "abducting" her son's girlfriend, Paula Jiménez, and bringing the girl back to her house for her son. In this case, the girl's parents objected to the match, and Faustina took the dramatic step of removing the young woman from her parent's home to compel them to change their minds.[43] Other mothers of desperate boyfriends intervened to protect the honor of the young girlfriends. Demetria of the Hacienda de Rosario had sent her fifteen-year-old daughter to work as a domestic in the city. She told the court that she had not heard from her daughter, Bibiana, in fifteen days, and that the *ama* (the lady in whose house Bibiana worked) had reported that the girl had run away one afternoon with a man who had been skulking around the house. Carlos admitted that he had taken Bibiana and brought her to his house, where he lived with his mother. Perceiving the grave consequences that the rapto would have for the young woman, his mother sent Carlos back to his place of work, telling him that he should sleep there with his coworkers. The mother testified that the girl slept with her, and the next day they took her to Bibiana's aunt's house. Bibiana corroborated the deposition and insisted that she was still a virgin.[44] The mother's presence during the elopement, as well as Carlos' absence from the home, certainly substantiated that Bibiana had remained honorable (virginal) as she had not been alone with an unrelated man.

Gifts and Money

Although the ritualistic exchange of gifts was a necessary precursor for marriage or amasiato, accepting food or money presented problems for single girls. Both connoted an illicit exchange—namely sex for a man's daily wage, or worse, prostitution. Gift exchanges were never refuted in court. Litigants acknowledged that they both gave and received prendas. Love letters, clothing, or jewelry represented romantic gifts that sealed the permanence of the relationship. Litigants and witnesses who testified to the exchange of love tokens supported the common expectation that ritual gift exchange between the betrothed and sometimes between their families solidified a commit-ment. Judges also looked at gifts as proof of a man's promise of marriage. However, to the couple, gifts could also constitute a commitment to cohabi-tate (consensual union). Juana and Melquiadez had such an arrangement. He gave her fabric, clothes, candles, and particularly food because Juana's mother did not support her. She stressed that her mother knew of these gifts, did not object to them, and for Juana, they were indications of their mutual decision to live together rather than to marry.[45] The testimonies rarely mentioned a girl's gifts to the boy. It was more important to know if gifts were given by the boy to the girl as it would obligate him to marry her.

Whether coached by court officials or not, many girls plainly stated that they did not receive money before their elopement or after sexual relations. For example, Narcisa Cortés and José García, both fifteen years of age, ran off together after her day of selling sweets by the Cathedral. She testified that she had had amorous relations with José for two months; José swore that it was only two days. Nevertheless, Narcisa stated that she left with José because her mother abused her and José had offered to marry her. She ada-mantly testified that she had not received money from José, an attempt to establish her honor. The defense attorney still labeled her a "*diabla*" (devil), and oddly, even though doctors concluded that Narcisa had lost her vir-ginity at an earlier date, the judge imprisoned José without explanation.[46] Perhaps it was the glaring inequity between the two families: Narcisa lived with her poor, single mother, whereas José hailed from a ranch outside of the city. Or perhaps it was his tender age of fifteen that compelled the judge to punish him, even though Narcisa was not a virgin and therefore unwor-thy of protection.

If a defendant could convince the judge that he had given a girl money before having sex, it would impugn the girl's reputation and influence the judge to drop the suit. Sometimes the girl's own admissions facilitated this. In 1897, sixteen-year-old Carmen Carreño walked one afternoon to the spot where she sold scarves. There she crossed paths with José Arías, her sweet-heart for the past year. He convinced her to follow him up the hill to a small rented room. When she went inside, she saw a bottle of liquor and a *petate* (sleeping mat) on the floor. She incriminated herself by admitting that she imbibed alcohol even though it was only after he persistently beseeched her to drink. Once inebriated, she agreed to have sex with him after he prom-ised to marry her. He then left while she was sleeping in the room. She brought the case of deflowering to the court herself, claiming to have been deceived with false promises and alcohol.

José had a dual strategy in his testimony. He first admitted that he had promised to marry her, thereby following the traditional pattern of betrothal. José confessed that they drank mescal together and had sexual intercourse, but he exonerated his actions with the usual defense: He had discovered that Carmen was not the virgin she claimed to be. So, he paid her a few pesos and left her. Noting that he paid her after sex could absolve him of any responsibility by making her appear to be a prostitute or, at least, a sexually experienced woman.[47]

A gift of money could also have different meanings for the involved parties. In 1857, seventeen-year-old María López testified that she had a one-year friendship with Don Manuel Noriega, a twenty-six-year-old philosophy scholar. She swore that she ran away with him because he promised to marry her. He took her to a house where they had sex for the first time. Since consummating the relationship, Noriega had given her two reales a day, and she fully expected him to keep his promise of marriage. When he failed to do that, she initiated the charge of rapto herself. In contrast, Noriega argued that he indeed gave her money and other gifts, but he said he never promised to marry her. In his eyes, their exchange of gifts and money for sex made her his *querida* or mistress. The judge agreed and dropped the case.[48] Money carried a lot of currency in society and in the courtroom. An exchange of money for sex between individuals could be likened to prostitution. Yet, amasiatos or consensual unions also involved an exchange of money or alimentos for access to female sexuality.

Indeed, economic realities combined with love and romance to figure prominently in decisions to elope or marry. The economic viability of the union was important to the betrothed, their parents, and the state. Marriage usually required a fiesta and then setting up a household. An amasiato required less money up front, and many couples lived consensually with the idea that they would marry when they had saved the needed financial resources. In fact, Francisco Mimiago told Primitiva Franco that they could not marry because he lacked the *recursos* (financial resources).[49] Matias Hernández also testified that he lived with his girlfriend and could not marry her because he lacked the funds.[50] In another case, nineteen-year-old Francisca, a domestic servant, brought a case of rapto against her boyfriend. They had often talked about their plans for marriage. One day she met him on the corner, and he led her to a room and then forcibly deflowered her. She presented the complaint to the court with the hope that the judge would compel Teofilo to marry her. Teofilo contradicted Francisca's testimony. He argued that they had had a two-year relationship. Although he had promised to marry her, he never forced her to have sex with him. He stated that he wanted to marry her, but lacked the money to do so. Nevertheless, in the courtroom, he offered to marry her within six months. Francisca's mother intervened and negotiated the term down to four months and she made it clear that she would initiate a new suit if he did not keep his word.[51] The case ends there. For Teofilo, Matías, and Francisco, a lack of funds could be an excuse, but it is more likely that this was the reason they chose an amasiato over marriage, at least until they could save the money for the wedding party, marriage fees, and costs of setting up a household. It should be noted that these men hailed from the working classes, laboring as a button maker, miner, and hatmaker, respectively.

Parents sometimes rejected suitors because they had no reliable income to provide a home and security for the daughter.[52] In fact, a common way that the girl's parents impugned the man's intentions was by questioning his ability to provide support. Josefa Calvo's mother made it clear that she highly doubted Manuel Vivas's ability to support her daughter, and she even called him a vagrant and implied that he did not earn a consistent income.[53] In their decisions, judges probably evaluated a young man's prospects for supporting a new family, as well. When it seemed that a couple could survive together on their own, judges also sanctioned their relationship by dropping the rapto case if both agreed to marry, a union that could take place at some indeterminate time in the future.

Bodies and Spaces: The Gestures and Scenes of Courtship

Gifts were only one indication of a betrothal. Litigants and witnesses have regularly testified to the physical and spatial expressions of courtship, especially remarking on the physical affection and gestures of young couples. Indeed courting couples ate off the same plate, fed each other, or played games together. One witness called in to testify in an 1869 case about the seduction of fifteen-year-old Atitana Cazonla observed something significant. She saw Vicente Jiménez purchase food from a street vendor and proceed to eat with Atitana off the same plate. To her and many others, this signified a level of intimacy appropriate to family members or lovers.[54] Witnesses also testified to seeing the couple drink alcohol together, another sign of romantic closeness. In 1887, in the case of José Ruiz and Margarita Morales, witnesses emphasized that the couple purchased mescal together, an act that signified a sexual relationship. They further swore that the couple behaved amiably together, thereby suggesting that Margarita accompanied her seducer willingly. In the eyes of the community, a woman who drank alcohol with a man also had sexual relations with him.[55]

Besides eating food off the same plate or imbibing spirits together, peers also described specific articles of clothing or body parts as symbolic of a sexual relationship, whether forced or consensual. If a man folded a woman in his serape, it symbolized sexual possession, as one witness remarked when she saw Teofila wrapped in a man's poncho outside a pulquería. Allegedly the man was inebriated and attempted to force the young girl. She escaped, and the man was charged with attempted deflowering.[56] Importantly, eye witnesses stressed that she was rendered immobile in his serape, an article of male clothing that connoted sexual intimacy or danger. A man's belt and hat also represented symbols of masculinity and their removal, sexual intentions. Ángela Ramírez described Aniceto Ramos's intention to ravish her in 1852, noting that he threw his sombrero on the ground and yanked off his belt. Luckily her mother arrived just in the nick of time, wielding a knife to fight off the would-be attacker.[57]

The rebozo or shawl showed up often as a sexual symbol or as evidence in the cases. Rebozos signified femininity and modesty. Women wore rebozos wrapped around their shoulders and upper arms to cover themselves, and mothers carried their babies in them. Some daring couples had sex under a rebozo as a measure of privacy even when in public.[58] Walking the street without a rebozo seemed scandalous to some, as it implied nakedness or vulnerability. Fifteen-year-old Trinidad Vásquez testified that two women in the neighborhood, Ramona García and Concepción Vargas, came to her home and told her they could get her a job working as a domestic for three pesos per month if she would just come with them immediately to arrange everything. She expressed concern about leaving without her mother's permission but reluctantly went with them anyway. When they arrived at another home, they locked her in the bedroom for two hours and took her rebozo, knowing that because she could not be seen without it, she would not attempt to escape.[59]

In an 1879 case, Manuela Mendoza conspired to help her friend Adelaida Cervantes elope with Benito Meixueire. Neighbors testified to seeing Manuela holding a bundle wrapped in a rebozo and Adelaida accompanying her, uncovered. The witnesses realized that two things were amiss. First, one of the girls' possessions was concealed in the rebozo and, second, Adelaida immodestly went out into the street without her rebozo covering her shoulders. They assumed that the two of them were accomplices in a scandalous act.[60]

Young women also testified that men grabbed them by the rebozo or by their braids to initiate the rapto. This act of grabbing also euphemistically meant that force was used in their abduction and deflowering. Casimira began her narrative of seduction by stating that her boyfriend grabbed her by the rebozo.[61] In a particularly dramatic case, a thirty-two-year old married woman, Mariana Hernández, defended her lover and countered charges that he had abducted her by force. Notably, to emphasize that she was not forcibly abducted, she told the judge that Joaquín did not pull off her rebozo, an act her husband had stressed when attempting to convey that force played a role in the event.[62] Her husband, Fernando García, and twelve-year-old daughter, María, were principal plaintiffs in this 1886 case of rapto and force against Joaquín Chávez, a twenty-four-year-old with a violent criminal history. According to the father and daughter, the family was walking home to their village one evening when four men assaulted them as they reached Mariano Lázaro's milpa. One of the men draped his arm around Fernando and told him, "Don't mess with these men; don't get involved." Two assailants wielded large sticks and taunted, "Are you brave? We will see!" Then, Joaquín grabbed Mariana by the rebozo and her daughter and ran off waving a knife. The father pointed out that the abductor hit his daughter in the face several times with a stick, injuring her. The aggrieved husband appealed to the mayor of Tlalixtac, who managed to apprehend a couple of the assailants but not the main target of Fernando's wrath. The husband, in court, admitted that Mariana had had sex with Joaquín on three occasions but, he claimed, not willingly, and he had forgiven her each time. As the case moved to the Oaxaca courts, the police apprehended Joaquín, who admitted to running off with Mariana, but he swore that she went with him voluntarily, as they were amasias. Probably in an attempt to justify his bold actions, he also testified that he did not remember everything that transpired, as he had drunk a lot of mescal, tepache, and aguardiente (alcoholic beverages). He also admitted that he had been arrested for assault before and sentenced to fifteen months, but he escaped incarceration. Mariana, Fernando's wife, testified last. Also pleading drunkenness, she claimed not to know how her daughter came to be injured during the abduction. She also stated that she was Joaquín's amasia, and on hearing this, her estranged husband dropped the charges.

It is clear that a rebozo ensured a woman's modesty when she went out in public, and its trespass also connoted sexual danger. Litigants and witnesses attested frequently to braid-pulling by the men to connote that they took the girls by force.[63] Men brandished knives, grabbed rebozos, and pulled on braids in the script of male sexual treachery, according to women of the rapto dramas. It is interesting that the terms rebozo and *trenzas* (braids) show up in many cases. If a man wanted to grab a woman, the rebozo or braids may have been a likely and effective target to overpower her. Yet, their symbolic meaning warrants further attention. Indeed, as noted earlier, community members publicly shamed women by cutting off their braids.[64] Male coworkers could react violently if one touched the other man's face or beard.[65] Clearly the head was a bodily representation of honor. In some rapto cases, a mother would lament that her daughter's suitor had a reputation as someone who cut women's faces. In two cases, girls claimed that they eloped with their boyfriends because they threatened to cut the girls' faces.[66] When a man scarred a woman's face or cut her hair, he marked her as an immoral and dominated woman. For some girls, abduction may have seemed less ominous than having their faces cut, marking them forever as disgraced women—a broken hymen was easier to conceal than a scarred face.

Men pulled women through the street by their braids. They grabbed the girls' rebozos as they tried to run away or wrapped them in their serapes to express affection, immobilize them, or claim sexual ownership. Onlookers witnessed these actions on the street. The street may have connoted a public arena of potential dishonor but it was in public spaces that girls rendezvoused with their suitors. The marketplace in particular was a site of peril but also opportunity. Ángela and Juana, discussed previously, both sold products in the marketplace and fled the site with their lovers. Ángela worked alongside her mother selling meat but once, when sent on an errand to purchase *enaguas* (underskirts), she seized the moment to take a walk with Aniceto. Although she refused to enter a pulquería with him, she willingly accompanied him to the river where her mother would later find her.[67] The market provided an escape route for Dolores Chagoya. She had left home with her eight-year-old brother to shop for food. Instead of taking him with her all the way, she told her brother to wait for her in the doorway of the Temple of San Juan de Dios. He stood there for hours but grew suspicious when a certain Francisco García walked by. A friend of the family also passed by, and the young boy, Enrique, asked her to alert his father. The boy stayed put until his father collected him. After a brief search through the marketplace that failed to turn up Dolores, he hurried to the court to file a charge of rapto against Francisco. Neighbors came forward to offer their opinions. They told the father that Francisco and Dolores had been alone in a part of his house, and they believed that she had lost her virginity to him more than a year ago.

Their testimony foiled the father's quest for justice, as the judge ruled that the case did not merit proceeding with an investigation.[68] In this instance, although witnesses testified for the father, they ended up spoiling his case, as the judge decided that since the daughter had presumably lost her virginity sometime earlier, no crime had occurred.

Although not a distinct physical space, running errands morphed into an act of rebellion for many girls. Venturing out of the house on an errand provided an opportunity to meet a loved one to exchange letters, steal a kiss, have sex, or even elope. One brave young woman, Julia Alcalá, admitted that she left home in 1876 on the pretext of delivering some clothes to a neighbor. Instead, she visited Romulo at the carpentry shop where he worked. She then agreed to accompany him to the river Ayotac, where "he enjoyed her." She attested that she was not a virgin when she left home, because a certain Antonio had taken her virginity some months earlier. Her mother thought she had been abducted, when in reality, Julia had sought refuge in her comadre's home because she feared her mother would beat her.[69] Fathers of Casimira Montaño and Soledad Blanco sent them out to buy sugar and candles, respectively, and grew worried when their daughters failed to return home. Instead of buying sugar, in this 1889 case, Casimira took the three pesos her father had given her and fled with Gaspar, a man from Teotitlán de Valle. They went to Jalatlaco, an eastern neighborhood of Oaxaca City. Casimira and Gaspar wanted to marry, but her parents and grandparents had rejected her suitor. Casimira's parents filed a rapto charge with the court against Gaspar. Doctors ruled that the couple had not consummated relations, and Gaspar Lázaro promised to marry Casimira, which resulted in the judge dropping the charge. In the end, the elopement planned on pretense of running an errand successfully earned the couple the right to marry.[70] Fifteen-year-old Soledad, on the other hand, stole away with her boyfriend, José Martínez, to the atrium of Temple of the Guadalupe. In this 1887 case, the young girl and the seventeen-year-old carpenter had sex three times in the atrium and vowed that they would marry. They did in fact wed three months later, as a marriage certificate was inserted into the court file.[71]

As seen here, church grounds served as another convenient space where lovers could engage in courtship. Church properties had historical significance as they had been important rallying sites for village rebellions in earlier times, and they were important landmarks to describe where particular events took place.[72] They were also official and legitimate spaces in their daily lives as individuals marked important moments in their life course, including baptism, first communion, marriage, and death. Telling of time revolved around the nightly *oración* (prayers), and it could be used to mark the timing of an elopement. Besides the chance to meet a lover at mass, a few couples even consummated their love on church property (like Soledad and José above). More commonly they met on church grounds as a starting point of their elopement. Josefa Calvo and Manuel Vivas, discussed briefly above, met at the Church of La Soledad before they rented a room and sealed their relationship.[73] Pascuala Camarillo and Simona Selís met their sweethearts at mass.[74] Margarita Fernández also arranged to meet Agustín Robles at a saint's day festival. He had been living in Mexico City and returned to town to arrange for their marriage. Meeting in the crowd of the festival allowed them a semblance of privacy amidst the throngs of festival goers. This couple was successful in marrying some months later.[75]

If we return to the real-life saga of Carmen and Inocente that initiated this chapter, several themes emerge. Many of the rapto trials became a scenario of "he said, she said, they said." Witnesses, whether neighbors or bystanders, played important roles in the private lives of couples who were dragged into court to face criminal prosecution. Courtships were public affairs and closely watched and commented on by all who witnessed it. Individuals noted signs of romance—the exchange of gifts and affectionate murmurings—and gestures of sexual possession—grabbing a woman's rebozo or wrapping her in a serape. They provided eyewitness testimony that a boy and a girl had conversed in the street, a doorway, or in the cemetery, as was the case for Carmen and Inocente. These conversations implied a relationship, and the community took notice. Witnesses warned that one or the other had a bad reputation in the community. Sometimes bystanders rescued girls in peril. Carmen's friends contradicted each other in their telling of events that led to her ravishment. Inocente's friends tried valiantly, whether they lied or not, to paint Carmen as a rash and calculating young vixen. Older villagers gossiped about the failure of the municipal president to adequately punish the young man. Carmen held fast to the traditional script—that she never acquiesced in going with Inocente. Rather, he forced her even when she resisted. When rituals seemed to have been violated the community sprang into action. They were more than willing to impugn the character of either boy or girl if they felt that the limits of community mores had been breached.

Finally, the exchanges of gossip and information, the surveillance of female sexuality, and the rituals of courtship unfolded in spaces that were both germane and symbolic in individuals' lives. Whether churchyard or marketplace, public spaces could be sites of romance, rebellion, and censure in the lives of Mexicans who had not yet reached their majority. Courtship was rarely a private affair. Unfortunately for Inocente, he was one of the few defendants who earned a prison term, for four years. The judge did not offer a reason. The facts that Inocente had stated that he was unwilling to marry Carmen and doctors determined that he had deflowered her may have influenced the judge in making his decision. In that case, the defendant had to pay even though witness testimony suggested that the victim had engineered the entire escapade. If it were possible to know each family's relative standing in the village that might have shed some light on the outcome of this particular case. Carmen's father may have been an important man in the community and able to influence the judge's decision to punish the young musician. The next chapter leaves the arena of the community and enters the courtroom, where parents, children, and state officials negotiated the parameters of appropriate sexuality and the parent-child bond.

CHAPTER FIVE

Disobedient Daughters and the Liberal State

Generational Conflicts over Marriage Choice

ॐ

For two years in a row, 1885 and 1886, Señora Teresa Montiel, a native of Oaxaca de Juárez, pleaded with the court to prosecute her daughter's suitors. The first time after seeing her thirteen-year-old daughter, Primitiva Franco, chatting with Juan Noriega in the street and finding his love letter in her home, she grew suspicious. When Primitiva disappeared around seven in the evening that same day, she hurried to the police station to accuse the young man of seducing and taking the girl. Primitiva testified that she was sixteen-years-old and had run away to her aunt's home because she feared her mother's wrath at discovering the love letter. She further stated that she had broken up with Juan some weeks earlier and that they had never had sexual relations.[1] The following year, Primitiva eloped with a different man, and her mother surfaces in the historical record again. This time she testified that she saw her daughter talking with Francisco Mimiago in the doorway of Teresa's house. After Primitiva ran away with Francisco, Teresa testified that he came by her house saying that "he took Primitiva because he was a man."[2] In both cases, Primitiva's mother asked the judge to prosecute her daughter's seducers to the full extent of the law, arguing that Primitiva lacked the maturity to choose her mate wisely. Police officers apprehended both young men, and they were charged with rapto in Oaxaca de Juárez's municipal court. In the second case, the judge sided with Señora Teresa's minor daughter, in effect emancipating her from parental authority by allowing her to begin family life with Francisco. As the preceding chapters have revealed, rapto could be a ritual step towards marriage or a ruse to force parental consent for the union. What is ironic is that judges actually fostered rapto as a preliminary step to a civil union and the emancipation of minors, even as official rhetoric was calling for the modernization of traditional and archaic Mexican customs, especially during the Porfiriato. The jurists condoned a traditional practice of bride stealing, and by siding with minors against parents, they also promoted liberal values of individualism and freedom. Our story continues to highlight how the advocates of civil legislation interacted and negotiated with parents and their minor charges over legal emancipation, family formation, and the boundaries of parental authority and filial obedience.

Rapto cases brilliantly illustrate the contentious nature of the parent-child relationship, as parents in the case files most often complained that daughters eloped because they refused to allow young people to wed. Notions of childhood changed over time and by the end of the nineteenth century an emerging concept of adolescence began to coalesce. Significantly, judges evaluated the rapto cases with care and considered the nascent rights of minor children. Of course, law and notions of *patria potestad* (legal authority of the patriarch) changed from the late colonial period to the early twentieth century in Mexico. A society's set of laws reveal plenty about that social order and how at least the state viewed parental authority and obligations vis-à-vis children.

Working-class parents like Primitiva's mother turned to the courts to manage rebellious children and contest their decisions to move out of the house to live with their boyfriends. Other parents pleaded legal cases to ensure that their daughters' suitors fulfilled their promises of marriage. Generational conflicts proved particularly serious in elopement cases, as many parents lamented that their adolescent children could not make mature judgments over the very important life-course decision of marriage. This was demonstrated when a parent leveled insults at a suitor in an attempt to impugn his reputation and prove that the young man was unworthy to marry the daughter. In practical terms, poor families also relied on each member's contribution, so losing a minor child's financial input when he or she married could spell economic hardship for a family, especially those headed by single mothers. Likewise, working-class families could not "shelter" their daughters.[3] Many young girls worked outside the home as domestic servants or marketplace vendors, or they ran errands for their working parents. Their presence in public places made them vulnerable to assault and deceit but also provided opportunities to carry on a romantic relationship and to rendezvous with their lovers. Certainly working-class parents had more difficulty in supervising and protecting their adolescent children under these circumstances, but as the previous chapter revealed, neighbors could certainly provide helpful intelligence.

At cursory glance, it seems that middle-class and elite professionals administered the judicial system to promote their agenda: to control what they viewed as unruly and unacceptable behaviors of working-class youth and their parents. Yet, rather than accept a social control thesis that looks at criminal records with a top-down approach to class and gender relations, we ought to view the various actors in the elopement dramas—children, parents, witnesses, medical personnel, and court officials—as actively participating in and negotiating an intricate web of struggles over sexuality, marriage, paternal and state authority, and children's rights and obligations.[4] Untangling this fascinating web of social relations reveals that, in truth, the elite had only a superficial interest in extirpating rapto and archaic courtship practices. Instead, their exoneration of male defendants and denial of parental wishes promoted the values of liberalism, including individuality and personal freedom. They wanted couples to marry and form families, but they required no proof of that marriage, perhaps because they realized that consensual unions were an appropriate (although it was to be hoped, only transitional) relationship for working-class couples. Indeed, judges only meted out fines and jail sentences to the seven of the 212 male defendants. In the end, the court perpetuated rather than discouraged the dramatic courtship practice of rapto among young working-class Mexicans.

The Social Construction of Childhood in Latin America

Scholars have valiantly attempted to reconstruct the lives of Latin America's children from a dearth of sources.[5] Much of what we know about children comes from official documents, including the papers of charitable organizations, such as *casas de cuna* (orphanages) and welfare institutions.[6] Occasionally, children's voices also emerge in criminal documents, as evidenced by the adolescent testimonies in the rapto cases. Yet, this did not mean that the elite neglected or ignored child welfare. The colonial Church singled out Indian children for special attention, and as early as the eighteenth century, the Crown displayed concern about the growing number of orphans in Latin American society. During the colonial period, patria potestad gave order to the family by guiding the relationship between a patriarch and his children. This system provided stability for society and the thirteenth-century authors of the Siete Partidas (seven-part law code) went to great lengths to outline procedures for marriage, inheritance, and other matters of family life.

Viewing childhood as a distinct phase in an individual's life cycle was the first step to conceptualizing Mexico's children as individuals worthy of expanded rights and concerns. The Spanish elite viewed children differently than did their European counterparts. Influenced by Jean Jacques Rousseau, European intellectuals believed infants and children were born innocent, without "ambition or social prejudices." Radical in his time, Rousseau proposed in his writings that the child was born in a state of innocence but vulnerable to the vagaries of "prejudices, authority, necessity, example, all the social institutions in which we find ourselves submerged."[7] He described the stages of childhood, noting that children possessed their own way of experiencing the world and that nature, rather than adults, ought to guide them. Later Romantics expanded on Rousseau's conception of childhood and depicted the child as a possessor of deep wisdom and morality, an individual who by their unadulterated nature could actually teach their parents a great deal about life.[8] Latin America came late to this view of children but nevertheless considered childhood as a distinctly different stage of life. No longer was the child considered a mini-adult or an apprentice to adulthood. A 1734 Spanish dictionary defined infancy and youth essentially as preparatory stages to adulthood. The Siete Partidas displayed a rudimentary concept of childhood by noting that individuals under the age of ten years and six months could not be tried in court. Minors between ages ten and a half and seventeen who committed crimes could be tried in court but still did not face the same level of punishment as adults. It was at that age range that minors supposedly knew the difference between moral and immoral actions but also deserved a lighter punishment for their crimes. Minors from ages seventeen to twenty-five also required a representative in court, but their penalty could equal that of adult criminals, since it was believed that at that advanced age, they possessed the maturity to know right from wrong.[9]

It has been argued that the Latin American elite's preoccupation with children is not a new phenomenon of the post-Independence period but rather one that manifested particularly in the nineteenth century when the elite became more interested in the welfare of children, as evidenced by the plethora of educational reforms and welfare institutions that emerged in many nations during the liberal era. This cultural change came about when the state ceased viewing children as minors simply needing education and protection, and instead saw them as "capable of actively confronting difficult situations and raising their voices, emphasizing their character as independent people with their own rights."[10] Thus, the clear delineation of childhood as an important life cycle stage coincided with the appreciation of children as actors, not mere receptacles for adult lessons and demands. Politicians and intellectuals also began to delineate a particular stage of childhood that would later be called adolescence.

Although terminology such as "childhood" and "adolescence" gradually entered the nineteenth-century Mexican lexicon, Rousseau's innocent child was nowhere to be seen. Official documents and attention centered on the problematic child: the juvenile delinquent, the abandoned orphan, the sickly child. The happy and healthy child did not evoke state intervention.[11] Not coincidently, these "problematic" children were from the popular classes, the very social group the liberal state targeted for their various reform and disciplinary programs.[12] In continuity with the colonial period, the state desired that families be harmonious, corporate entities, and they saw little reason to intervene unless they perceived that children were in danger or their actions jeopardized public order. Many scholars point out the state's rhetoric spoke to protecting children, but more accurately, its actions and programs reflected the primary concern of defending family honor and state prerogative.[13]

Clearly, in Latin America the nineteenth century heralded a watershed for new thinking about childhood, and this significantly affected the sanctity of patria potestad in family relationships. While a fundamental tension between Crown and family or the state and family has always existed, after independence and as Mexico consolidated as a liberal state, civil codes had the effect of weakening patria potestad and sanctioning the increased intrusion of the state into the private lives of families. Family life became a public arena where the state and individuals fought and parlayed over formerly ecclesiastical matters, such as marriage, birth, and the parent-child bond. In Mexico, liberal jurists pushed educational reforms, wrote new civil codes, promoted hygiene and eugenics, sought to understand criminality, and effectively transformed the relationship between the state and families, in particular, working-class families. Jurists focused their attention on mothers in an effort to promote patriotic or civic motherhood (see chapter 2). In their minds, exalting motherhood and training good mothers would lead to healthy generations of hardworking Mexicans.[14] Concurrent with their preoccupation with motherhood, the state viewed childhood as a distinct phase of life and did not hesitate to breach private home life to act as a surrogate parental authority, especially in poor families.[15]

The Development of Civil Law and the Reorganization of Family Power

Civil codes provide a window through which we can view changes over time in the laws regulating power within families and gauge legal prescriptions for the parent-child relationship. It is especially important to measure changes over time since the Mexican elite replaced ecclesiastical laws with secular legislation that regulated private life. After the foundation of Mexico as a republic and the planned and programmed secularization of society, politicians wrote civil codes that governed marriage, divorce, inheritance, and birth inside and outside of marriage, arenas that the Church formerly supervised. Colonial Hispanic law viewed the father or patriarch as the sovereign over his "subjects" (wife, children, servants, and slaves), although these personal relationships varied widely in practice. Wives, in particular, wielded private power within the household, and they could appeal to the courts and to the community to censure husbands who mistreated or abandoned them.[16] Patriarchs ruled over their families much as a king ruled over his kingdom, ideally with firm benevolence. In theory, single minor women and wives lived out their entire lives under patriarchal control. When a female child married, her tutelage transferred from father to husband, or to convent if she entered a religious order. Late colonial Hispanic law "circumscribed" the patriarch's power over wife and children. Fathers no longer had control over married children, and a father did not have the right to kill an adulterous daughter or sell his children in cases of extreme poverty.[17] The notion of patria potestad derived from Roman, Visigothic, and canon laws, but its application varied from locale to locale. The Spanish Crown desired uniformity but in reality, *audiencias* (district courts) applied laws differently. For example, in 1787, the Spanish king gave viceroys and presidents of district courts the authority to sanction marriages that parents objected to, but in Argentina, the district court chose to side with the parents rather than the children.[18]

By the second half of the nineteenth century, Mexico's civil codes heralded the unambiguous intervention of the state in family life. Mexico did not have its first national civil code promulgated until 1871, thus before that date, most Mexican judges relied on colonial-era laws to rule on family and domestic conflicts concerning inheritance and patria potestad. Between Mexico's independence in 1821 and 1871, "the imparting of justice and resolution of conflicts" in families operated under similar processes to the colonial period.[19] Indeed, the 1870 Civil Code for the Federal District and the Territory of Baja California, promulgated in 1871, incorporated most of the colonial laws that had excluded women from politics, maintained the sexual double standard, and reinforced patriarchal control over wife and children. However, it allowed for some weakening of the patriarch's absolutism. For example, the code granted single mothers who recognized their children patria potestad and allowed widows some parental authority over their children, a situation now codified but that some women had won through individual legal challenges in earlier eras. The code also granted the right to a divorce by mutual consent.[20]

The History of Oaxaca's Civil Codes

Oaxacan jurists created Latin America's first civil code in 1827–1828, under-lining the state's role as a crucible of Mexican liberalism.[21] Oaxaca enacted a second civil code in 1852, long before the nation's capital had its own in place.[22] Components of these civil codes inspired and influenced *Proyecto de Código Civil*, a body of legislation that Justo Sierra penned for the fed-eral district in 1861 at the request of liberal politician and Oaxacan native, Benito Juárez. In 1870, it was enacted as the *Código Civil del Distrito Federal y Territorio de Baja California*, and most states adopted the statute. Oaxaca joined other Mexican states in adopting the national code. Federal officials revised the code in 1884, and it remained in force until 1915.[23]

Oaxaca's Civil Code of 1827–1828, written during the time of partisan pol-itics in Oaxaca City, was progressive on women's rights in comparison with Nuevo Febrero and the 1870 Code.[24] However, it fell short on the issue of widow's right over children. Although they all recognized the importance of giving widows some control over their children, only the 1850 *Nuevo Febrero Mexicano* (a predecessor of Justo Sierra's 1861 Civil Code project) advocated giving the widow patria potestad even if she remarried.[25] The 1827–1828 Oaxacan code rescinded a widow's parental authority if she remarried and further restricted her ability to administer her children's property by man-dating the consent of a council comprised of local authorities and surviving family members. The code also allowed the father to name in his will a male advisor with whom his widow was obligated to consult when making deci-sions regarding their children.[26]

Oaxaca's 1827–1828 code required that children seek the father's *and* mother's approval for marriage, but if the parents disagreed, only the father's consent was necessary. Although the other two codes (Nuevo Febrero and the 1870 Code) gave patria potestad to legally separated mothers, the Oaxaca code also conferred it on the wife in her husband's absence. However the spirit of extending patria potestad to women in these carefully delineated cases did not endow them with public authority but merely domestic power over their children. In all three codes discussed, women could now defend themselves in a criminal suit without their husband's approval, but women were also required to get permission to accept encumbered or unencumbered inheritances. Specific to Oaxaca and reflective of the large proportion of female shopkeepers and market vendors, Oaxacan female entrepreneurs could enter into legal contracts related to their business without the authorization of their husbands.[27] Finally, the code recognized that respectable women over the age of fifty could be suitable guardians to unrelated children. This designation essentially recognized respectable, older women's capacity for "public ministries," and perhaps it was indicative of the prevalence of households headed by older women in Oaxaca.[28]

Regarding children, the 1827–1828 Oaxaca code allowed them more autonomy than did the other codes. Although the code set the age of majority for both genders at twenty-one, sons had to seek consent for marriage until age twenty-five, and daughters, age twenty-three. An additional article suggests that out of respect, adult children should always seek their parent's counsel and consent to contract marriage.[29] In addition, the code expanded the independence of children by prohibiting parents' usufruct rights over minor children's independently earned income.[30] Boys who were at least twenty-one and girls who were at least nineteen and who were not legally recognized, or whose parents had died or had refused consent for a marriage, were obligated to seek permission from the mayor or from an *ad hoc* tutor named by community authorities.[31] As was true in the colonial era, Oaxaca's first civil code maintained the power of an official, now the governor rather than the priest, to marry minors without the parents' consent.[32] The idea, in continuity with colonial practice, promoted the free will of sons and daughters to make their own marriage choices. This provision disappeared in later civil codes.

Oaxaca's first civil code continued the Greco-Roman tradition of noting different stages of childhood: infancy, from birth to seven years; *impuberes* (nonpubescent), from seven through thirteen; and *puberes* (pubescent), from fourteen to twenty-one.[33] It may be argued that the "puberes" noted in the civil code was akin to a newly emerging category of adolescence—a period when a person is no longer a child but is as yet not endowed with the full rights and responsibilities of an adult. These individuals, who had passed through puberty but had not fully matured in mind and body, were still a protected group. Although they could be prosecuted and held responsible for crimes, they were not punished the same as adults. Indeed, the law punishing rapto reinforces this notion. The law protected a girl under the age of sixteen if she had been seduced without violence by a man. However, if the girl was not a virgin, she was then categorized as an adult in terms of her sexuality, and she lost her right to the court's protection but without gaining the civil rights and autonomy that would come with majority. Girls, virgins or not, still had to seek parental permission to marry until the age of twenty-one. The code also dictated that with parental consent, sons could marry at age fourteen and daughters at age twelve, again reinforcing the notion of a transitional stage of adolescence between childhood and adulthood that recognized a limited level of maturity.

Further evidence of an emerging category of adolescence exists with Oaxaca's modifications to the national penal code. In 1887, jurists in that state revisited Mexico's national 1871 penal code, which had been adopted as Oaxaca's code, and they made some notable changes in the levels of punishment for certain crimes. Importantly, jurists desired to reconcile the penal and civil codes by raising the age of *estupro inmaturo* (deflowering of a pre-pubescent girl) from ten to twelve years. The national code categorized the severity of the crime based on the victim's age: younger than ten, older than ten but younger than fourteen, and older than fourteen. Punishment of the perpetrator lessened as the victim's age increased across the three categories. Oaxaca jurists emphasized that they recognized a difference between a twelve-year-old and fourteen-year-old girl, as the first might not be pubescent but the second was plainly pubescent and therefore more developed physically and morally. Moreover, the Oaxacan jurists note that the national codes inferred that girls under ten could consent to sexual relations, something they believed to be impossible. Therefore, the Oaxacan modifications determined that if a girl under age twelve had been deflowered, the punishment would be equal to rape and would merit a prison sentence of ten years instead of eight years, that was provided for by the national code. In the spirit of harmonizing the civil and penal codes for the state, Oaxacan politicians essentially extended the age of childhood for minor girls.[34]

Overall, Latin America's first civil code reflected the Oaxacan elite's penchant for liberalism and secularism. It widened an individual's guarantees by especially defending male citizens against the excesses of public power. Yet, it also allowed for greater rights for certain women, especially for widows and women over fifty years of age. Moreover, the congress at the time issued decrees that created the Escuela Normal del Estado in 1824 and the Sociedad de Amigos de los Niños in 1825. Ortiz-Urquidi contends that these decrees were the first institutional efforts in Mexico to significantly protect infancy.[35] Certainly, their creation supports the idea that children and their well-being were important to Oaxaca's liberal jurists.

The 1827–1828 Civil Code was replaced by the now-lost 1852 Code. It, in turn, was replaced with a code based on the 1870 Civil Code for the Federal District. This new code conferred patria potestad on the father and obligated him to provide alimentos (food, clothing, shelter, and education) to his children. The code continued colonial patriarchal prerogatives, sanctioning the father to rule over and punish his children with moderation and to enjoy usufruct rights to a child's remuneration.

The history of civil legislation in Mexico and Oaxaca reveals liberal politicians concern about what constituted legitimate families and the limits of parental authority over their children. The tone and provisions of the codes changed over time, but they are consistent in laying out guidelines for the parent-child relationship as well as for inheritance, succession, and division by classification of heir. Oaxaca produced Mexico's first civil code, a body of legislation that reflected liberal ideals from the state that produced two of Mexico's liberal presidents, Benito Juárez and Porfirio Díaz. Civil codes also provided judges and parties to the rapto cases a mutually comprehensible set of norms and values with which to challenge parental authority.

Maltreatment and the Emancipation of Minors

Civil legislation sought to define the parameters of the child-parent relationship, setting conditions for emancipation, consent to marriage, and rights to inheritance. It dismantled the absolutism of the patriarch and allowed plenty of space for the state to maneuver in the private lives of families. Court cases involving the elopement of minors is one illustrative example of the state acting as patriarch in settling family conflict. Children have always defied parental authority, but the characteristics of this rebellion have changed over time. In Oaxaca, minor children eloped with their sweethearts through all historical eras. Maltreatment was a commonly cited reason for elopement, and romantic love also continued to fuel the decision to defy parents. Indeed, Patricia Seed found that colonial Mexican minors often stated that they chose their betrothed and defied parental wishes out of love.[36] For the Oaxacan cases, maltreatment and love ring constant in the youngsters' testimonies, but increasingly, these same individuals claim their right to majority and the ability to forge a conjugal contract on their own. To the judges, parental abuse and young love were the perfect mix that motivated them to side with minors. Parents would have none of it. Even when some daughters reached majority age (twenty-one), parents or guardians still felt they ought to be able to control their children's life choices.

For example, twenty-three-year-old Tomasa Fuentes told the court in 1857 that she had informed her mother, Francisca Peña, that she wanted to leave home to be with her sweetheart, Eduardo Díaz. Tomasa swore that her mother retorted, "Do what you want!" So she went to a rented room that Eduardo had arranged for her. To the court, she argued that her more than year-long relationship with Eduardo was a serious one. Tomasa also reasoned that because her father had died and her mother mistreated her, she thought it wise to take such a dramatic step. Since her father died, her older brother, Amando Fuentes, had paternal authority in the family home, and he also mistreated her. She professed that Eduardo was the only man she respected as much as she had her father. Thus, she utilized this argument in court to convince officials that her move from one patriarchal situation to another was done in good faith. In effect, Tomasa did not challenge the patriarchal order that placed women under the control of male family members. She simply followed the normative script that had women trade one male authority figure for another. Yet she did this on her own rebellious terms. Her mother countered that she never mistreated Tomasa but alleged that her daughter had been "deceived with some frequency," and thus she committed "a dishonorable act" by running away with a man who would never marry her. For all intent and purposes, the mother wanted to make it clear to the court that Tomasa lacked maturity and had committed romantic follies on other occasions. In court, Tomasa's brother, Amando, defended his prerogatives as male head of household, arguing that it was right to confront Eduardo with a gun to avenge his family's and sister's honor.[37]

Like Tomasa, many daughters told the courts that they felt compelled to elope with their suitors because of the maltreatment they suffered at home. "Maltreatment" could mean they were being overworked, they had frequent arguments with their parents, they were neglected or physically or sexually abused. The evolving civil codes imparted guidelines that endowed parents and children with certain rights and obligations. Under the Napoleonic Code, a father had the duty to feed, clothe, and educate his children, and he had the right to discipline them and to refuse a child's decision to marry.[38] Children had to obey fathers or legal guardians, but the later civil codes also left room for them to outmaneuver that obligation, by charging a parent with *maltrato* (abuse). Limiting the severity of parental punishment harks back to the medieval law code of the Siete Partidas, which warned that patria potestad sanctioned only moderate punishment.[39] Thus, if a child pleaded maltreatment, the court would intervene to determine whether the "abuse" warranted the parent's punishment and potentially the removal of parental authority over the child. Children, honestly or sometimes dishonestly, used the allegation of parental abuse to both explain their actions and garner some credibility before court officials. The court attentively listened.

Juana Silva worked as a domestic servant but lived with her sister Adela. When Juana ran away with her lover in 1872, her single mother filed a court complaint that the girl had been forcibly abducted (*raptada*) by nineteen-year-old shoemaker Melquiadez Barzalobre. Because Juana did not live with her mother, Señora Ramírez, rather than talking about the dishonor to her house, lamented that Adela's house had been dishonored or corrupted (*estrajado*). When Juana provided her testimony, she stressed that her mother had full knowledge of her ongoing relationship with Melquiadez because she had seen his numerous presents, including a rebozo, votives, and bolts of calico fabric. She then told the judge that she ran away to his house because they had mutually agreed to live together and that her mother never helped her or her sister with food or any other of life's necessities. This charge fits with Oaxaca's civil legislation that denied parents patria potestad if they did not support their children. She further stated that Melquiadez gave her food, which she shared with her sister. The civil code dictated that children should share alimentos with their parents and with each other, if necessary.[40] These words fell on receptive ears because the judge continued the investigation. Finally, Juana emphasized that she did not elope from her mother's house but from the home of her sister, implying that she had not dishonored the parental home. For his part, Melquiadez supported her story by reemphasizing the neglect Juana suffered and stressed that the mother had never complained about the presents he had given Juana. While the case continued, rather than returning Juana to her mother, the judge sent her to a *depósito* (an institution or private home for temporary custody) and Melquiadez to prison. A few weeks later, the judge placed Melquiadez under the tutelage of a sponsor and *comerciante* (businessman), who could employ his services. Around the same time, Juana managed to escape the custody of the depósito, and the case file ends.[41]

Judges utilized depósito for the girls or "victims" only in cases involving members of the elite or when they believed that lower-class girls faced peril by returning to the parental home. In Juana's case, the judge probably agreed that the mother had neglected her daughters and felt it prudent to place her in safe custody. Juana's flight from her custodial home shows her strong desire to be independent and make adult decisions regarding whether she should marry and to whom.

Although we do not know the outcome of this case, Juana made it clear to the court using mutually comprehensible concepts that her mother had failed in her duty to support her daughters. Proving this alone would jeopardize her mother's patria potestad over her daughters and gain them sympathy and maybe even emancipation through a court order. The lover, Melquiadez, noted that Juana's mother had an opportunity to complain when he gave her daughter presents and food but she did not take it. The food and objects he gave Juana sealed their agreement to be amasias, which was, for many working-class Oaxacans, an acceptable alternative to marriage and one that came with just as many mutual obligations and rights.

Daughters ran away more than once to escape alleged child abuse and court officials willingly listened to their experiences. One widow, Josefa Ruiz, filed a complaint in 1886 that Jesús Pimentel had violently abducted her nineteen-year-old daughter, Porfiria Ramírez, from the central market of Oaxaca de Juárez over a month before. Josefa turned to the court after learning that Porfiria was staying at the home of a woman known as "the mother" who rented rooms to prostitutes and allegedly acted as their madam. Apprehended by the police and taken to court, Porfiria testified that she had run away from home three times with different men, whom she listed by name for the judge, and that she had done so to escape her mother's maltreatment. This time Jesús was her man, and they mutually agreed to marry in the future, which satisfied the judge and ended the case.[42]

Other daughters seemingly wrapped up in the pleasures of courtship lost track of time while strolling with their sweethearts and chose not to go home because they feared *bofetadas* (a good slapping). Fifteen-year-old Luz García claimed that she had met Basilio López at the Church of San Juan de Dios, and they proceeded to walk and talk throughout the city. At eight o'clock in the evening, she chose to go home with Basilio rather than face her mother's anger.[43]

In 1889, another young woman, Casimira Montaño, wanted to marry Gaspar Lázaro. Her maltreatment began when his parents brought her father and grandparents the present "that is custom in the villages" and asked their permission for the minors to marry. Casimira testified that ever since, she had received the mala vida. Both her father and grandparents forbade her to see Gaspar. Finally, she got out of the house on the pretext of buying cigars and sugar for her father, and she ran away with Gaspar.[44]

Some daughters detailed the abuse they received at home. Feliciana Sánchez told the court that she ran away with Pioquinto Aguilar in 1887 because her mother threatened to hire her out as a live-in domestic servant.[45] Three years later Rosa Martínez justified her elopement with Aurelio García, telling the court that she desired him even though he was poor, but her mother wanted her to marry a rich man, Ramón Martínez, whom she did not love, thus she chose elopement over an unhappy marriage with the rich suitor. When she told this to Aurelio, he agreed that she should run away from home, and she slipped out of the house at three o'clock in the morning to meet him under the tree in front of her house.[46] Eloping was Rosa's strategy to nullify her mother's intention to have her marry someone she did not love. Her excuse must have rung true with the judges since popular culture advised marrying for love and reason rather than money (see chapter 3).

Some young women feared sexual abuse and left home to avoid it. Stepfathers and male relatives posed the greatest risks to young women. Francisca Delgado and Anita Nicolás justified their elopements in the late 1800s by citing the mala vida their mothers gave them and their stepfathers repeated attempts to sexually assault them.[47] In the case of José Inés Caballero, recounted above, he related the story of a nefarious stepfather. The suitor claimed that he had to send his niece with burros to collect Candelaria before her stepfather could deflower her. Candelaria provided scant testimony, but the couple agreed to marriage, which the judge sanctioned, and consequently, he closed the case.[48]

In these cases of alleged sexual abuse or threats by stepfathers, there is no evidence that the judges initiated investigations of the elder men. Other girls were not so lucky to escape their stepfathers' predations. Fourteen-year-old Narcisa Rafaela Cortés walked from her barrio of Xochimilco to sell sweets in 1886 near the atrium of the Cathedral. Soon after she set up her wares, she decided to elope with fifteen-year-old José García. She told the court that in light of her one-and-a-half-month relationship with José and his offer of marriage, she chose to leave her mother's control. Almost as an afterthought or possibly to reinforce her case, she added that her mother mistreated her. José was more forthcoming in justifying their actions and his recollections of the events leading to their elopement. He swore that they had only had a romantic relationship for two days, but since Narcisa did not want to go home anymore, he ran away with her. According to his testimony, her mother frequently became inebriated and hit her, forcing her to flee from the home on many occasions. As the case unfolded, Narcisa had to explain to José and the court why she was not a virgin when the couple first had sexual intercourse. She stated simply that she had been deflowered by her stepfather in the patio of their home.

In a rare twist, the case ends unsatisfactorily for José. Doctors determined that Narcisa had lost her virginity at an earlier date and went to great clinical lengths to describe her vagina's capacity to accept something the size of a man's penis. This finding alone should have nullified the case, but the judge still sentenced the young man to one year and four months in prison and a fifty-peso fine, with no further comments or justification.[49] José's unusual sentence is difficult to understand. He hailed from the Rancho de Yacuí but at the time resided in Oaxaca City. Only fifteen years old, he did not have a father or paternal figure to vouch for his actions and to uphold his rights. The court assigned him a defense lawyer who called Narcisa and her mother "diablas" (she-devils), but he failed to influence the judge. Working as a brick mason may have been a decent occupation for a working-class man, but perhaps because the boy lacked a parent or guardian, the judge decided to make an example of him.[50] Incarcerating the young man certainly sent a message that men should not run off with girls. He may have also been incarcerated because he rescinded his promise of marriage, testifying that he had heard *"malas noticias"* (bad news or gossip) about Narcisa.

Citing maltreatment or a dereliction of parental duty was sure to gain the court's attention. Civil codes dictated that parents must be moderate in punishing their children, and when a parent could not or would not provide alimentos, the law allowed the state to intervene. Taking a cue from political discourse, runaway daughters cited mistreatment as a chief justification for eloping with their lovers. Judges listened attentively to these testimonies. Although it is impossible to know if indeed the girls suffered the frequency and level of abuse they attested to, it was a brilliant strategy to win the court's favor for emancipation and permission to marry or live with their sweethearts. In fact, citing maltreatment distinguished nineteenth-century cases from colonial cases over marriage choice.[51] Colonial-era couples in Mexico did not testify that maltreatment propelled them to elope or defy their parents and in the Oaxacan cases before 1870, only two young women cited mistreatment.[52] However, from 1870 to 1900, one quarter of the daughters testified they ran away because one of their parents (including stepfathers) abused them.[53] As pleading child abuse increasingly mobilized the court in children's favor, this suggests an increasing widespread notion in the modernizing nation-state that children and adolescents should be protected. Law has tempered the severity of parental castigation since medieval times. Yet in late nineteenth-century Mexico, an era characterized by various social and economic programs to modernize the nation, the spectacle of an abusive or neglectful parent was antithetical to the mission of promoting healthy, patriotic, and hardworking families. The civil code provided judges the justification to abolish, or at least, weaken, the authority of an abusive parent.[54] After all, the future of the nation rested in its children, Mexico's future workers.

For Reasons of Love

The parent-child relationship revealed in the elopement dramas was not all hardship and abuse. Love rang clear for both parties. In her study of conflicts over marriage choice in colonial Mexico, Patricia Seed showed that love was one of three cultural attitudes that shaped how the church intervened between parental objection and a child's will. Before 1690, the church sided more often with children than parents in prenuptial conflicts, effectively ruling in favor of will, love, and honor and against any motive a parent could contrive in opposition. The church also dramatically utilized the strategy of a secret marriage to dispense with the banns in order to protect young couples from parental abuse, which could extend to imprisonment or exile of a disobedient son or daughter. The church sided with love and will and also wished to protect female sexual honor. It was not until the seventeenth century that female sexual honor lost its potency and the notion of the irrevocable promise of marriage loosened its grips on young men's intentions and accountability for the words they uttered in passionate moments. In other words, extenuating circumstances like social distance between the couple or childish whim could supercede the need to protect female sexual honor. Conflict negotiation that turned on honor was replaced by the argument, offered by parents, that love and will were unstable emotions especially when professed by minor children. The church, and later the state, listened. In society, as love became less exalted and acquisitiveness more accepted, the self-interest and concerns of parents were given weight in the courts that adjudicated marriage-conflict cases. Seed found that even though cases declined during this period, parents usually won.[55] The Royal Pragmatic on Marriage implemented in Latin America in 1778 reinforced these trends, in particular the opportunity for parents to deny marriage permission if they could prove social inequality. In essence, class or racial inequality could trump free will in marriage.

Seed's formal lawsuits, which provide wonderfully detailed real stories of conflicts between parents, involve mostly people in the upper classes, because those families could afford the legal fees to proceed with an expensive court case. For this study that focuses on nineteenth-century working families, parents and children did not have to worry as much about having to divide assets to give a daughter or son their dowry or inheritance. In addition, the minors in these cases usually chose mates from their own social group, at least from the perspective of the elite judges. Hence, judges rarely cited social or racial inequality as a reason to side with the parent to prevent the union. Marriage between working-class youngsters clearly did not forge major financial alliances between families. Yet social historians have shown that the popular class had its own internal hierarchy, which ranked people in terms of status, reputation, and honor.[56]

Young adults eloped for reasons of love,[57] as proven by the love letters that were included in many of the case files (see chapter 3).[58] Testimonies by the various sweethearts also provide a glimpse into their inner lives. Even a few defense lawyers spoke eloquently about the defendant's love for the woman with whom he had eloped, arguably attesting to the continued cultural respect for love as a basis of marriage and family.

In 1872, Eulalia Vásquez complained that she had to work too much at home and that since she loved Pedro Clerín, she took off for the cigar factory where he worked and waited for him. She fled with him to San Felipe del Agua to the north of the city to have sex and begin life together, the customary step to constitute a conjugal unit in the face of parental opposition. Pedro corroborated her story. Doctors ruled that she had been recently deflowered and the defense lawyer prepared his case well. In his brief to the court, Pedro's lawyer wrote about the boy's grand love for Eulalia and their wish to begin married life together. Nowhere was there a hint of ridicule or the mention of the folly of fickle minors. Convinced, the judge dismissed the case and allowed the couple to plan their marriage.[59]

To the court, female minors declared love as their reason for eloping more often than their boyfriends, but this may have been because it was up to them to justify their "immoral" actions. Arcadia Benítes had been involved with police officer, Juan López, for four months in 1887, and he had promised to marry her. Her parents warned her not to talk to him anymore, but Arcadia stated that "because I have so much love" for him, she resolved to leave home. She took the first opportunity to meet him after work and go home with him, where he "destroyed (her) virginity." Juan did not use the verb *"querer"* (literally, to want, but meaning to love in this context), but he claimed that he wanted to marry Arcadia as soon as possible.[60] Another young woman, fifteen-year-old Soledad Blanco, told the judge that she ran away with seventeen-year-old carpenter José Martínez because "it is so much love I have for Martínez." They were the couple who had sex in the atrium of the Church of Guadalupe. Not professing love as a reason, José nonetheless responded that he wanted to repair her good reputation (*honra*) by marrying her. The judge agreed, and they married the next year (remarkably, the marriage certificate was inserted in their case file).[61]

The young male suitors, while not as likely to publicly profess love for their girlfriends in front of the judges, pined longingly for love and affection in the private letters they wrote to these girls. Remember Arcadio, the suitor literally caught with his pants down. He and several other suitors penned romantic and tender missives to their beloved girls (chapter 3). These letters attest to the importance of love in these illicit relationships. For their part, parents willingly submitted love letters in order to prove that their daughters' suitors either promised marriage or as evidence of a serious, romantic relationship.

Yet some parents, even though they provided the letters as evidence, had other intentions. In several testimonies, parents bemoaned the youth and inexperience of their daughters, reasoning that they were too immature to make wise choices in matters of love, which may be evidence of the existence of a notion of adolescence as a fickle and irrational stage. Citing immaturity may have also been a plausible way of expressing their distaste for the suitor to an elite judge. Undoubtedly, the judge categorized working-class Oaxacans as one undifferentiated group. Pleading social distance or inequality would have fallen on deaf ears. Even in those cases when the daughter had been deflowered and dishonored, some parents still opposed the marriage. Josefa Calvo's story illustrates this point. Her mother charged her intended, Manuel Vivas, with being a *"vago"* (vagrant), a word that could have several meanings, none of them positive.[62] She simply disapproved of him as marriage material for Josefa and attempted to block the relationship, first through beatings and threats and then through the court.[63] Another mother testified at length to her concern about her daughter's choice of a husband. In one 1873 case, Señora Rodríguez recounted that more than a year before, Manuel Mimiaga had asked to marry her twenty-year-old daughter, Guadalupe Ogarrio. The mother refused because, she claimed, his "poor public conduct foretold a bad future for her daughter." Some months passed, and Guadalupe continued to show signs of love and affection for Manuel. "Fearing the likelihood of a stain on the honor of her house," she agreed to let Manuel marry her daughter. But, she continued, he had tricked her and taken advantage of her good will to elope with Guadalupe rather than waiting for a proper marriage ceremony, so the mother could no longer give her permission for the union. Even though she "redoubled her vigilance," around 11:30 p.m., the night before the complaint was filed, when the mother was drinking chocolate, Guadalupe disappeared, an occurrence she blames on the evil intentions of Manuel and the immaturity of Guadalupe.[64]

Parental love was a valid reason for mothers and fathers to oppose their children's intended mates, but judges ignored it if the couple wished to marry and they shared equal social position. In an unusual rapto case, one more akin to rape, thirty-year-old laborer Victoriano Chávez abducted twelve-year-old Asunción Quevedo from the marketplace while she was shopping for tortillas. Taking her outside the city center first to Jalatlaco and then to Tlacolula, he forced himself on her with threats and lived with her for fifteen days before they were apprehended by the police. Interestingly, Asunción's father learned of her rapto from Victoriano's amasia, who told him that Victoriano had not returned home in several days. Victoriano tried to defend himself by testifying that Asunción had had amorous relations with him for a couple of months and that she told him she wanted to leave home because her father made her work too much. Marriage was the best solution for restoring honor and promoting social harmony, but Asunción's parents rejected Victoriano since he had lived with another woman for sixteen years and fathered six children. He also carried a large knife, something the parents could not accept. These factors, they pleaded, would only lead to la mala vida for their daughter, thus they were willing to accept family dishonor as the lesser of two evils.[65]

In 1852, one mother displayed her maternal love and instinct most forcefully: Señora Soto claimed that while she sold meat in the marketplace, she had sent Ángela Gabriela Ramírez on an errand to purchase enaguas (underskirts). When the girl did not return, she grew alarmed and began searching for her around the neighborhood. The daughter, Ángela, testified that she went to the pulquería to look for her injured father and met up with Aniceto Ramos. He invited her in for a drink, but she refused. He then began pushing her toward the river. Aniceto contradicted some of her testimony, telling the judge that she would not go into the tavern for a drink but did agree to go to the river with him to talk. The mother reenters the story at the river. According to Ángela, her mother arrived in time to save her as

Aniceto had just thrown his hat and sash on the ground. Noting these sexually fraught items of clothing was Ángela's way of alleging that Aniceto was on the brink of ravishing her. Aniceto testified that they only had a friendly conversation and nothing else. All the witnesses testified that Señora Soto was wielding a knife to protect her daughter from dishonor. Indeed, Señora Soto told the judge that it was her duty as a mother who loved her daughter to protect her from Aniceto, with violence if necessary.[66]

Fathers also displayed their paternal love and concern before the court. Pedro, resident and worker on the Hacienda de San José near Ocotlán, pleaded with court officials to intervene to help his daughter, Encarnación Arango, who had been seduced by Isaac Robles in 1906. He testified that he had heard she was being treated cruelly and kept against her will in neighboring Xochimilco and two women told him that Isaac beat Encarnación. The father's testimony became more and more desperate as he attempted to convince the court of her imminent danger. He even asked to be allowed to at least bring her bread or tortillas.[67] Unfortunately the case ends with no written resolution. Judges accepted romantic and paternal love as well as maltreatment as justifications for actions. Minor daughters defied patria potestad out of love and because they feared abuse. Parents opposed their children out of love and concern. These were rational arguments to explain behaviors with each participant trying to prove that they had the victim's (or their own) best interests and happiness in mind.

Parlaying Family Conflict: The Court Takes Sides

What did the court make of all these protestations and defenses? Judges and defense lawyers usually provided terse comments when their opinions were recorded at all. More often than not, judges refrained from providing lengthy justifications for their conclusions, or at least, they were not written down for posterity. If no legal impediments existed and the young couple was willing, judges preferred marriage to resolve the matter. Oaxaca's 1887 Penal Code dictated that a criminal case should not proceed if "the abductor married the offended woman."[68] In effect, law and its practitioners recognized and even endorsed rapto as a strategy for minors to defy parents and choose when to marry and to whom. Under these circumstances, the court routinely sided with children in their love matches over any parental objections that existed. However, judges and lawyers did contribute to discussions of honor, good parenting, liberty, and individualism in making marriage choices. In a particularly pointed decision, a judge ruled for the minor daughter after the father complained that she did not show him the proper respect due a father. In that 1875 case, the father, Julián Serna, felt disgusted that his twenty-two-year-old daughter, Dolores, had left home to live with her lover. He happened to pass her in the street, hurled some insults at her, and then began to hit her in the presence of several witnesses. Dolores testified that the fight ensued after she told her father to mind his own business. Julián saw these actions and words as a grave lack of respect and admitted to hitting Dolores several times. When he picked up a rock, however, witnesses intervened. The police arrived and escorted father and daughter to the police station. Julián argued before the judge that Dolores remained under his power as she lived in a house that he paid for and that even though she had a son born outside of marriage, she was still legally under his dominion. The judge decided to free Dolores, even though she had also struck her father but in self-defense. He sentenced Julián to twenty days of incarceration.[69] Clearly, the judge decided that either Dolores was old enough to make her own life choices or her father had crossed the line by using undue violence in public to correct what he perceived as his daughter's disrespectful behavior. The civil codes of 1870 required that single daughters seek permission to move out of the house until age thirty,[70] but the judge ruled that Dolores was an adult and could make her own decisions about when to move and with whom to live.

A judge felt compelled to explain his opinion on one particular case that involved a godfather seducing his goddaughter. The father of the girl, Francisco Jiménez, wrote to the court in 1875 that "a circumstance of notable infamy" had occurred when his closest spiritual advisor, and godparent to his daughter, fifteen-year-old Patrocinia, abducted her with force and deceit. He emphasized their close bond, noting that the perpetrator, Nicolás Flores, had been his closest confidante, and they had mutually helped each other's families on numerous occasions. The case took various twists and turns as witnesses provided testimony of seeing Nicolás and Patrocinia together outside the city. Nicolás testified that he had no other relationship with Patrocinia than one of spiritual mentor. Conversely, Patrocinia swore that he fell in love with her and had expressed this to her on one of his regular visits. She did not tell her father for fear of reprisal. She stated that her godfather returned another day, this time with a knife, and forced her to go with him under threats that he would harm her. Fearfully she acquiesced and stayed with him for fifteen days before she managed to escape. Witnesses testified that he had arrived at a farm in Xia with a young girl and on different occasions, referred to her as his daughter, maid, or lover. He ended up departing the farm with his brother, leaving Patrocinia behind to work as a maid for a resident until her father found her several weeks later. The judge believed the father and daughter and jailed Nicolás. In his judgment, he weighed in on honor, female vulnerability, and the bond of godparenthood:

> The seduction of the young Jiménez, making her abandon the paternal home and dishonoring it, causes a stain that is difficult to erase and darkens the future of the young woman. Using threats and a knife to intimidate her is the cruelest act. Her young age and the gender she belongs to made her naturally weak and vulnerable. In these acts, evil intentions and an unbridled sexual appetite disgraced a young girl and introduced into her family sadness and dishonor. Not satisfied with this and without reason, he abused the confidence and great responsibilities bestowed on him by the parents to be godparent. He violated good faith and the family bond by committing this crime.[71]

Judges elaborated on their rulings in these exceptional cases. Mostly, elopement cases revealed the various actors' testimony and the judge provided a brief conclusion. Remember the goal was familial and social peace and most cases ended without dramatic incident. Either the defendant agreed to marry his victim and she agreed, or the court nullified complaints for reason of age, the young woman's past sexual history, or lack of merit.

Conclusion

The court provided opinions on family relationships, paternal authority, and filial obedience. Court officials also laid out parameters of sexual behavior, especially for women. Indeed, with rare exceptions, the court only protected virgins.[72] Notably, the cases from Oaxaca attest to the fact that the liberal state limited parental authority in working-class families and used its power to adjudicate as an ad hoc patriarch. Only seven cases out of 212 resulted in a sentence or fine for the male defendants.[73] Unlike findings for Lima, judges never asked plaintiffs for betrothal documents to prove that an engagement had been set.[74] Love letters or witness testimony sufficed and essentially, judges accepted the practice of elopement as a strategy to overcome parental objection to a marriage. A daughter could justify her running away for reasons of maltreatment, sexual abuse, or love, and the judges listened. By

eschewing castigation for marriage at sometime in the future, court officials effectively emancipated minors of both genders by siding with them in
conflicts over marriage choices. Yet at the same time, there is no evidence
that judges required documentation that a marriage took place. It sufficed
that the couple verbally contracted to a marriage ceremony that could take
place at an indeterminate time in the future. This probably more closely
reflected the pattern of marriage among lower-order Oaxacans. Young couples, like their colonial counterparts, eloped with a view toward marriage but
it could be preceded by months or years of a consensual union. Marriage
rituals and ceremonies were expensive undertakings. Some couples actually testified that they planned to marry as soon as they saved the necessary
resources. The judges' decisions maintained this tradition. Remember they
ignored parents' demands of incarceration and fines for the boys, instead
adjudicating for the marriage of minor daughters rather than the restora-
tion of parental authority. Of course, the complicating factor was also that
many of these young women had been deflowered, a fact the court, at least
in theory, sought to repair through matrimony. More likely, judges acted
on behalf of minor, working-class couples by sanctioning their sexual and
conjugal wishes but, more importantly, overruling parental opinion. Both
officials and youngsters supported virginity as a normative value. Yet the
young women also knew that virginity could be wielded as a bargaining chip
not only with their suitors but also with parents and the state in order to
achieve their aims of independence and the desire to forge a new family.
Like nineteenth-century Cubans, couples rebelled against parents and community, asserted their individuality, and claimed their freedom and right to
make autonomous choices.[75] Playing out the script of seduction, daughters
lost virtue by running away with their sweethearts but also vividly brandished
this loss of honor to achieve their desired outcome, a new life with their
lover and legal emancipation. Authorities conceded in these cases because,
to them, no social distance existed between the betrothed. By siding with the
young sweethearts, court officials proved that sexually mature minors could
be emancipated from patria potestad if they desired to marry and no impediment stood in their way. This reality meshed with the civil codes that allowed
minor children at age fourteen for boys and twelve for girls to marry with
paternal consent. In essence, judges recognized a transitional stage (that
would later be defined as adolescence) between childhood and adulthood in
which they felt comfortable emancipating minors who were capable of forging families or who had suffered maltreatment from their parents or guardian. Yet, once children were emancipated, they became adults. Girls received

special protection and judges did not hesitate to allow them to marry their suitors even in the face of parental opposition. Marriage emancipated them, and they became full-fledged adult women. Even girls that chose consensual unions outside of wedlock won a measure of autonomy, as they were no longer under the authority of a parent or a husband. If the minor girls married their sweethearts, they enjoyed freedom from parental authority. Yet their new husbands now had commensurate power over their daily lives. The laws still dictated that the father or husband had the official clout to rule over his household, including a disproportionate power over his children as well. Nonetheless, the conjugal bond, or what Steve J. Stern has coined the "patriarchal pact," like the parent-child contract, could be negotiated.[76] Wives were not powerless to defend their rights before the courts and in their communities. Although a double standard continued to exist in Mexico during a period of expanded rights for children and women, courts regularly intervened as proxy patriarchs to occasionally side with minor daughters and wives. Judges' actions legally emancipated girls from parental authority and in some cases, this action saved them from the sexual predations of stepfathers or the physical abuse by mothers. Freedom from parental authority was not altogether liberating for these minor girls, as female adulthood could also be rife with violence and abuse. Nonetheless by emancipating minor girls and allowing them either to marry their suitors or cohabit with them, judges also curtailed their childhood by essentially shortening the period of adolescence. Now women, these girls lacked childhood protection but could seek justice as adult women in domestic-violence cases. In the end, poor girls embroiled in rapto cases were both sexualized at a younger age and reached womanhood at an earlier age than their elite sisters.

Girls who either chose or accepted a consensual union may have lacked the legal security of an official marriage, but they also were not legally bound to their male partner. Stated differently, girls who abandoned the family home to live but not marry their lovers escaped paternal guardianship and control but also did not transfer their official tutelage to their male cohabiter. This placed girls in a unique position. Newly emancipated from parental authority but not yet under the legal authority of a husband, they may have been able to carve out a degree of autonomy not afforded their married sisters. A woman unsatisfied with her common-law husband could dissolve the union more easily and possibly even have more success in censuring abusive partners.[77]

The novelty for the nineteenth century was that judges accepted maltreatment as a reason to allow young, rebellious couples to marry. The liberal state wished to promote civil marriage, but through leniency in elopement cases, the state perpetuated the traditional practice of elopement as a clandestine courtship practice that sometimes led to marriage and the disregard for parents' opinions. Therein lies the irony. In essence, adolescent minors recognized their status as individuals with rights and guarantees and could wield these concepts effectively in their depositions and arguments before the judge. At the same time, judges and especially lawyers waxed eloquent about love and honor when they defended a couple's elopement or ruled in favor of youthful romance rather than parental authority. Likewise, I do not want to romanticize the situation and suggest that judges were without prejudice when dealing with working-class individuals. Liberal norms predicated that all Mexicans, regardless of class or ethnicity, ought to have equal treatment before the law. However, rapto, while addressed in the penal code, was not the same sort of crime as theft, homicide, or infanticide. I see no evidence the judges looked at this behavior as criminal. Judges appeared unwilling to incarcerate the suitors who had either seduced or run off with their girlfriends. In the minds of the judges, these were underage couples acting in a very calculated manner to get what they wanted. Judges recognized that their romantic actions were tempered by rationality and in the end, ruled in their favor. While in colonial times young couples sometimes found an ally in the Church, in nineteenth-century Mexico, the state aided and abetted them in forming nuclear families based on civil marriage and the values of liberalism and individualism. The next chapter delves more deeply into the inner lives and bonds between lovers, with special attention to the female protagonists of the rapto dramas.

CHAPTER SIX

Runaway Daughters

Sexual Honor and Sources of Female Power

☙❦☙

EARLY ON A WEDNESDAY EVENING IN 1899, JOSEFA CALVO ELOPED WITH her boyfriend, Manuel Vivas. The steps leading up to her flight and its aftermath followed the script of seduction and elopement. Just fourteen-years-old and a seamstress like her mother, Josefa had been seeing Manuel, an eighteen-year-old shawl maker, for four months. The minors hoped to marry, but Josefa's mother refused to give her permission. Manuel wanted to follow proper channels and offered to send his father to ask the single mother for permission. Josefa, however, vehemently rejected his suggestion, stating that the abuse she was suffering at home would only escalate. Instead, Josefa threatened her suitor, saying that if he would not run off with her, she might "feel obligated to go away with someone else." Manuel gave in and agreed to elope with Josefa. What set her apart from most of the other girls in these cases is that she assumed the assertive role in the elopement script by setting the date, time, place, and plan of execution for their clandestine tryst. A few days later, she bundled up her clothes and other personal effects and ran off with Manuel.[1]

The romantic relationship of Josefa and two contemporaries, Francisca and Luz Esther, introduced below, are exemplary of many of the struggles and personal choices that runaway daughters faced in nineteenth-century

Oaxaca. They are stories of minor girls making striking choices that often turned out in their favor. On the precipice between childhood and adulthood, they fled the relative safety of their parental home to build a conjugal relationship with the boys or men they professed to love. For whatever reason—love, lust, or abuse at home—the girls made the bold but also very calculated move to be "seduced" by their suitors. The runaway daughters gambled their honor, because to run off with a man implied that he sexually possessed her. In the official script, she lost honor and this reflected a loss of honor for her family as well. Their stories are in the archives because their mother or father protested their maneuvering to leave home and begin life anew with their boyfriends. While eloping to overcome parental objection seemed like a simple process, it was rife with conflict and contradictions that especially impacted the runaway daughters. Unraveling the rapto dramas of Josefa, Francisca, and Luz Esther reveals their personal dilemmas that shared certain attributes, but also exhibit noteworthy differences, based on their class and ethnicity. Importantly, focusing on the girls themselves reveals much about the complex machinations and meanings of a working-class honor code in nineteenth-century Mexico, especially as it defined appropriate female sexual honor. As previously discussed, working-class litigants in the rapto dramas wielded the language of honor before the judges and lawyers to good effect.

Josefa and Manuel

Let us return to the courtship of Josefa and Manuel. She chose the church named after Oaxaca City's patron saint, the Templo de la Soledad, for their rendezvous. Josefa, accompanied by her best friend, thirteen-year-old Teresa Hernández, arrived at 7:00 p.m., and they probably milled around with the people leaving the nightly service. After Josefa stashed a small bundle with her possessions under some rocks in the garden, the two girls searched for Manuel, and once they found him, the three discussed plans to find a private room in which to spend the night so that the couple could consummate their union. When they went to retrieve Josefa's belongings, the gardener accosted the unsuspecting trio and alerted a police officer. The gardener and the officer accused the minors of stealing the clothes and then hiding them in the church garden, and they quickly carted them off to a nearby police station. Imagine the anxiety and fear of the three as the police interrogated them about their plans and actions. Police officers grilled them on the sequence of events that led them to church that night and their relation to each other. Eventually the police decided that the clothes did, in fact, belong to Josefa. They also believed her lie that the three of them were siblings, and so they let them go. Now free of the police, the three rushed north several blocks to Xochimilco, a barrio at the city limits, where they again posed as siblings as they rented a room. In later court testimony, the landlady testified that she was reluctant, but since it was late and they obviously needed shelter for the night, she relented and rented them a room. Once safe inside, Josefa and Manuel had sexual intercourse, while Teresa slept in the front vestibule. The next morning, the landlady opened the door and surely to the youngsters' dismay, there stood Josefa's mother, Juana, and a police officer. The officer arrested Manuel, and the livid mother filed a criminal complaint against the boy.[2] Josefa went home with her angry mother. What happened to Teresa is unknown, but she provided a deposition in subsequent days.

In the court documents, Josefa testified that she loved Manuel and that he had promised to marry her. She had also sent him five letters, which Manuel submitted to the court as evidence of their serious relationship. Josefa had to pass her letters through Teresa because her mother constantly watched her every move. She swore that her mother threatened to kill her if she carried on with Manuel. She told the judge that she had wanted to marry Manuel, but because her mother disapproved, she eloped instead. Josefa also promised that she was a virgin before her night with Manuel, a claim that Manuel would later contradict. In her testimony to the judge, Juana tempered her passion for Manuel with reason, by emphasizing that she had no other recourse to escape her mother's abuse and be with her beloved.

For his part, Manuel confirmed the seriousness of the relationship and his promise of marriage. The love letters he had submitted, he suggested, showed that the couple's relationship had developed through proper steps. He also stated that Josefa had engineered their elopement, and he doubted that she was a virgin at the time of their first sexual encounter. This statement by Manuel complicated Josefa's testimony that she was indeed a virgin, which staked her claim to official honor. Manuel testified that she did not "show blood" after sexual intercourse, and he had interrogated her on this point. According to him, she admitted that she had been "deceived" at a young age, but even though he had heard rumors that a certain Alfredo was the author of her disgrace, it was untrue. Conflicting statements aside, the judge ordered government doctors to examine the girl. At the close of his deposition, Manuel professed that he still wanted to marry Josefa regardless of whether Alfredo or someone else took her virginity. Why would the boy who loved the girl impugn her reputation in the public arena of the court? He must have known that the rapto law did not protect nonvirgins.

Francisca and Filomeno

In 1872, fifteen-year-old Francisca Pérez ran away with Filomeno Ruiz, an eighteen-year-old weaver, and they lived together for almost one month. The girl's widowed father, Antonio, had sent her on daily rounds to collect money for the bread he supplied to local haciendas. Francisca had not returned home, and the baker became concerned when his oldest daughter, Petrona, told him she had seen Francisca chatting with Filomeno. This led to the father filing a complaint against the young man. Petrona testified that at one point, the alleged seducer had visited her house and told her, "The bakers say that I have stolen your sister, but I can do whatever I like, wherever I like." The judge sent policemen to search for the couple, and they found them living together in Bonifacia Jiménez's house. Once in custody, Filomeno told the judge that he had every intention of marrying Francisca but had wanted to make sure she was a virgin first, a rationale the judge could understand. Eloping with her allowed him to "test her honor," but, he promised, he would arrange a civil marriage as soon as he had the money.

Francisca was more garrulous with the judge. She explained her actions in mutually comprehensible terms. Being in love with Filomeno, she had agreed to live with him until they could save the money to marry, implying that she bargained her virginity for a promise of marriage. Remarkably, the now deflowered girl rejected her suitor and went home with her father and sister. She stated that after more than a month with Filomeno, "Now, I am not disposed to marry him any longer because . . . I have quarrels [*disgustos*] with his family, and whereas before I could not stand to be separated from him, now I want to go with my father, Antonio." She also promised that she was not pregnant. The judge closed the case since the father had achieved his aim of getting his daughter back and he did not want to pursue the case against Filomeno.[3]

Luz and Manuel

One afternoon in 1899, Luz Esther, a daughter from a well-to-do family, left home on the pretense of going to her piano lessons. Instead, she headed for her boyfriend's store on the zócalo. She found herself in court because a set of confusing events resulted in her mother charging her alleged boyfriend,

Manuel Canseco, with rapto. Luz Esther testified that she and Manuel had been sweethearts for eleven months, and he had asked her to marry him. She also testified that she had been in Mexico City the previous month, and when she returned, Manuel had asked her to prove that she was not a "*mujer común*" (promiscuous woman). Luz Esther swore she had gone to his shop to discuss marriage arrangements. According to the girl, Manuel instead proposed that she be his lover until they could marry. She protested, but he beseeched her and repeatedly offered to take her to a hotel in "*un coche bien cerrado*" (a closed carriage). She refused all his offers, and they quarreled.⁴ Manuel grabbed her arms and told her to wait in his office while he finished some business in the store. Luz Esther then claimed that his brother, Agustín, came to the store, offered her wine, and told her to wait for Manuel. She also testified that she sent one of the store employees to alert her mother of her abduction.⁵

For his part, Manuel stated that his relationship with Luz Esther was only that of shopkeeper and customer, and he had never promised to marry her, as they had not shared a single romantic exchange. He also accused Luz Esther and her mother of forging the eight love letters that were included in the legal complaint as evidence of the betrothal (see chapter 3). Specifically, he claimed to have been away from the store on the day in question, and he returned after closing only to discover that an "*escandalito*" (small scandal) had occurred during his absence. Moreover, he professed to be mortified by the accusations of the young woman and her mother. The brother, Agustín, testified next, stating that he never offered Luz Esther wine and that Manuel never proposed marriage to the plaintiff's daughter.

Witnesses had their turn in court next. On that fateful afternoon, a young couple had taken refuge under the portal in front of Manuel's shop during a rainstorm, and they saw Luz Esther run out of the rain and into the store. Deciding to look over the merchandise, they also entered the store, and they noticed Manuel and Luz Esther talking in raised voices at his desk. After a few minutes, they saw Manuel leave the store, while Luz Esther stayed behind. Another witness, a personal friend and associate of the defendant, stated that he met Manuel at the store, before going to a tavern where they drank beer until late in the afternoon. A store employee also vouched that Manuel had gone to drink with a friend, leaving the brother Agustín in charge of the store. The worker also stated that Manuel did not return to the store until ten o'clock that night. He also claimed that Luz Esther had entered the store and talked excitedly with Agustín, not Manuel. Upset by the argument, she jumped over the checkout counter and went into the back room, and she refused to leave until Manuel returned! The worker then stated that Luz Esther's mother arrived, summoned the girl, and left with her in tow. The judge accepted the various witness and litigant testimonies, but in the end, he dropped the case because Luz Esther was nineteen-years-old and the use of force could not be established.

Altering Traditional Scripts of Passive Femininity

Consider the case of Josefa whose story introduced this chapter. She tried to be the master of her own destiny but some things were beyond her control. She rejected Manuel's request to follow the proper channels for marrying because she claimed her mother would only abuse her more. She wrote him a series of letters to express her feelings as she found it difficult to meet Manuel in person because of her mother's constant surveillance. She set the date, time, and place for her own "abduction" and threatened Manuel if he did not consent to her plan. She also convinced her best friend, Teresa, to fund the entire escapade. In effect, Josefa asserted her desires and mobilized available resources to get her way. She wished to begin conjugal life with Manuel (or another man if he refused) and escape the torment and oppression inflicted by her mother. Whether her mother mistreated her or not, it was clear that Josefa either wanted to be emancipated or she expected that her mother would accept Manuel if the daughter's honor was jeopardized. Clearly, she acted assertively by engineering her own elopement. She turned the tables on official gender norms and "seduced and abducted" her male sweetheart. Assertiveness, persuasion, cunning, and action were all traits associated with men, but Josefa employed them in her plan to elope with Manuel.[6] Equally, Manuel admitted his passive role in his seduction, noting in his testimony that Josefa calculated every detail of their escape and even borrowed the money to rent the room for the night. If Josefa's letters had not confirmed these facts, one might have thought that the young man had conspired to impugn her reputation in order to exonerate his actions.

The baker's daughter, Francisca, openly denigrated Filomeno's honor by rejecting him after first losing her virginity to him and then living with him and getting to know his family for a month. Her own understanding of elopement as a step towards marriage is clear in her testimony. Francisca knew that consensual unions frequently led to marriage, once the couple had saved the necessary resources for the ceremony, civil fees, gifts exchanges, and the fiesta. She testified that she initially intended to marry Filomeno when she ran off with him. One month must have been all she could take, as she told the judge that because of the unbearable conflicts with Filomeno's parents she decided to return to her father's home. Her lost honor was a small price to pay for not having to endure the life she envisioned with her potential in-laws. In her case, familial harmony trumped any concern about her lost honor and virginity.

Luz Esther's alleged boyfriend, Manuel, the storeowner, mustered an arsenal of weapons to damage the reputation of the allegedly aggrieved girl. He and his allies—brother Agustín and the store employees—portrayed Luz Esther's actions in decidedly dishonorable ways. They depicted her as argumentative, dramatic, and calculating. Indeed, the spectacle of a young woman arguing in a public place, jumping over the counter to disappear into the back room of the store owned by a man who was not her kin, and her forging love letters to trick him into marriage must have seemed uncouth to the judge, especially for an upper-class daughter. Nonetheless, he listened to all the witness testimonies, including those of the couple who observed the alleged argument between Luz Esther and Manuel. With the various testimonies in hand, the judge ruled on the case, stating that all the witness statements possessed merit (even though they contradicted each other), but the charge of rapto could not be proven because Luz Esther voluntarily went to Manuel's store to discuss their supposed marriage plans. Moreover, she was nineteen, and a charge of *rapto de seducción* in the absence of force could not be litigated when it involved a girl over fifteen years of age. The judge dismissed the case, and the story ended there. Although Luz Esther had no legal recourse, like Francisca and Josefa, she displayed a strong personality in attempting to achieve her aims. All of these girls transgressed prevailing social norms of proper feminine behavior by attempting to take control of their romantic and sexual lives.

What is remarkable is that these girls understood the parameters and official scripts of the rapto drama, its consequences, and how the courts would interpret the law to either censure their behavior or support their desire to form a new family with their boyfriends. Of course they eloped when a parent denied them permission to marry. That initial step of running off with their suitors was an age-old method to overturn parental objection. At the same time, however, they understood how judges would approach the ensuing investigation. They not only had to prove their honor in order to be taken seriously, they also understood what physical signs were important to emphasize.

For example, Dolores Garcés lived with her fifty-year-old widowed father, Manuel, a carpenter, and she wanted to marry twenty-two-year-old José Rios

Nateret, a shoemaker. Dolores took advantage of her father's absence from home and went with José to the house of a mutual friend. José and Dolores admitted they had sex, and the young man swore he would marry her to restore her honor. She told the judge that because she was "chaste and honest" and a virgin before their sexual tryst, she had "all the signs of deflowering" after consummating their union. In other words, she stressed that doctors would find the telltale signs of her recent loss of virginity. Probably to her dismay, physicians ruled that the bloodstains on her clothes were from past menstrual cycles and that she had lost her virginity at an earlier date. Nevertheless, and even though José promised to marry her, the judge sentenced him to more than five years in jail, justifying his decision by stating that José had corrupted a girl of *buenas costumbres* (good customs).[7] This incongruent sentence is hard to explain. Carpenters and shoemakers were both lower-status artisans, but Dolores's father, Manuel, may have run his own shop, giving him more status in the eyes of the judge.

Sexualizing Poor and Indian Girls

The judges and lawyers of the cases certainly viewed the runaway daughters in contradictory ways. Although they listened to the girls assert their honorable intentions, they also subjected the poor girls to humiliating virginity tests, in effect sexualizing them at a young age.[8] In an 1855 case of the deflowering of a domestic servant, the mistress of the home charged a male servant with raping eleven-year-old Policarpia. He claimed consensual sex; the young girl swore that she had gone to the kitchen to get a tortilla, and he took her by force on the floor there. Doctors negated the young man's testimony because the girl had not reached puberty, so, in their opinion, it was not possible for her to give her consent. They determined that her hymen had been destroyed, but she had not developed breasts nor had she begun menstruating. The judge sentenced the perpetrator to more than a year of labor on public works but not before his defense attorney tried to exonerate the servant's actions. The lawyer argued that the prepubescent girl—an orphan, poor, and indigenous—consented to sex with twenty-two-year-old Manuel. It was simple fornication, he said, rather than deflowering of an immature girl. And he reminded the court that a girl has "a thousand resources to resist like her voice, legs, and any movement of the body," implying that she must have been willing. Policarpia testified that she did not resist because he covered her mouth and threatened to kill her. The lawyer also blamed the blood on her genitalia on a fever, and he explained her loss of hymen by arguing that "in the most common [poor] communities they lose it by any sort of movement and very early" in life. He went on to question the thoroughness of the experts who examined the eleven-year-old and highlights her ethnicity, hoping to convince the judge to apply different standards:

> It is not surprising that an indigenous girl, like Policarpia, should be lacking beauty [pubic hair], like all people of her class, who go to their grave after sixty to eighty years of life, the men without beards to shave and the women without beauty [pubic hair] in their parts. Likewise, it is blind to believe that the lack of development of the breasts is a sign that she has not achieved puberty.[9]

Although the lawyer's strategy did not work, officials generally presumed that pubescent poor girls had sexual experiences at a younger age than their richer sisters. The onset of puberty meant the likely commencement of sexual relations, and when a birth or baptismal certificate could not be produced, doctors went to great lengths to determine age by assessing the development of the breasts, hips, and genital organs. Their goal was to establish if the female victim was younger than sixteen, but also to determine if her body was physically developed enough to engage in sexual relations, which in their terms meant a vagina that had the capacity to accept entry of a penis. Puberty implied the capacity for sexual relations for all girls, but poor and Indian girls, it was presumed, gave their consent to said relations at an earlier age. Permission could mean just failing to resist. Likewise, in depositions, court scribes more commonly noted working-class or indigenous girls as *soltera* (single) or *libre* (free) rather than *doncella* (virgin). Doncella was reserved for the few elite girls represented in the body of cases.

While puberty marked the age of consent for girls, the state of the hymen defined for the judge whether they were virgins or not. Manuel mentioned to the judge that he had heard rumor in the community that Josefa had been already been deflowered by a certain Alfredo. Josefa claimed to be a virgin, but the magistrate required "scientific" proof. Doctors from the main hospital examined the young girl in order to assess her virginity by judging the integrity of her hymen and looking for signs of violence or force. Midwives had performed this role in the earlier cases, with the first medical doctor, a man, cited only in 1850. In later decades, especially the 1880s, medical exams or virginity tests occurred in every case, as Porfirian politicians, judges, and technicians increasingly championed everything scientific. In

Josefa's case, physicians determined she had engaged in sexual intercourse, but because she possessed what they termed "an elastic hymen," they could not conclude that she had been recently deflowered. In cases involving girls with this type of hymen, it was impossible for the doctors to determine whether the subject was or was not a virgin.[10] Judges deemed girls in this liminal state to have been sexually active and therefore not candidates for legal protection.

Luz Esther did not undergo a virginity exam for two reasons. First, her mother pressed a charge of attempted seduction and abduction, arguing that she frustrated Manuel's ploy by rescuing Luz Esther from his lecherous clutches. The mother still demanded marriage to repair the family honor, but she never claimed that Manuel deflowered her daughter. Significantly, Luz Esther had remained in a public place, in the presence of other people, rather than under Manuel's power, in his home or a hotel. More importantly, the family's class status exempted them from having government-paid doctors examine the minor girl. The elite cases represent only 4 percent of the total, but in only one of these cases did the girl undergo a virginity exam, at the instigation of her father.

In another elite case, Enriqueta's father, Leonardo Selle, had his personal doctor tender a certificate of virginity to the court to publicly prove his daughter was still a virgin even if she had rashly eloped one night with her suitor, Luis Labadie. The father did not want to force a marriage. Significantly, he paid his family physician to do the exam rather than have the same doctors who treated prostitutes and the indigent in the city's hospital set their hands on his beloved Enriqueta.[11]

Although it is difficult to know what factors might have excused a medical evaluation, middle- and upper-class families probably could avoid the embarrassment and humiliation of having their daughters examined by male doctors. If the young women were found not to be virgins, the families had more to lose in terms of honor and cultural power than their poorer counterparts in the rapto dramas. It was paramount that elite daughters maintain their virginity until marriage or at least the public façade of that condition. Working-class girls had more flexibility on this matter. Francisca did not have a gynecological exam because she rejected Filomeno, and the judge saw no reason to go further as her father did not want to force the marriage. However, her case was unique as poor girls suffered exams even when the boys desired to marry them, a promise that should have made a virginity test unnecessary. Judges and lawyers sexualized working-class indigenous girls, believing them to be sexually active at a young age. Why go ahead with a genital exam if the male defendants promised to marry the girls? Evidently, judges had no qualms in subjecting poor girls to further shame or allowing doctors to further their investigations of female sexuality and the diversity of hymen types.[12] Proving that a poor girl was not a virgin when the "abduction" occurred would quickly bring the court proceedings to an end. It was not culturally appropriate to have middle- and upper-class daughters subjected to forced gynecological exams. What if doctors found that she had lost her virginity long ago? What damage would that wreak on Oaxaca's elite families? Señor Selle, who contracted his private physician to prove his daughter's virginity, needed to publicly pronounce his own honor by proving his daughter's virtue. Excusing elite girls from examination by strange men set them apart from the masses that suffered constant scrutiny during the liberal nineteenth century. After all it was not the sexuality of the elite that required inspection and modification, but the working class and their alleged promiscuity and sexual deviancy.

Notions of honor and shame have shaped the lives of women from all classes.[13] The popular classes accepted an elite-defined honor code and fine-tuned and refashioned it for their purposes.[14] They were also very vocal and insistent about their possession of honor in their communication with each other. Recall the love letters of Enrique to Carmen. He wrote: "I don't want to overlook my obligations as a married man," and "Darling, you also ask me if I will use you like all men use women. My love, I will never betray you. You very well know how much I love you, and I would never use you."[15] His letter and testimony go on to claim that he always had honorable intentions in his love for Carmen. Additionally, fourteen-year-old laundress, María, testified that Francisco approached her on the street and attempted to talk to her several times. To prove her honorable reputation, she informed the judge that whenever she met Francisco on the street, she resisted his attempts at conversation and pelted him with rocks in hopes of spurning further entreaties.[16] Resisting his overtures proved that María possessed honor, since speaking to men who were not one's relatives implied either coquetry or worse, promiscuity. If working-class girls could not be sheltered in their homes, they could at least carry that sense of enclosure with them in the streets.[17]

The rapto dramas of Josefa, Francisca, and Luz Esther reveal a complex honor code in nineteenth-century Mexico. Although elite and working class alike shared many values in this code, the rapto cases disclose important differences. Josefa's mother, Juana, acknowledged to the magistrate that marriage would be the likely solution but protested that her daughter was only fourteen years old, and Manuel had no resources or anything else to prove him a responsible man. Furthermore, she called the young man a vagrant and asked for the full prosecution of the law. Her daughter's virginity had been taken, and dishonor rained down on her home, but nevertheless, Josefa's mother did not want them to marry and had opposed their relationship from the outset. Francisca's father, the baker, Antonio, wanted his daughter back, too. He never asked for the couple to marry, and even the dishonored girl rejected marriage in favor of returning to her widowed father and elder sister. She admitted losing her virginity to Filomeno, but in the end, she chose her family over la mala vida with his. She did not accept the traditional script's ending of repairing her honor through marriage to a suitor she decided was unsuitable for whatever reason.

As far as we know, Luz Esther did not achieve her aim of marrying Manuel. Nonetheless, her testimony reveals traditional aspects of elite honor that contrasted with the cases of Josefa and Francisca. Certainly Luz Esther was bold to skip piano lessons and go to Manuel's shop on the zócalo. Likewise, it was remarkable that she walked the city streets alone, upsetting the stereotype that all honorable women should be accompanied by chaperones. Luz Esther played on feminine vulnerability and masculine power by describing how Manuel forcefully grabbed her arms and ordered her to await his return. She also inferred that Manuel commissioned his brother to keep her in the store, even plying her with wine to play on her vulnerability. In Luz Esther's testimony and alleged behavior, she acted in ways that fit traditional gender roles—superior morality, chasteness, and sexual vulnerability. She refused to be his lover outside of marriage, turned down an offer of wine, and depicted herself as a prisoner in the store until her mother rescued her.

Luz Esther declined to be Manuel's amasia and rejected a consensual union as an acceptable stage before marriage. This set her apart from many of the runaway daughters who recognized an amasiato as a prelude to marriage or even a satisfactory type of permanent relationship. As discussed previously, marriages were expensive affairs that required the poor to save for the fees and festivities. At the same time, the working class recognized consensual unions outside the civil registry as legitimate conjugal arrangements. This is proven by the number of marital disputes litigated between amasios as well as between *esposos* (legal spouses).[18] However, as a member of the elite, Luz Esther's stake to honor required her to reject an amasiato in favor of marriage. Only the poor cohabited outside of marriage. Even though Manuel promised to protect her reputation by discreetly conveying her to a hotel in a closed carriage to presumably test her virginity, she certainly gained points with the judge by refusing this ruse. Poor couples living together outside of civil marriage were a different matter. Judges condoned consensual unions for the popular classes, as seen in their decisions in the rapto cases. Although they never directly promoted consensual unions in their written decisions, in the end, the judges' exoneration of defendants without requiring proof that a marriage took place endorsed these unofficial unions as legitimate relationships.

Even though the law dictated, however murkily, the distinction between dishonest and honest or prostitute and virgin, the discourse revealed in the testimonies of deflowered young women, their parents, and witnesses challenged the official version of female respectability and honor. In effect, the young women possessed a modified sense of morality and honor that did not entirely mimic the conceptualizations held by their boyfriends, parents, or court officials. In their eyes (as well as in the eyes of some of the boyfriends), a girl not being a virgin when she ran off with her current lover did not diminish her honor and marriageability. Although the law may have labeled them dishonorable and therefore not worthy of protection under the penal code, the women asserted their worth through accounts of their comportment in daily life, work, and relationships. For example, Josefa claimed honor when she wrote in a love letter to Manuel that even though she was poor and had to go out in the street, she maintained her good reputation by her modest conduct. Specifically, she avowed that she never talked to strange men.[19] In the cases, alternative constructions of moral behavior emerged that in effect muted polar distinctions between virgin and whore. Non-virgins could still possess honor in their own eyes and in the eyes of their sweethearts and families. Young women could also display assertive traits, such as brazenness and cunning, and not suffer the censure of their peers. Hence, the popular classes asserted their own version of morality and social norms that sometimes paralleled, and at other times diverged from, the elite's rendition.[20] These diversions may not have been dramatic, but they certainly draw a more complete portrait of how honor worked in nineteenth-century Mexican society. These alternate values may have been based on class and also ethnicity considering Oaxaca's unique historical trajectory. It is probable that indigenous gender relations had a bearing on these cases. Zapotec culture recognized female assertiveness and indigenous women embroiled in conjugal disputes had a plethora of defenses for protecting themselves, including appealing to values of social peace and harmony in the community, enlisting the help of male elders, and relying on the support of their families and female allies (see chapter 1). Recognition of female power and assertiveness also informed the community response to conjugal disputes. Self-assured and forceful women, like Josefa, may not have been that unusual among ethnic Oaxacans. In any case, indigenous women displayed these attributes to affirm and fight for their own decisions and wishes. Virginity, honor, and marriage were prized in indigenous communities, but indigenous women also had a more flexible honor code than did their elite counterparts in the rapto dramas. This flexibility played out in the identities and roles pursued by the runaway daughters. Importantly as well, a publicized loss of virginity was not as damaging to working-class girls as it was to their elite counterparts. Elite women who sexually transgressed the norms of virginity and modesty by bearing children out of wedlock still managed to maintain honor as long as the transgressions stayed private. A public breach of the transgression could irreparably damage her honor and status in the community.[21] For poor women, the sexual transgression of childbearing or sexual relations outside of wedlock had fewer grave consequences. Marriage and legitimate childbearing may have been a desired norm, but, clearly, other conjugal forms were accepted as legitimate and respectable by the working class.

The assertive young women of the rapto dramas frequently acted one way in private and then expressed those actions very differently in court, each time hoping to get their way. Their actions, therefore, were based on the situation they found themselves in. At the same time, the youthful actions of the couples and the responses of their families occurred within the context of the capital city. Their behaviors were not as neatly circumscribed as they might have been had they lived in outlying, indigenous villages, where presumably everyone knew everyone else's business. Indeed, although we lack official statistics, it is probable that elopement to overcome parental objection to marriage was more common and effective in urban areas than in rural pueblos. This may account for the few cases where parents appealed to Oaxaca City courts because they failed to receive the desired justice in their villages. In the case of Inocente and Carmen discussed previously, the mayor incarcerated the abductor for three days, a cursory sentence that Carmen's parents rejected and which propelled them to turn to the capital's justice system.[22] The city itself not only provided more opportunities to develop a romantic liaison but it also provided some semblance of anonymity outside the pueblo. Parents may have had more trouble watching the movement and actions of their children, as it is likely that each family member had to work in order to maintain the household. In a large number of cases, the girls eloped while on errands or while working for their parents, also indicating an economic imperative that resulted in the children not being completely supervised. As discussed previously, the traditional script required that the female victims of seduction be passive. Yet girls received conflicting messages. The official norms and the ideology that undergirded the law defined women as passive in romantic and sexual relations (chapter 2). However, popular culture advised girls to actively create the conditions for them to be chosen by a suitor (chapter 3). While the boy thought he chose the girl, in reality, popular culture advised girls to make sure they were chosen.[23] Girls also adeptly and shrewdly wielded the classic language of the dominant culture when speaking of threats to family order and stains on their honor. Presumably lawyers, judges, and even notaries may have influenced the girls' testimonies and defenses through suggestion and leading questions.

The state, through its judges and their rulings in the rapto cases, also emitted contradictory messages. Judges viewed poor and indigenous girls as sexual beings and subjected them to medical exams to prove their virginity while they exempted middle- and upper-class girls. For the first, sexual experience was expected; virginity had to be proven. For the second, innocence was assumed and more importantly, these families had to be spared the humiliation of virginity tests. However, the contradictions went beyond medical proof. The state assumed the role of patriarch to emancipate runaway daughters and censure abusive parents, or at least, parents who could not control the girl's behavior (chapter 5). Generally, courts sanctioned the elopement as the first step toward a future marriage at an indeterminate time. These girls were pubescent and over the legal marriage age of twelve. In the cases, the median age was sixteen for the girls; twenty-one, for their suitors. However, although political agendas told judges that rapto was a practice needing extirpation, they never required proof that a marriage had occurred after the court trial. They emancipated girls from paternal authority, but patria potestad transferred to no one until they legally married. Although the judges prized paternal authority in theory, they trespassed that power in cases involving working-class families. The state could both protect minor girls from alleged abuse by emancipating them but also propel them from protected childhood to adulthood. Adolescence was still a nascent and fleeting concept for working-class girls, as those who did marry their suitors immediately came under their dominion.

In reality, while consensual unions could be short-lived and fraught with insecurity, girls who became amasias may have had greater autonomy than their married counterparts. They surely suffered when they paired with men who abused or abandoned them, but they also had more leeway to throw them out and take up with someone else—a necessity for many working families who relied on income from all members of the household. Not legally bound to their men, they never faced adultery charges for proceeding to another consensual union. Girls who chose consensual unions over civil marriage, however, had little legal recourse to make an estranged lover support his children. However, as a practice that was condoned in especially urban working-class neighborhoods, this may have been the best arrangement for many girls. Effectively emancipated from parental authority as a minor, she entered a stage of independence and autonomy, not legally under her amasio's power but with the power of the courts to censure him if he abused her. At the same time, the girls who married their suitors at least escaped their intolerable situations at home. Many of them charged child abuse or that their stepfathers made constant sexual advances. Some parents it seemed simply refused their daughters' suitors because they abhorred losing a source of family income as customarily she moved out of the house to either live with his family or on their own. Parents citing economic reasons for their rejection of their children's marriage choices surfaced in colonial and modern cases. Elite parents did not want to divide up their assets and issue the customary inheritance when a son or daughter married.[24] Poor families of nineteenth-century Oaxaca feared the loss of labor and income when their daughters moved out of the house. For elite and poor families, the trepidation of economic devastation overruled their concerns about the happiness of their sons and daughters.

The Semantics of Working-Class Honor

In the cases, several working-class participants utilized the word "honra" before elite court officials, which perhaps proves that these words had entered their lexicon as verbal tools to defend their actions and stake their claim to respectability.[25] Others simply employed the concepts without uttering the word itself. Parents wielded notions of honor to impugn the reputation of their daughters and their suitors and assert their authority as respectable parents. For example, Macaria pleaded with the judge to punish her adolescent daughter's seducer, Jesús García. She and another witness recounted that Jesús had a history of attacking women and seducing young innocent girls, noting that they had heard he had cut one unfortunate victim's face with a knife.[26] Young men also utilized the honor concept to assure the court that they would marry the women they had dishonored and thus prevent their own punishment. Young women either employed honor as a reason for deciding to reject suitors or to force the court to demand marriage or compensate them for their lost honor. Occasionally, court officials also entered the fray and discussed honor openly in their official discourse.

In 1890, Señora Francisca Reyes appeared before the court, incensed that her daughter had been seduced and kidnapped by a teacher at her school, Andrés Flores. Feeling shamed by the scandal, Señora Reyes asserted her honor, telling the court "that even despite my poverty, I have always instilled honor and morality in my children and until him, she [her daughter] had not had any relations with any man nor did she provoke gossip of any kind." The mother continued to speak of the scandal of a teacher bringing darkness to the school and village as "a real-life example of deceiving the innocent and playing with the honor of another's charge."[27]

Another mother reached a point of desperation and turned to the court to force her daughter's seducer to marry her now-pregnant and disgraced child:

> As I am a widow, but honest and modest, I have had to work to support my orphaned children and send my daughter, Andrea, every day to this city from my village to sell the product of my labor, and he fraudulently deflowered her with treachery and seduced her with gifts and an offer to transport her and her cargo to town on his donkey.[28]

Andrea's mother who lived in San Pedro Yatlahuac brought in several witnesses to testify to her daughter's respectable conduct before this incident. Unfortunately for this family, Andrea's age of twenty-three precluded any court intervention, and her fate is unknown.

Another mother invoked honor and her status as a good mother when filing a complaint of abduction and rape against one Reinaldo. Washerwoman Manuela had a friend write the court on her behalf:

> I have a seventeen-year-old daughter named Rosa . . . and naturally, she lives with me and I have fulfilled my obligations as a mother. After making many small investigations, I have discovered that Señor Reinaldo seduced her with lewd intentions resulting, at last, in her abandoning my home.[29]

One Sebastiana also emphasized her honor as the moral guardian of her daughter Mariana. Apparently a doctor seduced Mariana, and when Sebastiana demanded that he marry the girl, he told her that a "professional" could not marry *"una hija del pueblo"* (an Indian girl). Mariana disappeared from home, and Sebastiana stressed to the court "that the disappearance of a child warrants a search by the mother."[30] As a single mother, no doubt Sebastiana felt she had to emphasize her good mothering skills to the judge.

Ponder the case of Arcadio again, the boy caught red-handed with his pants around his ankles. He stood accused of deceiving Anastacia, and her father was boiling mad. This father, Juan Delgado, carefully laid out his prerogatives as honorable man and father. He told the court that Arcadio had contracted marriage with Anastacia, several months before the boy broke into the Delgado home. The father complained that Arcadio took advantage of his absence from home to deflower his daughter without her consent. The father assured the judge that "fully realizing what had occurred, I thought about getting a pistol to defend my honor, but this man [Arcadio] and my two daughters got down on their knees and begged me to relent." After his fury subsided, he reluctantly agreed to meet Arcadio's parents to arrange a solution. But Arcadio's parents never initiated the meeting, so Juan Delgado resorted to a criminal complaint.[31] Anastacia's father believed that he had to prove his dignity and respectability as an honorable and dutiful patriarch. Hence, he probably did threaten to shoot Arcadio for dishonoring his home, yet he also showed restraint in noting that his daughters and Arcadio fell to their knees to beg forgiveness and leniency from the patriarch. His behavior prevented him from "losing face" as a strong father and defender of family honor. Like this father, most parents laid out their prerogatives and status as honorable and dutiful guardians of their minor children to argue that their complaint should be heard fairly by the court.

Parents and their children also wielded constructions of honor to impugn the reputation of the young men in court. One mother, Encarnación, lamented the seduction of her daughter, Herlinda Mendoza, at the hands of a serial lothario in her pueblo. Apparently, Mateo Pérez seduced and deflowered the girl with a false promise of marriage, a strategy he had employed earlier with another young woman of the pueblo who also became pregnant. Encarnación took the opportunity to comment on the libertine nature of young men in general. Calling for Mateo's incarceration, she argued that his "punishment would serve as an example to those in my village who say we are in a time of greater freedom and because of this, they decide they can spoil and disgrace young girls and disrupt family peace."[32] Another mother stated outright that "Crisóforo was a man of bad conduct . . . who would not fulfill the obligations that he contracted with my daughter." She also charged that he and her daughter had stolen 22 pesos from her market stall. She further denigrated his character and unsavory motivations by declaring that he had to get her daughter drunk first in order to seduce her.[33] In effect, she accused both minor children of robbery and bad conduct in an attempt to have the judge deny them the right to marry.

It is telling that parents like Encarnación lamented the increasing libertine culture of Mexico's youth. She called on the judge to punish her daughter's seducer, not only to restore her own sense of justice but also to send a message to the roguish, young men of her village. Her complaint and others point to a subtle undercurrent of the rapto cases. Through the centuries, parents had sued in court to make their daughters' seducers marry them in order to restore family peace and honor. Conversely, in lieu of a forced marriage, they fought for the punishment of the seducer and the return of their daughters to the family home. These motivations are clear and regularly substantiated through a myriad of cross-cultural studies. In the Oaxacan cases, there is a contradiction between working-class support of the practice of amasiato and parents suing to prevent their minor children from entering a consensual union. If lower order Oaxacans recognized such unions as a legitimate marriage form, then why did so many parents seek court intervention after their daughters eloped? Recall that the greatest proportion of rapto complaints occurred in the 1870s and 1880s. Better record keeping may have been a factor, but more likely, the liberal discourse promoting civil marriage and regular unions may have motivated parents to fight their daughters' romantic decisions hoping they would make a better match, marry in a civil ceremony, or at least grow older before they left home. Perhaps a generational gap operated in late nineteenth-century Oaxaca as some parents felt that their children neither sought their counsel nor respected the honor code of families. In many ways, all the classes had the same honor code, but it may have been negotiated between generations in ways that generated substantial quarreling between parents and their children. While Encarnación placed the onus on male libertines, other mothers criticized their daughters for making rash decisions with little thought to their consequences. For the daughters' parts, they maneuvered to assert their rights and guarantees as Mexican minors. Parents were both a threat and source of support to them. They may have embraced the circulating liberal discussion of individual guarantees and freedoms and acted boldly to run away and start their next life stage as wife or amasia. Moreover, single mothers who fought to have their daughters' suitors marry them may have wanted the security of a civil marriage for their daughters for the presumably honorable distinction it bestowed on them as legal wives. Surely, some of them must have been influenced by the official rhetoric that promoted civil marriages as the most respectable and patriotic marital form and desired this ideal for their daughters. What is clear is that families were rife with conflict during the late nineteenth century, belying the façade of social peace during the Porfiriato.

Clearly, the working class had a keen sense of honor, a fact that elite society sustained in court. Judges listened to these individuals discuss how their honor had been threatened or assaulted by the actions of minor daughters and their suitors. Nineteenth-century Oaxacans, whether elite or working-class, shared a structure of language and meaning surrounding honor and sexuality to communicate effectively with each other, although they differed as to the behaviors purported by these ideas. Certainly female virginity was upheld by all participants, but hard work and modest behavior were other determinants of working-class honor.[34] Parents as well as the sons and daughters in the cases had to lay claim to honor to both defend and justify their actions.

An alternative code of honor and sexuality existed for working-class Oaxacans. Their notions of female respectability and honor proved to be flexible. Honor and virtue did not rest solely on female virginity. In fact, most of the girls voluntarily left with their sweethearts and testified that they had not been deceived by them. Girls like Josefa asserted an active sexuality and a forceful strategy of eloping with their lovers. In many ways, some of them switched roles with the men by masterminding their elopement and persuading (seducing) their lovers to run away with them. Yet, before the court, they also displayed a passive, traditional femininity and attempted to prove their honor by appealing to traditional notions of female respectability. They could have sex before marriage as long as they had a promise of betrothal from their boyfriends. When it came to describing the actual sexual acts, the girls described their participation as passive, language that was possibly scripted by the lawyer or their consciousness of traditional female sexual roles.[35]

Courtroom narratives combined familiar, meaningful themes and a litany of individual details. The narratives plied by men and women served to affect legal outcomes, but as stories or performances, they also had their own meanings and motivations. Outside the court, these stories reflected the conflicts of gender relations in society. Participants aimed to be plausible and comprehensible, and to achieve that, their verbal performances were shaped by prevailing norms and morals. Hayden White has commented that "every fully realized story . . . is a kind of allegory, points to a moral, or endows events, whether real or imaginary, with a significance that they do not possess as a mere sequence . . . narrativity is intimately related to the impulse to moralize reality."[36] These narratives of everyday life were told and retold using universal complaints, characters, and themes. Gender informed each and every attempt at moralizing a complaint or a defense. In effect, both parties to the trial performed an archetypal version of gender relations. The young virgin was either deceived or forced by the man. The man was justified in abandoning the woman because she was not a virgin or he had been manipulated by an aggressive, calculating temptress. The testimonies were based on stock stereotypes of man and woman, and it seemed that every participant relied on them to make their cases plausible. The underlying legal meanings supported these archetypal machinations as well. Only virginal women were protected by the rapto law. Even the proof of the use of force in the encounter was insufficient if the man could convince the judge that the girl was not a virgin and therefore unworthy of protection.[37] Inocente and his friends who provided testimony followed this ruse, stressing Carmen's assertive, sexual nature in an attempt to depict her as the architect of her own deflowering and an archetype of a treacherous, worldly woman. However, it backfired, as he was one of seven young suitors sentenced to prison.

Is it useful to think of depositions as gendered performances? Like a more traditional performance in a public protest or a theater, the skill of testifying at court required that participants provide a coherent and plausible message. It was up to them to select the details to highlight, to stress particular times and spaces, and fix attention on certain themes. Like an actor, those who provided testimonies played out a role modeled after male or female archetypes—to show that they were honorable men or women and therefore, believable, they hoped, to the judge. Although these narrative acts were not entirely contrived, it is useful to see them as verbal performances where men and women played out traditional expectations of masculinity and femininity but also sometimes admitted non-archetypal attributes. Hence, Josefa could be assertive in the engineering of her own abduction while also playing the role of a deceived and vulnerable young woman before the judge. The father, Juan, who found his daughter's suitor with his pants around his ankles, assumed dual masculine roles. First, he assured the judge that he would have been justified in shooting Arcadio because that was his prerogative as a patriarch protecting his honor and family.[38] Secondly, he played the role of a civilized man who desired to be reasonable with his daughter's seducer. Juan placed himself in the company of other liberals, like the judge, who believed in the supremacy and universal application of the law. The patriarch eschewed the use of violence and agreed to settle the matter properly by agreeing to the couple's marriage if Arcadio's parents came to request the girl's hand on their son's behalf. Juan stressed to the judge that a legal complaint was necessary because Arcadio and his family did not fulfill their responsibility to arrange the betrothal. These small performances point to the fact that gender identity was not fixed across time and space and could readily be manipulated for different purposes and audiences.

Conclusion

There are several issues that jump out from the dramas of Josefa, Francisca, and Luz Esther. First, as a caveat, my aim is not to conjure up women's power out of a set of documents. The reality is that vis-à-vis men, women and girls held the short straw when it came to politics and public life. Undeniably, the bargaining power between lovers in the process of courtship and rapto was anything but even. Women gave up their virginity in return for the man's commitment to marry or live in a consensual union. They had more to lose if their suitors had a change of heart, abandoning them now deflowered or worse still, pregnant. Yet, scholars have overemphasized virginity as the main determinant of female honor, especially for the working class. As the cases from Oaxaca attest, female honor and respectability did not always depend on sexual purity. Men and women negotiated and renegotiated the patriarchal contract.[39] The word "contract" is important because the two parties, man and woman, each had responsibilities to fulfill. Many women sought legal redress if their husbands abandoned or abused them, reasoning that the men had not fulfilled their duties as a husband and/or father. Women did hold power in these cases, and the court often decided in their favor. The term "contract" is also crucial because these actors, no matter how lowly they might have been in the eyes of the elite, considered themselves to be a part of the social contract or body politic. Thus, they creatively maneuvered through the world of laws and politics to achieve their goals and exercise their rights as citizens. If we return to the story of Josefa that began this chapter, we might say that she and many other working-class Mexican girls performed multiple gender identities to defend and regain their honor and rights. The many faces of Josefa show that she, like her compatriots, displayed dynamic traits that neither conformed to, nor simply deviated from, the dominant honor complex that laid out gender norms. This alternative structure displayed in the rapto cases shows that masculinity and femininity did not rest on binary poles. In fact, in the preceding stories, female agency was masculine in this time and place.

Likewise, the female protagonists' rapto dramas reveal that family conflict was an important characteristic of nineteenth-century Mexico. Daughters resisted their parents placing them as domestic servants in elite homes, complained about excessive workloads, feared the sexual advances of stepfathers at home, and believed themselves worthy enough to make the decision of when and with whom to run away. They may have desired legitimate marriage most of all, but many accepted consensual unions as an acceptable alternative. Their mothers lamented the girls' seduction at the hands of local lotharios and grumbled over the disintegrating morals of the time, but daughters stood at a nexus between the old and new generations. Elopement is a timeless strategy of minors to overcome parental objection to marriage, but in these cases, runaway daughters manipulated elite judges' understanding of liberal ideals to achieve their goals. Unfortunately, their strategy led to some humiliating outcomes, such as virginity tests, but for these young women, virginity was also a form of capital that they could wield effectively with paramours and jurists alike.

Conclusion

❦

Fifteen-year-old Marina sat with her younger brother, Rafael, on a park bench in the town square. She rested after joining fellow villagers in celebrating their patron saint's festival for three days. The town band played in the gazebo, while vendors hawked bags of spiced fruit, religious trinkets, and squash-blossom quesadillas. Marina had assisted other girls in her neighborhood with preparing the flowers for the church's altar. During the festival, she had spurned the advances of José, an older man from a neighboring village who had a bad reputation for drinking and fighting. She spotted him several times during the festivities, and her mother warned her not to talk to him. As the nighttime fireworks ended, Marina left the plaza with her younger brother and headed home. As she rounded the corner, José grabbed her by the braids and pulled her into his car while she screamed and her brother ran off crying toward home. An hour later, Marina found herself in José's house, whereupon he forced her to have sex with him. She did not scream because she abhorred the idea of creating a scandal among villagers. The next day her family rescued her, but they did not initiate a suit against her rapist. Indeed, she never had her day in court to tell her version of events. Instead, her parents negotiated with José's family to arrange a quick marriage. Marina protested, but dreading her impending marriage, she acquiesced to her parents' wishes.

Marina and José are fictional characters, but since every chapter has begun with a real-life story, I thought that I would offer this tale as one that might easily be found by historians delving into twentieth and twenty-first century archives if her parents had decided to prosecute. Although the present study focused on the elopement of minor children, currently, controversy revolves around a variation of rapto more akin to rape, bride stealing, or abduction of an unwilling girl for sex than to the elopement scenarios from the late nineteenth century. The distinction between seduction, rape, and voluntary elopement continues to be murky. Mexican men could rape girls and not face charges of rape or rapto as long as they agreed to wed their victims until Mexico revised its rape law in 1991.[1] Like their nineteenth-century counterparts, victims still must prove that they are chaste and pure in order to sue their offenders in court. Some girls succumb to family and community pressure and agree to marry their rapists to restore harmony and honor to the family.

In Juchitán, Oaxaca, in the Isthmus of Tehuantepec, rapto persists as a ritualistic prelude to marriage. In that Zapotec community, there is much pomp and circumstance around the stylized abduction of a girl, who is taken to her future in-laws' home. As part of the ceremony, the bride-to-be lies in a bed with white linens surrounded by a ring of red flowers that represent her virginity or perhaps more literally, her hymen. After the wedding night, the groom is expected to show his parents proof of his bride's virtue, usually the bloodstained undergarments or sheets. The difference is that both the girl's and the boy's families agree to the bride-stealing ritual. Parents and children are willing participants in this rapto drama. Moreover, while a ritual of the post-Columbian Zapotec community, this was never a traditional indigenous custom in pre-Columbian Mexico.[2]

Various women's groups and activists rather than Porfirian politicians have led the crusade against the sexual victimization of girls and women in contemporary times. In 2001, the Oaxacan Women's Institute convinced the state legislature to increase the penalty for rapto from four years to ten years in prison, noting that older men kidnapped young girls to marry them or simply to deflower them, and families pressured the girls to marry their rapists to restore honor. The measure's advocates highlighted the cases of several teenage girls who were first forced sexually and then compelled to marry the men who had kidnapped and deflowered them. The legislature agreed that, especially in rural communities, girls were victims of sexual crimes and needed increased protection. The women's group did not relish its victory for long, because the next year, the legislature reneged on its promise to pass the amendment, with one legislator calling the historical practice of rapto "romantic." Those criticizing the lawmakers countered that they were not concerned about elopement when free will was evident all around. Rather they hoped to prosecute a man who could "spot a woman he fancies sitting in a park, pick her up, and carry her away to have sex with her."[3] The stealing of a girl still implies dishonor and the subsequent familial shame, so like nineteenth-century parents, many present-day families settle the matter with the attacker, rather than reporting the event as a crime.

Nineteenth-century Mexican society sent many messages to girls like Josefa, Anastacia, and Carmen, as well as to young men like Arcadio, Manuel, and Melquiadez, that influenced their daily decisions. No doubt family members had the most influence in children's socialization, but abundant moral fables, legends, and stories also warned them of the pitfalls of corrupting influences and deviant behaviors. Parents and children had normative scripts to follow that sometimes coincided with elite prescriptions. Parents had the duty to feed and care for their children, and were justified when castigating them moderately. In turn, children obeyed and respected parents and consulted them in matters of marriage. Yet neglected or abused children could gain the sympathy of community members and, importantly, the judges in the elopement dramas. The law intervened at times, but neighbors or community members could also sanction bad parents just as they would rebellious children. Mistreatment, whether real or concocted, served as an effective excuse for elopement in nineteenth-century Oaxaca—a charge that gained currency with liberal judges who sought to uphold individual guarantees and liberties.

Elopement succeeded as a marriage strategy in the Mexican cases for two reasons. First, in the eyes of the court, little or no social distance existed between the young lovers. Indeed, working-class families did not have as much to lose as did their elite counterparts when a child eloped "unwisely." Many of the mothers who instigated the cases were not married themselves, which may explain their wish for their daughter's economic security. Indeed, although they felt disgrace or dishonor at having a daughter "seduced," the picture may be more complex. What other complicating factors led these mothers to spurn their daughters' suitors? Loss of family labor or a real concern about the ability of the young man to support the daughter must surely have entered some parents' minds. Secondly, elopement succeeded because judges did not incarcerate the young men. Since race and class were not a key issue, they would dismiss cases when the couple and their families agreed to a marriage or if the girl was older than fifteen and the use of force could not be proven. Moreover, in their minds, a crime had not occurred unless the girl was a virgin. Judges provided the loophole by dismissing these cases in exchange for a promise of marriage that allowed young adults to defy their parents' wishes and steer their own destinies in forming unions and families. The state, in theory, wished to punish rapto as a backward rite that threatened public order and morality, but in practice, judges upheld principles of liberalism and free choice by allowing minors to continue clandestine courtships practices *and* freely choose their spouses as individuals. And even though most of the couples were minors, the seduction often resulted in the desired outcome: marriage or a consensual union of minor children without full parental support. Likewise, working-class Mexicans employed concepts of honor to assert their rights as citizens and worthy litigants. Indeed, judges and lawyers agreed that their lower-order compatriots possessed honor, an honor that could be likened to expanded definitions of citizenship in Mexico's liberal century. A person's merit came to define honor, a merit even the poor could claim.[4]

Rapto when both parties willingly participated (elopement) still presented more risks for females. After all, they bargained their virginity (honor) for the economic security of marriage or a consensual union. Sweet words and promises could lead to sexual ravishment and abandonment, and while the man could suffer criticism, his honor remained intact. A young girl deceived by her deflowerer found herself doubly dishonored: First, she had defied her parents, which transgressed the expectation of filial obedience. Second, as a deflowered victim, her chances for marrying were lessened. Undoubtedly, female virginity was highly prized by elite and workers alike. For individual girls like Petrona and Josefa, it was a form of capital that provided them power. As virgins, they were protected by law, and they could trade it for economic security. Unfortunately for many, "science" confounded the asset of female virtue, especially when doctors encountered the elastic or complacent hymen, which made a medical determination of virginity impossible.

Virginity continues to be a prized commodity in many societies. Many gynecologists and plastic surgeons in the United States offer hymenoplasty, a procedure known as "revirgination" that restores a membrane to the vaginal opening. Hymenoplasty involves scraping the upper layer of the tissues that made up the hymen to stimulate their growth once they are stitched together. Doctors endeavor to recreate the star-shaped "ring" as it was prior to sexual relations. Once healed, the revirginized woman will experience tearing, bleeding, and pain upon intercourse—an imagined scenario of what a real virgin would experience. Some doctors also supply their patients with a small vial of animal blood to pour on the wedding night linens just in case they fail to bleed sufficiently to leave the telltale stain. The procedure costs a few thousand dollars. Although clearly not "real" virgins after surgery, the cost and pain are a small price to pay for being "virtuous" on the wedding night.[5]

As shown in the saga of Petrona and Mariano that began this book, parents and youth suffered family conflicts that sometimes attracted official intervention in nineteenth-century Mexico. In the elopement cases, the actors were the same—mothers and fathers, minor daughters and their suitors, court officials, medical doctors, and witnesses—all brought together in the arena of the courtroom where they discussed marriage, honor, sexuality, parental authority, and filial obedience. All of these concepts also formed, in part, nineteenth-century liberal precepts of merit, liberty, and individual rights. The discord sprang from the same source in most of the cases. Parents lamented that their households had been violated by sexual trespasses on family honor. Specifically, they protested that their minor daughters had illegally eloped with their sweethearts or that they had been seduced, deflowered, and possibly even abandoned, resulting in an indelible stain on family honor and, sometimes, pregnancy. Fathers and mothers, however, did not always plead for marriage to expunge the stain. For some, the mere act of filing a criminal complaint provided a veneer of justice that partially offset the effects of public dishonor. To litigate in court upheld their personal honor, but it also distinguished them as individuals protecting their nascent rights as citizens. For example, Cipriana wanted Mariano incarcerated rather than have him marry her daughter. She never mentioned a broken promise of marriage. Yet parents may have been surprised at the court rulings, as the state sided more and more with minors over family heads (fathers or mothers). By extension, protecting the virginity of minor daughters shielded the honor of her father and other family members. By siding with children, however, the state reinforced the efficacy of rapto as a strategy to marry without a parent's consent, in effect, emancipating minors from parental control.

In summary, a teenage pubescent girl sat at a unique point between girl-child and woman, a time that was not yet termed adolescence. The sexual-crime dossiers reveal more than just relations between parents and children and families and the state. Popular understandings of gender norms and honor infuse the testimonies offered by all participants. Indeed, as the courtship of Mariano and Petrona reveals, working-class individuals defined honor differently than did the elite. For them, diligent work habits raised a man's reputation while virginity may not have been the sole determinant of a young girl's marriageability. In some of the cases, even though the girl had been deflowered, the suitor still wished to marry her or the girl spurned the suitor. Marriage to recoup honor was not always their objective.

Notes

Introduction

1. *Código Penal para el Distrito Federal y Territorio de la Baja California sobre delitos del fuero común y para toda la República sobre delitos contra la Federación* (Mexico City: Imprenta de Flores y Monsalve, 1874), 194. Oaxaca later adopted this code, with only a few modifications that are discussed in chapter 4. See *Código Penal para el Estado de Oaxaca* (Oaxaca City: Imprenta del Estado, 1888), chapter V (Rapto).

2. El Marquesado was a working-class community on the capital's northern limits, which the elite believed was populated with beggars, thieves, and unruly workers. It was annexed by Oaxaca City in 1909 to bring this troublesome district under centralized control. See Mark Overmyer-Velázquez, *Visions of the Emerald City: Modernity, Tradition, and the Formation of Porfirian Oaxaca, Mexico* (Durham: Duke University Press, 2006), 45–47.

3. A promise of marriage was considered a sacred pledge between a couple that was upheld by church authorities. Sexual relations and even the birth of children during a period of engagement occurred regularly during the colonial period even for elite couples. The Catholic Church expected that the marriage would occur and thus legitimize children and repair the honor of both the man and woman who had engaged in premarital sex. See Patricia Seed, *To Love, Honor, and Obey in Colonial Mexico: Conflicts over Marriage Choice, 1574–1821* (Stanford, CA: Stanford University Press, 1988) and Ann Twinam, *Public Lives, Private Secrets: Gender, Honor, Sexuality, and Illegitimacy in Colonial Spanish America* (Stanford, CA: Stanford University Press, 1999).

4. *Código civil del Distrito Federal y territorio de la Baja California* (Mexico City: Imprenta dirigida por José Batiza, 1870), Art. 396, and Silvestre Moreno Cora, *Código civil: promulgado en marzo de 1884* (Mexico City: Herrero Hermanos, 1904), Art. 370.

5. Prendas and love letters, in particular, were signs in society and before the court that a couple intended to marry. William E. French, "Prostitutes and Guardian Angels: Women, Work, and the Family in Porfirian Mexico," *Hispanic American Historical Review* 72 (1992). Love letters from the rapto cases are discussed in more detail in Chapter 3.

6. *Contra Mariano Cruz por rapto de seducción en Petrona Vásquez*, Oaxaca, 1886, Juzgado Primero de lo Criminal, Archivo Histórico Municipal de la Ciudad de Oaxaca (AHMCO).

7. Criminal testimonies may present conflicting facts, and as Pablo Piccato notes, "their claims to truth may be suspect even today, but they referred to socialized norms about veracity and justifications of individual behavior." See *City of Suspects: Crime in Mexico City, 1900–1931* (Durham: Duke University Press, 2001), 8.

8. For a discussion of rapto in Porfirian Chihuahua, see William E. French, "'Te Amo Muncho': The Love Letters of Pedro and Enriqueta," in *The Human Tradition in Mexico*, ed. Jeffrey M. Pilcher (Wilmington, DE: Scholarly Resources Inc., 2003). Ira Beltrán-Garibay is working on a dissertation that includes an examination of rapto in twentieth-century Mexico City. Laura Benítez-Barba has researched rapto in Guadalajara. For works that address rapto in colonial Spanish America, see Verena Stolcke, *Marriage, Class, and Colour in Nineteenth-Century Cuba: A Study of Racial Attitudes and Sexual Values in a Slave Society* (Ann Arbor: University of Michigan Press, 1989), and Ramón Gutiérrez, *When Jesus Came, The Corn Mothers Went Away: Marriage, Sexuality, and Power in New Mexico, 1500–1846* (Stanford, CA: Stanford University Press, 1991). For nineteenth-century studies in other parts of Latin America, see Christine Hunefeldt, *Liberalism in the Bedroom: Quarreling Spouses in Nineteenth-Century Lima* (University Park: The Pennsylvania State University Press, 2000) and Tanja Christiansen, *Disobedience, Slander, Seduction, and Assault: Women and Men in Cajamarca, Peru, 1862–1900* (Austin: University of Texas Press, 2004). Also see Kathryn A. Sloan, "Disobedient Daughters and the Liberal State: Generational Conflicts over Marriage Choice in Working-Class Families in Nineteenth-Century Oaxaca, Mexico," *The Americas* 63, no. 4 (2007).

9. Daniela Traffano, "En torno a la cuestión indígena en Oaxaca: La prensa y el discurso de los políticos," in *Historia, sociedad y literatura. Nuevos enfoques*, ed. Carlos Sánchez Silva (Oaxaca: Fondo Editorial IEEPO, 2004), 125.

10. William B. Taylor, *Landlord and Peasant in Colonial Oaxaca* (Stanford, CA: Stanford University Press, 1972) and *Drinking, Homicide, and Rebellion in Colonial Mexican Villages* (Stanford, CA: Stanford University Press, 1979).

11. Steve J. Stern, *The Secret History of Gender: Women, Men, and Power in Late Colonial Mexico* (Chapel Hill: University of North Carolina Press, 1995), 238–51. For an argument that gender complementarity prevailed in Zapotec and Mixtec cultures, see Lisa Mary Sousa, "Women and Crime in Colonial Oaxaca: Evidence of Complementary Gender Roles in Mixtec and Zapotec Societies," in *Indian Women of Early Mexico*, ed. Susan Schroeder, Stephanie Wood, and Robert Haskett (Norman: University of Oklahoma Press, 1997), 86.

12. Oaxaca's ethnic history is discussed in chapter 1. Stern (*The Secret History of Gender*, 241) claims that in Indian Oaxaca, "assertive female styles" were accepted. He also found, through a reading of conjugal disputes in criminal courts, that indigenous women claimed sexual ownership of their husbands. Ronald Spores, *The Mixtec in Ancient and Colonial Times* (Norman: University of Oklahoma Press, 1984), 10–11; for the Zapotec Valley, see Taylor, *Landlord*

and *Peasant*, 28; Joseph Whitecotton, *The Zapotecs: Princes, Priests, and Peasants* (Norman: University of Oklahoma Press, 1977), 155–56; for the Villa Alta, see John Chance, *Conquest of the Sierra: Spaniards and Indians in Colonial Oaxaca* (Norman: University of Oklahoma Press, 1989), 128–31.

13. Seed, *To Love, Honor, and Obey*, 89.

14. Ibid., 5. The Royal Pragmatic on Marriage of 1776 was extended to Spain's colonies in 1778. It allowed parents to successfully block the marriage of their children based on race. In practice, marriages were prevented when parents objected for reasons of social distance based on economics or social status. See Seed, *To Love, Honor, and Obey*, 200–215.

15. Jeffrey Shumway, *The Case of the Ugly Suitor and Other Histories of Love, Gender, and Nation in Buenos Aires, 1776–1870* (Lincoln: University of Nebraska Press, 2005), and Stolcke, *Marriage, Class, and Colour*.

16. Stolcke, *Marriage, Class, and Colour*, 109–10.

17. Stern, *The Secret History of Gender*, 34, 241; Sousa, "Women and Crime."

18. Race was not recorded in criminal cases after Mexican Independence. The working-class participants appear to be mestizo and indigenous descent, judging by their villages of origin. Yet, an indigenous ethnic heritage did not mean that a person's values and customs were not evolving, especially for people who had moved to the capital. The state of Oaxaca was primarily indigenous during this period. I will discuss other potential markers of race, such as attire, in later chapters. Although class is never clearly delineated in court records, I surmised economic status from occupation. There are only a handful of cases where participants are referred to as Don or Doña, honorifics sometimes indicating elite status.

19. Many scholars attest to the reformulation of the family during the liberal era of the nineteenth century. See Mark Szuchman, "A Challenge to the Patriarchs: Love among the Youth in Nineteenth-Century Argentina," in *The Middle Period in Latin America: Values and Attitudes in the Seventeenth to the Nineteenth Centuries*, ed. Mark Szuchman (Boulder: Lynne Rienner Publishers, 1989); Barbara Potthast and Sandra Carrera, eds., *Entre la familia, la sociedad y el estado: Niños y jóvenes en América Latina (Siglos XIX–XX)* (Madrid: Iberoamericana, 2005); Hunefeldt, *Liberalism in the Bedroom*; French, "Prostitutes and Guardian Angels"; Donna J. Guy, "Lower-Class Families, Women, and the Law in Nineteenth-Century Argentina," *Journal of Family History* 10, no. 3 (1985); Silvia M. Arrom, "Changes in Mexican Family Law in the Nineteenth Century: The Civil Codes of 1870 and 1884," *Journal of Family History* 10, no. 3 (1985); Ann S. Blum, "Conspicuous Benevolence: Liberalism, Public Welfare, and Private Charity in Porfirian Mexico City, 1877–1910," *The Americas* 58, no. 4 (2001).

20. Shumway, *The Case of the Ugly Suitor*.

21. Many scholars have noted this effect of liberalism on patria potestad (parental authority). See Arrom, "Changes in Mexican Family Law"; Elizabeth Dore and Maxine Molyneux, eds., *Hidden Histories of Gender and the State in Latin America* (Durham: Duke University Press, 2000); Guy, "Lower-Class Families"; Hunefeldt, *Liberalism in the Bedroom*; Carmen Ramos Escandón, "Entre la ley y el cariño. Normatividad juridical y disputas familiares sobre

la patria potestad en México (1873–1896)" in *Entre la familia, la sociedad y el estado: Niños y jóvenes en América Latina (Siglos XIX–XX)*, ed. Barbara Potthast and Sandra Carrera (Madrid: Iberoamericana, 2005); Szuchman, "A Challenge to the Patriarchs."

22. Francie R. Chassen-López, *From Liberal to Revolutionary Oaxaca: The View from the South, Mexico 1867–1911* (University Park: The Pennsylvania State University Press, 2004), 3.

23. My concept of hegemony is derived from Antonio Gramsci, *Selections from the Prison Notebooks, 1929–1935* (New York: International, 1971), and Susan Kellogg, "Hegemony Out of Conquest: The First Two Centuries of Spanish Rule in Central Mexico," *Radical History Review* 53 (1992). Hegemony is a type of domination that implies a measure of consent from below.

24. Eileen J. Suárez Findlay, in her study of working-class *ponceños*, argued that rapto was a customary courtship practice (*Imposing Decency: The Politics of Sexuality and Race in Puerto Rico, 1870–1920* [Durham: Duke University Press, 1999], ix–xii).

25. Sarah C. Chambers also argues for continuity (*From Subjects to Citizens: Honor, Gender, and Politics in Arequipa, Peru, 1780–1854* [University Park: The Pennsylvania State University Press, 1999], 6).

Chapter One

1. Like many streets and towns, after the Revolution, this market would lose its connection to Porfirio Díaz. Visitors to Oaxaca today will see it is now called "Juárez Market."

2. Charles Berry, *The Reform in Oaxaca, 1856–1876* (Lincoln: University of Nebraska Press, 1981), 3.

3. On the holdings of Hernán Cortés, see Lolita Gutiérrez Brockington, *The Leverage of Labor: Managing the Cortés Haciendas in Tehuantepec, 1588–1688* (Durham: Duke University Press, 1986).

4. María de los Ángeles Romero Frizzi, ed., *Lecturas históricas del estado de Oaxaca, vol. 2, Época colonial* (Mexico City: Instituto Nacional de Antropología e Historia, 1990); Taylor, *Landlord and Peasant*.

5. John K. Chance, *Race and Class in Colonial Oaxaca* (Stanford, CA: Stanford University Press, 1978), 38.

6. Alicia Barabas, "Rebeliones e insurreciones indígenas en Oaxaca. La trayectoría histórica de la resistencia étnica," in *Etnicidad y pluralismo cultural. La dinámica étnica en Oaxaca*, ed. Alicia Barabas and Miguel Bartolomé (Mexico City: Consejo Nacional para la Cultura y las Artes, 1990), 222–23.

7. For a discussion, see Mercedes Olivera and María de los Ángeles Romero Frizzi, "La conquista de las armas," in Romero Frizzi, ed., *Lecturas históricas*; Chance, *Conquest of the Sierra*; and Taylor, *Landlord and Peasant*.

8. Arthur D. Murphy and Alex Stepick, *Social Inequality in Oaxaca* (Philadelphia: Temple University Press, 1991), 18.

9. Taylor, *Landlord and Peasant*, 196.

10. Ibid., 195.

11. Manuel Toussaint, *Oaxaca* (Mexico City: Editorial "Cultura," 1926), 80.

12. Ibid., 81.

13. Ibid., 82.

14. Ralph L. Beals, *The Peasant Marketing System of Oaxaca, Mexico* (Berkeley: University of California Press, 1975); Whitecotton, *The Zapotecs*; Bronislaw Malinowski and Julio de la Fuente, *Malinowski in Mexico: The Economics of a Mexican Market System*, ed. Susan Drucker-Brown (London: Routledge and Kegan Paul, 1982).

15. Stern, *The Secret History of Gender*, 30–31; Marcelo Carmagnani, "Local Governments and Ethnic Government in Oaxaca," *Essays in the Political, Economic, and Social History of Colonial Latin America*, ed. Karen Spalding (Newark: Latin American Studies Program, University of Delaware).

16. Several Nahuatl-speaking allies followed Cortés to Antequera. Some four thousand probably resided in barrios around Antequera but were soon acculturated to Hispanic society. In 1790, Antequera grew to eighteen thousand residents. Of this number, seven thousand were mulattos and Indians and eleven thousand were Spaniards and mestizos. See Whitecotton, *The Zapotecs*, 183–84.

17. Ibid., 187.

18. Eric Wolf, *Sons of the Shaking Earth: The People of Mexico and Guatemala—Their Land, History, and Culture* (Chicago: University of Chicago Press, 1959), 214–42; Inga Clendinnen, "Yucatec Maya Women and the Spanish Conquest: Role and Ritual in Historical Reconstruction," *Journal of Social History* 15, no. 3 (1982); Holly F. Mathews, "Sexual Status in Oaxaca: An Analysis of the Relationship between Extradomestic Participation and Ideological Constructs of Gender" (PhD diss., Duke University, 1982); Beverly Chiñas, *The Isthmus Zapotecs: A Matrifocal Culture of Mexico*, 2nd ed. (Fort Worth: Harcourt, Brace, Jovanovich, 1992); and Laura Nader, *Harmony Ideology: Justice and Control in a Zapotec Mountain Village* (Stanford, CA: Stanford University Press, 1990).

19. William B. Taylor, *Drinking, Homicide, and Rebellion*, 116.

20. Guardino, *The Time of Liberty: Popular Political Culture in Oaxaca, 1750–1850* (Durham: Duke University Press, 2005), 268.

21. Cacica is the female term of cacique, an Indian political leader presumably descended from elite lineages.

22. Whitecotton, *The Zapotecs*, 155–56.

23. For the Mixteca Alta, see Romero Frizzi, *Epoca colonial*, 90; Ronald Spores, *The Mixtec*, 10–11; for the Zapotec Valley, see Taylor, *Landlord and Peasant*, 28; Whitecotton, *The Zapotecs*, 155–56; for the Villa Alta, see Chance, *Conquest of the Sierra*, 128–31.

24. Sousa, "Women and Crime," 201.

25. Stern, *The Secret History of Gender*, 237.

26. Ibid., and Sousa, "Women and Crime."

27. See Stern's discussion of the patriarchal contract, *The Secret History of Gender*, 97–98, 110–11, 283–84. For a discussion of a more even cultural terrain to negotiate gender relations in Oaxaca, see ibid., 238–51.

28. Sousa, "Women and Crime," 211–12. Also see Chiñas, *The Isthmus Zapotecs*.

29. Stern, *The Secret History of Gender*, 239.

30. Susan Kellogg, *Weaving the Past: A History of Latin America's Indigenous Women from the Prehispanic Period to the Present* (New York: Oxford University Press, 2005), 105.

31. Juan Bautista Carriedo, *Ensayo histórico-estadística del departamento de Oaxaca* (Oaxaca: Imprenta del Estado, 1889), 50.

32. Manuel Martínez Gracida, *Las razas indígenas de Oaxaca* (Mexico City: San Jacinto, 1919), and José Antonio Gay, *Historia de Oaxaca* (Mexico City: Imprenta del Comercio de Dublán, 1881), 129.

33. Martínez Gracida, *Las razas indígenas*, 121.

34. Robert McCaa, "Marriageways in Mexico and Spain, 1500–1900," *Continuity and Change* 9, no. 1 (1994). McCaa found that family forms during the colonial period departed dramatically from Iberian and Native American patterns.

35. Ibid., 12.

36. Rodolfo Pastor and Elías Trabulse, *Fluctuaciones económicas en Oaxaca durante el siglo XVII* (Mexico City: El Colegio de México, 1979).

37. Ana Carolina Ibarra, *Clero y política en Oaxaca: Biografía del Doctor José de San Martín* (Oaxaca: Instituto Oaxaqueño de las Culturas, 1995), 90–91. Ibarra recounts the life of the cleric José San Martín and his history as an insurgent during the War of Independence.

38. Guardino, *The Time of Liberty*, 153.

39. Ibid., 172.

40. Ibid., 174. Guardino also cites an article that admonishes women to embrace religious tolerance, which will lead to increased immigration and "many good young men and there will be many weddings."

41. Guardino, *The Time of Liberty*, 194.

42. Michael C. Meyer, William L. Sherman, and Susan M. Deeds, *The Course of Mexican History*, 6th edition (New York: Oxford University Press, 1999), 360.

43. Ibid., 217.

44. Guardino, *The Time of Liberty*, 220.

45. Berry, *The Reform in Oaxaca*, 145.

46. Ibid., 165.

47. Whitecotton, *The Zapotecs*, 221.

48. Francie R. Chassen and Hector G. Martínez, "El desarollo económico de Oaxaca a finales del Porfirato," *Revista Mexicana de Sociología* 48, no. 1 (1986).

49. James Greenberg, *Santiago's Sword: Chatino Peasant Economies and Religion* (Berkeley: University of California Press, 1981).

50. Chassen and Martínez, "El desarollo económico," 285.

51. Francie R. Chassen, "Los precursores de la Revolución en Oaxaca," in *La Revolución en Oaxaca, 1900–1930*, ed. Victor Raúl Martínez (Oaxaca: Instituto de Administración Pública de Oaxaca, 1985), 35–37, 39.

52. Chassen and Martínez, "El desarollo económico," 292.

53. María de la Luz Parcero, *Condiciones de la Mujer en México durante el siglo XIX* (Mexico City: Instituto Nacional de Antropología e Historia, 1992), 75–84.

54. Chassen-López, *From Liberal to Revolutionary Oaxaca*, 267–68.

55. *Estatutos de la Sociedad de Obreros Católicos*, quoted in ibid., 269.

56. Chassen-López, *From Liberal to Revolutionary Oaxaca*, 270.

57. Ibid., 423.

58. A traveling reporter for the *Diario del Hogar*, quoted in Chassen-López, *From Liberal to Revolutionary Oaxaca*, 422.

59. Overmyer-Velázquez, *Visions of the Emerald City*, 53.

60. Chassen-López, *From Liberal to Revolutionary Oaxaca*, 423. Baseball was the sport of the *gente decente* (upper class) in Porfirian Oaxaca, and soccer was associated with unruly and unhygienic workers. See Overmyer-Velázquez, *Visions of the Emerald City*, 31–34.

61. In *Alone before God: The Religious Origins of Modernity in Mexico* (Durham: Duke University Press, 2002), Pamela Voekel has argued that modernity had religious origins. More specifically to Oaxaca, the 1826 constitutional legislature, half of whose members were priests, founded the Instituto de Ciencias y Artes whose curriculum included courses not only in ecclesiastical history but also in civic law, the sciences, mathematics, ethics, and political economy. Benito Juárez graduated from the institute, and it competed with the seminary for the minds of Oaxaca's male youth. Indeed, some priests referred to the institute as a "house of heretics . . . and prostitution." See Berry, *The Reform in Oaxaca*, 12. Edward Wright-Rios also makes a case for the piety of Oaxaca's indigenous population ("Piety and Progress: Vision, Shrine, and Society in Oaxaca, 1887–1934" [PhD diss., University of California, San Diego, 2004]).

62. Guardino (*The Time of Liberty*, 159–61) makes this case for pre-1850 Oaxaca and effectively argues that Oaxacan liberalism before the 1850s and 1860s was not anticlerical. See also Chassen-López, *From Liberal to Revolutionary Oaxaca*, 423–44, and Wright-Rios, "Piety and Progress," 130–47.

63. W. E. Carson, *Mexico: Wonderland of the South* (New York: MacMillan, 1914).

64. Wright-Rios, "Piety and Progress." For an interpretation that argues that subalterns contested the messages of civic ceremonies, see Richard Warren, *Vagrants and Citizens: Politics and the Masses in Mexico City from Colony to Republic* (Wilmington, DE: Scholarly Resources, 2001).

65. Guardino, *The Time of Liberty*, 163.

66. Guardino, *The Time of Liberty*, 165.

67. Chassen-López, *From Liberal to Revolutionary Oaxaca*. See also Carlos Sánchez Silva, "Don José Zorrilla Trápaga (1829–1897): El 'Tenorio oaxaqueño,' in *Formación empresarial, fomento industrial y compañías agrícolas en el México del siglo XIX*, ed. Mario Trujillo Bolio and José Contreras Valdez (Mexico City: CIESAS, 2003); Chassen and Martínez, "El desarrollo económico de Oaxaca"; and Overmyer-Velázquez, *Visions of the Emerald City*.

68. Governor Porfirio Díaz addressing the Mexican Congress, September 17, 1882, quoted in Overmyer-Velázquez, *Visions of the Emerald City*, 63.

69. Ibid., 40.

70. Ibid., 41.

71. For a discussion of legalized prostitution in Oaxaca, see Kathryn A. Sloan, "Runaway Daughters and Dangerous Women: Work, Sexuality, and Gender Relations among the Working Class in Porfirian Oaxaca, Mexico" (PhD diss., University of Kansas, 2002). Overmyer-Velázquez (*Visions of the Emerald City*)

also discusses prostitution within the framework of modernization and discipline during the Porfiriato.

72. Overmyer-Velázquez, *Visions of the Emerald City*, 83. Of the 11,605 textile workers in the state, only 570 worked in factories in 1910. Ibid., 82. In 1895, the central district had a population of 66,381, and the capital city had 32,437 residents in 1896. See Chassen-López, *From Liberal to Revolutionary Oaxaca*, 241–42.

73. "La mujer en Oaxaca," *Periódico Oficial del Gobierno del Estado de Oaxaca*, Oaxaca de Juárez, no. 23, March 18, 1888, 1.

74. Chassen-López, *From Liberal to Revolutionary Oaxaca*, 392–99. For other recent studies that look at popular liberalism, see Chambers, *From Subjects to Citizens*; Guardino, *The Time of Liberty*; and Robert H. Jackson, ed., *Liberals, the Church, and Indian Peasants: Corporate Lands and the Challenge of Reform in Nineteenth-Century Spanish America* (Albuquerque: University of New Mexico Press, 1997).

75. Chassen-López, *From Liberal to Revolutionary Oaxaca*, 395.

Chapter Two

1. Love letter contained in the case file *Contra Enrique Martínez por rapto en la joven Carmen Llaguno*, Oaxaca, 1892, Juzgado Criminal Segundo, Archivo Histórico Municipal de la Ciudad de Oaxaca (AHMCO). Whether Enrique penned the letter himself, I cannot determine with certainty. Some lovers relied on scribes or friends who could write. Enrique was literate enough to sign his name to his deposition. This letter is also discussed in chapter 3.

2. For a discussion of these crimes as a reproduction of male power and domination, see Gutiérrez, *When Jesus Came*, 215–16. As a faint-hearted response that attempts to challenge dominant culture, see Martínez-Alier, *Marriage, Class, and Colour*, 100–141.

3. The seduction genre in literature has received ample scholarly attention. Patricia Seed discusses seduction in Spanish literature and theater in her "Narratives of Don Juan: The Language of Seduction in Seventeenth-Century Hispanic Literature and Society," *Journal of Social History* (1993). For Europe and Canada, see Susan Holloway-Ramírez, "Seducers as Agents of Social Change: A Selected History of the Discourse of Seduction in European and Canadian Writing" (PhD diss., University of Manitoba, 2002).

4. Martínez-Alier, *Marriage, Class, and Colour*; Ramón Gutíerrez, *When Jesus Came*; Shumway, *The Case of the Ugly Suitor*; French, "'Te Amo Muncho.'"

5. Sonya-Lipsett Rivera, "The Intersection of Rape and Marriage in Late-Colonial and Early National Mexico," *Colonial Latin American Historical Review* 6, no. 4 (1997).

6. Martínez-Alier also found that nineteenth-century Cuban couples eloped with the goal of forcing the parents to consent to the marriage (*Marriage, Class, and Colour*, 105–6).

7. See Silvia M. Arrom, *The Women of Mexico City, 1780–1850* (Stanford: Stanford University Press, 1985); Elizabeth Anne Kuznesof, "The History of the Family in Latin America: A Critique of Recent Work," *Latin American Research Review* 24, no. 2 (1989); Elizabeth Dore, "The Holy Family: Imagined Households in

Latin American History," in *Gender Politics in Latin America: Debates in Theory and Practice*, ed. Elizabeth Dore (New York: Monthly Review Press, 1997); and the special issue of the *Journal of Family History* 16, no. 3 (1991).

8. I determined the social group based on the person's occupation or when the *expedientes* (case files) contained references to people with titles that indicated elite status, such as "Don" and "Doña."

9. Susan Migden Socolow writes that elite families in colonial Buenos Aires avoided criminal proceedings in dealing with wayward wives and daughters. A public lawsuit would only damage the patriarch's reputation by revealing his lack of control over his women's behavior. See "Women and Crime: Buenos Aires, 1757–1791," *Journal of Latin American Studies* 12, no. 1 (1980): 52.

10. Definitions of homosexuality are more complex in Mexico than in the United States. Mexicans distinguish between men who are the active partner (those who penetrate another) and the maricón or *puto*, the passive partner (those who are penetrated). For further discussion, see Octavio Paz, *The Labyrinth of Solitude: Life and Thought in Mexico*, translated by Lysander Kemp (New York: Grove, 1961); Geoffrey Spurling, "Honor, Sexuality, and the Colonial Church," in *the Faces of Honor: Sex, Shame, and Violence in Colonial Latin America* (Albuquerque: University of New Mexico Press, 1998); and Michael James Higgins and Tanya L. Coen, *Streets, Bedrooms, and Patios: The Ordinariness of Diversity in Urban Oaxaca: Ethnographic Portraits of the Urban Poor, Transvestites, Discapacitados, and Other Popular Cultures* (Austin: University of Texas Press, 2000).

11. Paz, *The Labrinth of Solitude*, 75.

12. Marit Melhuus, "Power, Value, and Ambiguous Meanings of Gender," in *Machos, Mistresses, Madonnas: Contesting the Power of Latin American Gender Imagery*, ed. Marit Malhuus and Kristi Anne Stolen (New York: Verso, 1996), 239.

13. For generations of scholars striving to understand sex and gender and the national character of Mexico, Octavio Paz's book, *The Labyrinth of Solitude*, has been most influential and controversial. For Paz, gender is central to Mexican identity. In his construction, men are closed, impenetrable, protected against the world, while women are open, unprotected, thus weak and penetrable. Utilizing a discussion of the verb *chingar*, which among many definitions means to forcibly penetrate another, Paz lays out the dualisms of *el chingón* (the one who opens or penetrates) and *la chingada* (the passive one who is penetrated or opened). Hernán Cortés represents the original *chingón*, while Malinche exemplifies the original *chingada* and foremother who lives on in Mexico's master narrative. Like the consequences of Eve's consumption of the apple in the Old Testament, Malinche's treachery resulted in a particular Mexican character, according to Paz. In essence, a woman's vulnerability to seduction (and penetration) would have treacherous implications in both master narratives. The gender imagery of Mexican culture has been researched and discussed by several authors: Paz, *The Labyrinth of Solitude*; Roger Bartra, *The Cage of Melancholy: Identity and Metamorphosis in the Mexican Character*, translated by Christopher J. Hall (New Brunswick, NJ: Rutgers University Press, 1992); Debra A. Castillo, *Easy Women: Sex and Gender in Modern*

Mexican Fiction (Minneapolis: University of Minnesota Press, 1998); and Melhuus, "Power, Value, and Ambiguous Meanings of Gender."

14. Gutiérrez, *When Jesus Came*, 221.

15. *Contra Arcadio Ortega acusada de fuerza en Anastacia Delgado*, Oaxaca, 1875, Juzgado Tercero de lo Capital, AHMCO.

16. *Contra Francisco Mimiago por rapto de seducción en Primitiva Franco*, Oaxaca, 1886, Juzgado Primero Criminal, AHMCO.

17. Judith Butler, *Gender Trouble: Feminism and the Subversion of Identity* (New York: Routledge, 1990), 163–81. Butler's theories are useful for understanding identity and how hegemonic discourses shaped gender and how gender is defined by repetition. Scholars interested in applying her theory of performativity sought the "slippages" that effectively displaced dominant discourses and opened up a space for political and social change and for individuals. Some critics of Butler argue that her ruminations do not allow for conscious action by individuals. See, in particular, Lise Nelson, "Bodies (and Spaces) Do Matter: The Limits of Performativity," *Gender, Place, and Culture* 6, no. 4 (1999), 338. Butler attempts to address agency in *Bodies That Matter: On the Discursive Limits of "Sex"* (New York: Routledge, 1993). For another work that addresses the theatricality of gender, see Judith Halberstam, *Female Masculinity* (Durham: Duke University Press, 1998).

18. Lynn Stephen, "Sexualities and Genders in Zapotec Oaxaca," *Latin American Perspectives* 29, no. 2 (2002): 41.

19. Ibid., 43.

20. Several scholars support Edward Shorter's concept of "manipulative sexuality" or the female strategy of exchanging virginity for security. See "Illegitimacy, Sexual Revolution, and Social Change in Modern Europe," in *Journal of Interdisciplinary History*, vol. 2, no. 2 (1971), 241–42. Also see Elizabeth A. Kuznesof, "Raza, clase, y matrimonio en la Nueva España: Estado actual del debate," in *Familias Novohispanas: Siglos XVI al XIX*, ed. P. Gonzalbo (Mexico City: El Colegio de México, 1991), 213; and Hunefeldt, *Liberalism in the Bedroom*, 190.

21. Several scholars have studied elopement and clandestine marriage. See especially the studies of the Gretna Green and Fleet markets, including Roger Lee Brown, "The Rise and Fall of Fleet Marriages," and T. C. Smout, "Scottish Marriage, Regular and Irregular, 1500–1940," in *Marriage and Society: Studies in the Social History of Marriage*, edited by R. B. Outhwaite (New York: St. Martin's Press, 1981).

22. *Contra Exiquio Morales por el rapto de seducción de la menor Beatriz Ramírez*, Oaxaca, 1888, Primero Juzgado Criminal, AHMCO.

23. Findlay also surmises that plebeian *ponceños* often chose serial monogamy over marriage (*Imposing Decency*, 40).

24. Brian Donovan, "Gender Inequality and Criminal Seduction: Prosecuting Sexual Coercion in the Early Twentieth Century," *Law and Social Inquiry: Journal of the American Bar Foundation* 30, no. 1 (2005): 64.

25. Jane E. Larson, "Women Understand So Little, They Call My Good Nature 'Deceit'": A Feminist Rethinking of Seduction," *Columbia Law Review* 93, no. 2 (1993): 383.

26. Ibid., 386.

27. James R. Farr, *Authority and Sexuality in Early Modern Burgundy, 1550–1730* (New York: Oxford University Press, 1995), 102.

28. Rachel G. Fuchs, "Seduction, Paternity, and the Law in Fin de Siècle France," *Journal of Modern History* 72, no. 4 (2000): 946.

29. Ibid., 958. Fuchs notes that the Civil Code of 1804 forbade paternity searches, with the underlying ideology that this measure would force women to act more morally and carefully. Between 1878 and 1912, an unlikely alliance of conservative Catholic, socialist, and radical representatives introduced a series of proposals and exceptions that would allow women to initiate paternity suits.

30. Leah Leneman, "Seduction in Eighteenth and Early Nineteenth-Century Scotland," *The Scottish Historical Review* 78, no. 205 (1999): 39. See also Smout, "Scottish Marriage."

31. Leneman, "Seduction," 40.

32. Seed, *To Love, Honor, and Obey*, 205–15.

33. Robert McCaa, "Marriageways," 20–21. For a discussion of civil codes, see Arrom, "Changes in Mexican Family Law."

34. The 1884 revision of the 1870 civil code reiterated many of existing tenets, especially concerning the paterfamilias as the de facto authority in the family. Both codes reflect what Arrom has called values of the modern family and the liberalism of the educated elites ("Changes in Mexican Family Law").

35. A Oaxacan state decree (November 23, 1861) ruled that only civil marriages bestowed the accompanying civil rights (legitimacy, inheritance, patria potestad) on the couple. It also implied that those unhappy with their church marriage could contract marriage with another in a civil ceremony. See *Colección de leyes, circulares, y resoluciones referentes al estado civil personas* (Oaxaca: Imprenta del Estado en el Instituto, 1873). In a case of bigamy, the defendant reasoned that he had been married in the church to one woman, and after she left him for another man, he contracted civil marriage with another woman. See *Contra Julian Díaz vecino de esta ciudad acusado del delito de bigamía*, Oaxaca, 1866, Juzgado Segundo de la Capital, AHMCO.

36. *Código penal para el Distrito Federal*, Article 809.

37. William E. French, "Rapto and Estupro in Porfirian and Revolutionary Chihuahua" (paper presented at the IX Reunión de Historiadores Mexicanos e Norteamericanos, October 1994), 2. Usually, the man acted as abductor, but I found one case in which a mother was charged with abducting a young woman for her son. See *Contra Faustina Medina por atentados contra el pudor y rapto en Francisca Martínez*, Oaxaca, 1896, Juzgado Primero Criminal, AHMCO. In many cases, women took on the role of seducer or abductor in practice by engineering their own seduction, but before the courts, they portrayed themselves as innocent participants.

38. This claim is based on findings for colonial Latin America, but this belief continued into the national period. See Susan Socolow, "Acceptable Marriage Partners: Marriage Choice in Colonial Argentina, 1778–1810," in *Sexuality and Marriage*, ed. Asunción Lavrin (Lincoln: University of Nebraska Press, 1989), 234. Lipsett-Rivera found that colonial officials in rape cases sexualized

girls at a young age and blamed women for sexual temptation. See "The Intersection of Rape," 578.

39. *Contra Manuel de la Cruz por estupro cometido en perjuicio de Policarpia Marea ambos de esta ciudad*, Oaxaca, 1855, Juzgado Primero Criminal, AHMCO.

40. Odem, *Delinquent Daughters*, 178.

41. Larson, "Women Understand So Little." See also Odem, *Delinquent Daughters*.

42. See chapter 3 for a discussion of love and morality in popular culture.

43. "Rodolfo Gaona es el presunto seductor de M. Luisa Noecker," *El Diario*, December 7, 1909, 1. http://www.paperofrecord.com/paper_view. asp?PaperId=617&RecordId=1&PageId=6036828&iDateSearchId={B0EE5 E05-4FC8-473B-BE02-EFBD92243D99}. The type of examination doctors performed is not known, but presumably his "ailment" would prevent him from having sexual intercourse with the girl.

44. "Tras una noche de afrentas fue segada su vida en flor," *El Diario*, December 4, 1909, 1.

45. "Rodolfo Gaona es el presunto seductor."

46. "En el suicidio de la Srita. Nocker [*sic*] se inclupa a Rodolfo Gaona," *El País*, December 6, 1909, 1.

47. Ibid.

48. Indeed, some called for the abolition of bullfighting, or at least, the ritual slaying of the beast after the fight. Oaxaca City's liberal politicians outlawed bullfighting in the 1820s.

49. "Hay que capitular los cargos contra el presunto culpable," *El País*, December 14, 1909, 1. Felix Díaz was the nephew of president, Porfirio Díaz, and would go on to lead a rebellion against Francisco Madero in the first years of the Mexican Revolution.

50. "Public Indignation over Noecker Suicide," *The Mexican Herald*, December 7, 1909, 2.

51. "Rodolfo Gaona, Idol of Bull Ring, Arrested Again over Suicide," *The Mexican Herald*, December 8, 1909, 1.

52. "Noecker Asks Court for Time Extension," *The Mexican Herald*, January 28, 1910, 4. "Fuero" was a colonial-era special privilege reserved for clergy and military personnel and other social groups. A fuero exempted them from civil suits, taxes, and so forth. In modern times, it may be compared with diplomatic immunity.

53. *Contra Francisco Cruz acusado por Néstora Cruz de los delitos de injurias, difamación, calumnias, atentado contra el pudor, rapto de seducción, estupro no violento y separación de su virginidad*, Oaxaca, 1893, Primero Juzgado Criminal, AHMCO.

54. *Contra Luciano Nuñez por rapto en la menor Juana González*, Juzgado Primero de lo Criminal, Oaxaca, 1887, AHMCO.

55. Stern, *The Secret History of Gender*, 97–98, 110–11, 112–14.

56. Community social spaces became symbolic meeting places for lovers. Several witnesses testified to lovers talking in doorways, through windows, or on church or market grounds. Body parts and clothing also seemed to be symbolic of intimacy (or proof of force, in some cases). For example, young

women were seen wrapped in the man's serape as either evidence of amorous relations or violation. Young women testified to being pulled by their trenzas (braids) or rebozo in cases of estupro or violation. See chapter 4 for a fuller discussion of the space and symbols of courtship in working-class communities.

57. For studies that examine prostitution in Mexico, see Katherine Elaine Bliss, *Compromised Positions: Prostitution, Public Health, and Gender Politics in Revolutionary Mexico City* (University Park: The Pennsylvania State University Press, 2001); Overmyer-Velazquez, *Visions of the Emerald City*; and Kathryn A. Sloan, "Runaway Daughters and Dangerous Women."

58. Passage in *La Mujer*, quoted in Carmen Ramos Escandón, "Señoritas porfirianas: Mujer e ideología en el México progresista, 1880–1910," in *Presencia y transparencia: La mujer en la historia de México*, ed. Carmen Ramos Escandón (Mexico City: El Colegio de México, 1987), 151. Passage translated by Kathryn A. Sloan.

59. *El Hijo del Trabajo*, April 9, 1878, quoted in Escandón, "Señoritas porfirianas," 154–55. Translated by Kathryn A. Sloan.

60. "La mujer en Oaxaca," *Periódico Oficial del Gobierno del Estado de Oaxaca*, Oaxaca de Juárez, no. 23, March 18, 1888, 1.

61. Ibid.

62. Nancy Leys Stepan, *"The Hour of Eugenics": Race, Gender, and Nation in Latin America* (Ithaca, NY: Cornell University Press, 1991).

63. Tulio Halperín Donghi, "1880: Un nuevo clima de ideas," in *El espejo de la historia. Problemas argentinos y perspectivas latinoamericanas* (Buenos Aires: Sudamericana, 1987).

64. Karen Mead, "Gendering the Obstacles to Progress in Positivist Argentina, 1880–1920," *Hispanic American Historical Review* 77, no. 4 (1997).

65. "La mujer del pueblo," *La Mujer*, cited in Verena Radkau, *"Por la debilidad de nuestro ser": Mujeres del pueblo en la paz porfiriana* (Mexico City: Centro de Investigaciones y Estudios Superiores en Antropología Social, Secretaria de Educación Pública, 1987), 10.

66. "Economía doméstica," *El Correo de las Señoras*, cited in Radkau, *"Por la debilidad de nuestro ser,"* 9.

67. "Los Científicos," *El ideal semanario para los obreros y el pueblo*, October 23, 1910, 1.

68. Carlos Roumagnac, *Crímenes sexuales y pasionales: Estudios de psicología morbosa*, vol. 1, *Crímenes sexuales* (Mexico City: Librería de la Viuda de Ch. Bouret, 1906), 91.

69. Luis Lara y Pardo, *La prostitución en México* (Mexico City: Librería de la Viuda de Ch. Bouret, 1908), 120–21.

70. Passage from Manuel E. Guillén's 1903 bachelor's thesis, quoted in Cristina Rivera-Garza, "'She neither Respected nor Obeyed Anyone': Inmates and Psychiatrists Debate Gender and Class at the General Insane Asylum La Castañeda, Mexico, 1910–1930," *Hispanic American Historical Review* 81 (2001): 672–73.

71. For example, physician Román Ramírez wrote *El Manicomio* (Mexico City: Oficina Tip. de la Secretaría de Fomento, 1884), a report that surveyed U.S. and European models of construction, management, and treatment programs

for insane asylums. Cited in Rivera-Garza, "'She neither Respected nor Obeyed Anyone,'" 660–61.

72. Rivera-Garza, "The Criminalization of the Syphilitic Body: Prostitutes, Health Crimes, and Society in Mexico City, 1867–1930," in *Crime and Punishment in Latin America*, ed. Carlos Aguirre and Gilbert M. Joseph, (Durham: Duke University Press, 2001), 157.

73. A passage from Guillén's bachelor's thesis, quoted in Rivera-Garza, "The Criminalization of the Syphilitic Body," 160.

74. Rivera-Garza's article, "The Criminalization of the Syphilitic Body," is an discussion of studies produced in the medical institutions during the Porfiriato, such as Francisco Flores, *El hímen en México* (Mexico City: Oficina de la Secretaría de Fomento, 1885) and "Las poluciones de la mujer," published in the medical magazine, *La escuela de Medicina* 1, no. 1 (1889).

75. Julio Guerrero, *La genesis del crimen en México. Ensayo de psiquiatría social* (Mexico City: Librería de la Viuda de Ch. Bouret, 1901).

76. Quoted and translated by Ira Beltrán Garibay, "A State of Danger: Sexuality in Criminological and Judicial Discourse in Mexico, 1900–1940" (paper presented at the Third International Colloquium on Gender and Mexican History, Salt Lake City, Utah, September 2005), 718, fn 10.

77. Arrom, *The Women of Mexico City*.

78. Guerrero, *La genesis del crimen en México*, 164–68.

79. Beltrán Garibay, "A State of Danger," 11.

80. Silvia Arrom argues that by excluding married women, these reforms effectively increased their subordination to their husbands (*Women of Mexico City*, 93–96). Also see Elizabeth Anne Kuznesof and Robert Oppenheimer, "The Family and Society in Nineteenth-Century Latin America: An Historiographical Introduction," *Journal of Family History* 10, no. 3 (1985), and Arrom, "Changes in Mexican Family Law." Donna Guy found the same result for Argentina ("Lower Class Families, Women, and the Law in Nineteenth-Century Argentina," *Journal of Family History* 10, no. 3 [1985]).

81. Arrom, "Changes in Mexican Family Law," 95.

82. Elizabeth Dore, "One Step Forward, Two Steps Back," in *Hidden Histories of Gender and the State in Latin America*, ed. Elizabeth Dore and Maxine Molyneux (Durham: Duke University Press, 2000), 22.

83. Martínez-Alier, *Marriage, Class, and Colour*.

84. Dore, "One Step Forward, Two Steps Back," 23.

85. Arrom, "Changes in Mexican Family Law," 305–17; Socolow, "Women and Crime," 52.

86. *Código Penal para el Estado de Oaxaca*, chapter VI, article 810, I and II.

87. Manuel C. Brioso y Candiani, *Catecismo político de los oaxaqueños: Obra destinada a las escuelas de enseñanza primaria* (Oaxaca: Imprenta del Estado, 1889), 27.

88. W. E. Carson, *Mexico*, 266–68.

89. *El Ideal Semanario para los obreros y el pueblo*, November 16, 1910, 2.

90. Andrés Portillo, *La Hija del Cielo: Estudios Poéticas sobre el destino de la mujer* (Oaxaca: Imprenta de San-Germán, 1899), 120–22. Translation by author.

91. For example see *Contra Mariano Cruz por rapto de seducción en Petrona Vasquez*, Oaxaca, 1886, Juzgado Primero de lo Criminal, AHMCO; *Contra José García por rapto y estupro en Narcisa Rafaela Cortés*, Oaxaca, 1886, Juzgado Primero de lo Criminal, AHMCO; *Contra Enrique Martínez por rapto*, Oaxaca, 1892, Juzgado Primero de lo Capital, AHMCO.

92. See Gutiérrez, *When Jesus Came*, 224–25, for a discussion of an upper-class woman who had a male notary present during her exam to prove her honorable condition. The judge in the case accused the notary of depraved and dishonest behavior and the woman of being common for allowing the notary in the room while she was being examined.

93. In more than one case, doctors could not determine whether a young woman had lost her virginity because she had what they termed an "elastic hymen." In such cases the court dismissed the case because deflowering could not be proven. In a case involving two men engaging in sex in the northern door of the Cathedral, the judge ordered a medical exam, which found signs of recent sodomy. In the end, the judge dropped the case, noting that the act was not a crime. But, clearly, in this instance, a homosexual man was feminized by being subjected to the same humiliating medical examinations as the poor girls in the rapto cases. The active partner, Rafael, admitted to the act, while José, the passive partner, denied any illicit acts. See *Contra José Luz Valencia y Rafael Castellanos por ultrajes a la moral pública*, Oaxaca 1889, Juzgado Primero Criminal, AHMCO.

94. Sueann Caulfield, *In Defense of Honor: Sexual Morality, Modernity, and Nation in Early Twentieth-Century Brazil* (Durham: Duke University Press, 2000), 35–38.

95. Flores, *El hímen en México*, 20.

96. Ibid., 7–9.

97. *Contra Manuel de la Cruz por estupro cometido en perjuicio de Policarpia Marea ambos de esta ciudad*, Oaxaca, 1855, Juzgado Criminal Segundo, AHMCO.

98. José S. Unda, *Prontuario de los delitos ligeros de que habla la sección 8 tit. 3 del Código de Procedimientos Criminales* (Oaxaca: Imprenta del Estado a cargo de I. Candiani, 1887).

Chapter Three

1. *Contra Arcadio Ortega acusado de fuerza en Anastacia Delgado*, Oaxaca, 1875, Juzgado Tercero de la Capital, AHMCO. This case is discussed in more detail in chapter 5.

2. This is also evident in the letter-writing manuals of the era that provided examples of how to ask for the return of letters and prendas from a former love interest.

3. Today in the Juárez market, there is still an *"escritorio público"* (public scribe) who residents can hire to fill out forms, pen letters, or write pleas. The nineteenth-century public scribe, Jesús Sosa, penned the initial letter of complaint in the case *Contra Pedro Escobar por estupro en Andrea Pacheco*, Oaxaca 1876, Juzgado Primero Constitucional, AHMCO.

4. Martyn Lyons, "Love Letters and Writing Practices: On *Escritures Intimes* in the Nineteenth Century," *Journal of Family History* 24, no. 2 (1999), 233.

5. Lawrence Stone and other family historians have correlated the exchange of love letters between husband and wife with the rise of the modern family. The writers express affection and other subjective feelings, leading scholars to cast the modern family as intimate and close. See Stone, *Uncertain Unions and Broken Lives: Marriage and Divorce in England, 1600–1857* (Oxford University Press, 1995); Ralph Houlbrooke, *Church Courts, and the People during the English Reformation, 1520–70* (New York: Oxford University Press, 1975); and J. A. Sharpe, *Early Modern England: A Social History, 1550–1760* (Baltimore, MD: E. Arnold, 1993).

6. Fay Bound, "Writing the Self? Love and the Letter in England, c. 1660–c. 1760," *Literature and History* 11, no. 1 (2002), 5.

7. William Rowe and Vivian Schelling stress that popular culture was anything but homogenous, and that it connotes a distinct space or sphere of culture, which could also be included within a larger context like mass culture (*Memory and Modernity: Popular Culture in Latin America* [New York: Verso, 1991], 2). Also see Néstor García Canclini, *Transforming Modernity: Popular Culture in Mexico* (Austin: University of Texas Press, 1993). He unites the theoretical perspectives of Antonio Gramsci and Pierre Bourdieu to examine culture within a capitalist market.

8. Elisa Speckman Guerra, "De amor y desamor: ideas, imágenes, recetas y códigos en los impresos de Antonio Vanegas Arroyo," *Revista de Literaturas Populares* 1, no. 2 (2001), 70.

9. Although rates are difficult to determine, one historian, Juan Bautista Carriedo (*Estudios históricos y estadísticos del Estado Oaxaqueño*, vol. 2 [Mexico City: Adrián Morales S., 1949], 174) estimated that 14 percent of the population of Oaxaca City was literate, based on school attendance records in 1845. Cited in Stephen A. Kowalewski and Jacqueline J. Saindon, "The Spread of Literacy in a Latin American Peasant Society: Oaxaca, Mexico, 1890 to 1980," *Comparative Studies in Society and History* 34, no. 1 (1992), 116. The overall rate for the city may have been higher, since other authors estimated a literacy rate of 14 percent in El Marquesado, the workers' barrio to the north of the city center, where many of the people involved in the rapto cases resided (ibid., 116). Given that the census listed six teachers working and residing in that barrio (ibid., 122), and that a number of the lovers in the rapto cases penned their own letters, this figure seems reasonable.

10. There are several interesting studies of Mexican popular culture. See William H. Beezley, *Judas at the Jockey Club and Other Episodes of Porfirian Mexico*, 2nd ed. (Lincoln: University of Nebraska Press, 2004); William H. Beezley and Linda A. Curcio-Nagy, eds. *Latin American Popular Culture: An Introduction* (Wilmington, DE: Scholarly Resources, Inc., 2000); William H. Beezley, Cheryl English Martin, and William E. French, eds. *Rituals of Rule, Rituals of Resistance: Public Celebrations and Popular Culture in Mexico* (Wilmington, DE: Scholarly Resources, Inc., 1994); and García Canclini, *Transforming Modernity*.

11. An issue of *El Imparcial* also cost one centavo but Speckman Guerra doubts that the popular class perused that government mouthpiece as much as the presses of Vanegas Arroyo and Eduardo Guerrero.

12. María Elena Díaz, "The Satiric Penny Press for Workers in Mexico, 1900–1910: A Case Study in the Politicization of Popular Culture," in *Molding the Hearts and Minds: Education, Communications, and Social Change in Latin America*, ed. John A. Britton (Wilmington, DE: Scholarly Resources, Inc., 1994), 70. In comparison, Díaz states that *El Imparcial*, the most important semi- or government subsidized official daily, had a circulation that ran from 40,000 to 100,000 copies.

13. Ericka Kim Verba, "Las Hojas Sueltas (Broadsides): Nineteenth-Century Chilean Popular Poetry as a Source for the Historian," *Studies in Latin American Popular Culture* 12 (1993), 141.

14. Ibid., 141.

15. Speckman Guerra, *Crimen y Castigo*, 10, and Speckman Guerra, "De amor y desamor." She agrees with Georges Duby who surmised that the content of popular literature had to resonate with its reader, thus it had to reflect their values and attitudes. See Duby, *El amor en la edad media y otros ensayos* (Madrid: Alianza, 1990).

16. Elisa Speckman Guerra, *Crimen y castigo: Legislación penal, interpretaciones de la criminalidad y Administración de Justicia (Ciudad de México, 1872–1910)* (Mexico City: El Colegio de México, 2002), 204; see fn. 18.

17. Posada is best known today for popularizing the *calavera* or skeletal figure often used in Day of the Dead celebrations. In his time, he was the artist of the people, toiling hours in the workshop to produce animated illustrations of sensational crimes, children's stories, and devotional tracts. He worked from 1888 to 1913 for Vanegas Arroyo in Mexico City. Speckman Guerra, *Crimen y castigo*, 201.

18. Speckman Guerra, *Crimen y Castigo*, 6. Patrick Frank (*Posada's Broadsheets: Mexican Popular Imagery 1890–1910* [Albuquerque: UNM Press, 1998]) states that Posada's broadsheets did not reflect ordinary news but human-interest stories, some of which were based on real-life crimes. More than half of his broadsheets narrated and illustrated sensational crimes.

19. Frank, *Posada's Broadsheets*, 4–5.

20. Frank, *Posada's Broadsheets*, 6.

21. Guerrero, *La génesis del crimen en México*, 235.

22. Daniela Traffano, "En torno a la cuestión indígena en Oaxaca," 129.

23. Frank, *Posada's Broadsheets*, 31.

24. Speckman (*Crimen y Castigo*, 206) states that homicide represented only 2 percent of all crimes committed in the Federal District and cases where children murdered their parents were even rarer.

25. *Terrible y verdadera noticia del espantoso ejemplar ocurrido con Norberta Reyes, y que cerca de la ciudad de Zamora asesinó a sus padres el día 2 del mes pasado del presente año* (Mexico: A. Vanegas Arroyo, 1910), Caroline and Erwin Swann Caricature and Cartoon Collection, Library of Congress. For other discussions of this broadsheet, see Frank, *Posada's Broadsheets*, 31–32, and Speckman Guerra, *Crimen y Castigo*, 209.

26. *¡Horrible y espantosísimo acontecimiento! Un hijo ínfame que envenena a sus padres y una criada en Pachuca* (Mexico City: A. Vanegas Arroyo [n.d.]) is discussed in Frank, *Posada's Broadsheets*, 34–36.

27. Frank, *Posada's Broadsheets*, 34.

28. Ibid., 35–36.

29. Speckman (*Crimen y Castigo*, 210, fn. 36) lists some of the sheets including *Espantoso suceso. Pedro Lara fue arrebatado por un huracán* (1911), *Asombroso suceso. Acaecido en San Miguel de Mezquital. ¡Espantoso huracán!* (n.d.), and *¡Horrible asesinato! Una vil hija le quita la existencia a sus padres. Justo y ejemplar castigo del cielo!* (n.d.).

30. *Contra Mateo Pérez acusado de rapto y estupro en Herlinda Mendoza*, Oaxaca, 1886, Juzgado Criminal Segundo, AHMCO.

31. *Muy interesante noticia de los cuatro asesinatos por el desgraciado Antonio Sánchez en el pueblo de San José Iturbide, estado de Guanajuato, quien después del horrible crimen se comió los restos de su propio hijo* (Mexico: A. Vanegas Arroyo, 1911) is discussed in Speckman Guerra, *Crimen y Castigo*, 211.

32. *El crimen de la Bejarano, El linchamiento de la Bejarano, y Guadalupe Bejarano en las bartolinas de Belén. Careo entre la mujer verdugo y su hijo* (Mexico City: A. Vanegas Arroyo, 1892) is discussed in Speckman Guerra, *Crimen y Castigo*, 212–13, and in Frank, *Posada's Broadsheets*, 23–26.

33. *¡Espantoso crímen nunca visto! Mujer peor que las fieras!! Una niña con la ropa cosida al cuerpo* (Mexico: A. Vanegas Arroyo, n.d.), Mexican Popular Prints Collection (MPPC), Center for Southwest Research, University of New Mexico. This broadsheet is also reprinted and discussed in Speckman Guerra, *Crimen y Castigo*, 213.

34. *Doloroso y triste ejemplo que paso el 20 del presente en el pueblo de San Juan cerca de Puruándiro, en las personas de dos hermanos llamados Tomás y Cleofás Urrutia* (n.d.), Mexican Broadsides Collection (MBC), Center for Southwest Research, University of New Mexico.

35. *La prisión de Rodolfo Gaona y suicido de la Srita. María Luisa Noeker* (Mexico City: A. Vanegas Arroyo, 1909), discussed in Frank, *Posada's Broadsheets*, 154–57. Speckman Guerra also analyzes this broadsheet ("De amor y desamor," 88). The popular press misspells the victim's last name, Noecker, as "Noeker."

36. *Sufrimientos, reflexiones y consejos de la suicida de María Luisa Noeker: en la otra vida* (Mexico City: A. Vanegas Arroyo, 1909) discussed in Frank, *Posada's Broadsheets*, 158. Another broadsheet contained three songs, and reporting that Gaona was gored on July 5, 1909, it considers whether or not he was cheating death. See "Amor cuando muere, canción moderna. Gaona se muere y no," *El cancionero popular*, no. 5 (Mexico City: A. Vanegas Arroyo, 1909), CESCCC. Available at http://hdl.loc.gov/loc.pnp/ppmsc.04541 (last accessed on February 26, 2008).

37. Frank, *Posada's Broadsheets*, 158.

38. "Bullfighter Gaona Released from Belen," *The Mexican Herald*, December 31, 1909, 1.

39. Speckman Guerra, "De amor y desamor," 88. Another chapbook depicted a woman in a love triangle with two bullfighters. See *Una corrida de toros o el amor de Luisa* (Mexico City: A. Vanegas Arroyo, between 1890 and 1913), CESCCC. Available at http://hdl.loc.gov/loc.pnp/ppmsc.03361 (last accessed on March 1, 2008).

40. Stern, *The Secret History of Gender*, 343–44. Stern suggests that La Llorona may be a more suitable female archetype than Malinche for women of the popular classes who seek reconciliation with spouse or lover or those who have lost a child.

41. Manuel Martínez Gracida, *Las razas indígenas de Oaxaca* (San Jacinto, Tacuba, D.F.: 1932), 107. He notes that this rendition of the Matlacihua legend is probably post-Columbian.

42. Martínez Gracida, *Las razas indígenas*, 104.

43. *El grillito valeroso* (Mexico City: A. Vanegas Arroyo, between 1890 and 1913), CESCCC. Available at http://hdl.loc.gov/loc.pnp/ppmsc.04530 (last accessed on March 1, 2008).

44. *¡Horrible Asesinato!* (Mexico City: A. Vanegas Arroyo, 1910), MPPC.

45. *Contra Nicolás Flores por rapto y estupro en la joven Patrocinia Jiménez*, Oaxaca, 1885, Juzgado Primero Criminal, AHMCO. This case is discussed in detail in chapter 5.

46. Both hojas are discussed in Speckman Guerra, *Crimen y Castigo*, 214–15.

47. Ibid., 218.

48. Ibid., 208.

49. Ibid., 208.

50. *La vida de un borracho y su familia* (Mexico City: A. Vanegas Arroyo, n.d.) discussed in Speckman Guerra, *Crimen y Castigo*, 208. Translated by Kathryn A. Sloan.

51. *Suicidio causado por envenenamiento y celos de dos señoritas en el bosque de Chapultepec á inmediaciones del castillo* (Mexico City: A. Vanegas Arroyo, between 1890 and 1909), CESCCC. Available at http://hdl.loc.gov/loc.pnp/ ppmsc.04494 and http://hdl.loc.gov/loc.pnp/ppmsc.04495 (last accessed on February 26, 2008).

52. *La última nota, triste canción* (Mexico City: Antonio Vanegas Arroyo, between 1890 and 1909), CESCCC. Available at http://hdl.loc.gov/loc.pnp/ppmsc.04528 and http://hdl.loc.gov/loc.pnp/ppmsc.04529 (last accessed on February 26, 2008).

53. Socolow, "Women and Crime," 49. Also see chapter 4 for an additional discussion of marking women by cutting their hair or face.

54. *Tristes quejas de un amante que se encuentra hoy en Belem, con fuertes grillos atado por causa de una mujer* (Mexico City: A. Vanegas Arroyo, n.d.), MBC.

55. *Pleito de casados que siempre están enojados* (Mexico: A. Vanegas Arroyo, n.d.), MPPC.

56. *Vaya un pleito divertido entre mujer y marido* (Mexico City: A.Vanegas Arroyo, n.d.), MBC.

57. *Loa dicha por una cocinera y un aguador, en honor de Nuestra Señora del Rosario* (Mexico City: A. Vanegas Arroyo, between 1890 and 1909), CESCCC. Available at http://hdl.loc.gov/loc.pnp/ppmsc.04454 and http://hdl.loc.gov/loc.pnp/ ppmsc.04455 (last accessed on February 26, 2008).

58. *Plata* means "silver," and Ricardo sounds like *rico* or rich.

59. "*Jedentinita*" is a diminutive version of *jedentina* which means intense odor. Her last name, "Rabos," has several connotations, including the tail of an animal or a camp follower.

60. "Los dicha por una tortillera y un catrín en honor de San Felipe de Jesús," *Colección de Loas Publicadas,* Notebook no. 1 (Mexico: A. Vanegas Arroyo, 1897), MPPC. San Felipe de Jesús is the patron saint of Mexico City and the first Mexican-born saint. Born Felipe de las Casas Martínez in 1572, he eventually joined the Franciscans in Mexico City. He left the order and moved to Manila to be a silversmith and soon after, he joined the Franciscans again. He set sail for Acapulco in order to be ordained, but the ship was blown off course and wrecked on the coast of Japan. Felipe de Jesús and twenty-five other shipmates were detained by the authorities and then marched to Nagasaki where, by order of the Shogun, they were crucified in 1597. A papal bull beatified the martyr in 1629. See José María Montes de Oca, *Vida de San Felipe de Jesús Protomartir de Japón y Patrón de su Patría México* (Mexico City: Montes de Oca, 1801).

61. Speckman Guerra, "De amor y desamor," 75–76.

62. *Colección de Cartas Amorosas,* no. 1 (Mexico: Antonio Vanegas Arroyo, illustrated by José Guadalupe Posada, n.d.), Mexican Chapbook Collection (MCC), Center for Southwest Research, University of New Mexico. The date is not indicated on the chapbook, but no. 4 of the series was published in 1893 and reprinted in 1909, and no. 6 was published in 1893 and reprinted in 1907.

63. Speckman Guerra, "De amor y desamor," 72.

64. Ibid., 78–79.

65. *El Secretaria de los Amantes o Sea el Lenguaje de las Flores, Frutas, y Paneulo* (Mexico City: A. Vanegas Arroyo, n.d.), MCC.

66. The Vanegas Arroyo press published several love-letter-writing manuals between 1892 and 1905.

67. *Contra Arcadio Ortega acusado de fuerza en Anastacia Delgado,* Oaxaca, 1875, Juzgado Tercero de la Capital, AHMCO. This letter predates the love-letter-writing manual referred to below, but I would argue that the structure of appealing for love and commitment in the manuals reflected existing knowledge of how to write a love letter.

68. Bound (*Writing the Self,* 6) suggests that letter-writing manuals in particular "helped shape the development of a romantic epistolary 'self.'"

69. *Colección de Cartas Amorosas,* no. 5 (n.d.), MCC.

70. Love letter contained in the case *Contra Arcadio Ortega acusado de fuerza en Anastacia Delgado,* Oaxaca, 1875, Juzgado Tercero de la Capital, AHMCO.

71. Ibid.

72. The first selection of lyrics is from "¡Ausencia!" and the second from "Adoración." Both songs are published in the chapbook titled *Cantares Oaxaqueños: Nuevo colección de canciones modernas para 1903,* Notebook no. 2 (Mexico: Vanegas Arroyo, 1903), MCC.

73. "Serenata," *Cantares Oaxaqueños.*

74. "La cubanita," *Colección de canciones modernas,* no. 22 (Mexico: Vanegas Arroyo, 1893), MCC.

75. Love letter, translated by Adriana Natali Sommerville, from the file *Contra Juan González por rapto en Tomasa Rivera,* Oaxaca, 1889, Primero Juzgado Criminal, AHMCO.

76. *Colección de Cartas Amorosas*, no. 5.

77. *Contra José María Palacios Sargento del Batallón Auxiliares por rapto en María Quiróz*, Oaxaca, 1885, Juzgado Primero de lo Criminal, AHMCO.

78. *Contra Roque Cabrera por rapto y estupro de que lo acusa María Rafaela Carrasco*, Oaxaca, 1905, Juzgado Segundo Penal, AHMCO.

79. *Contra Enrique Martínez por rapto*, Oaxaca, 1892, Juzgado Criminal Segundo, AHMCO.

80. *Contra Manuel B. Canseco for conatos de rapto de seducción de que lo acusa Adela Valle*, Oaxaca, 1899, Juzgado Primero de lo Criminal, AHMCO. "Teresita" is the nickname of Luz Ester. In one of the few elite cases, Señora Valle charged that Manuel attempted to seduce Teresita by containing her in his store on the zócalo. He countercharged that she arrived at the store and refused to leave even when he was out on business. Teresita swore that he offered to take her to a hotel in a covered carriage, but she refused be his amasia because she was chaste and honorable. She was only freed when her mother arrived to rescue her from potential dishonor.

81. Speckman Guerra, "De amor y desamor," 84.

Chapter Four

1. See *Contra Manuel de la Cruz por estupro cometido en perjuicio de Policarpia Marea ambos de esta ciudad*, Oaxaca, 1855, Juzgado Primero Criminal, AHMCO. In that case, the lawyer argued that estupro (deflowering) without violence ought to be deemed fornication "because a woman who is violated against her will has a thousand recourses to free herself, such as her voice, hands, legs, and so many movements of the human body." His rationale failed to convince the judge, and the defendant who raped an eleven-year-old girl received a one-year sentence of labor on public-works projects.

2. This friend and the municipal president have the same last name, Santos, but I could not determine if they were related. If they were, it may explain why Mariña's testimony contradicted Carmen's deposition.

3. Contra *Inocente Zárate por rapto en Carmen Falledos*, Oaxaca, 1888, Primero Juzgado Criminal, AHMCO.

4. Many scholars have addressed the role of gossip and insult in regulating community life: Laura Gotkowitz, "Trading Insults: Honor, Violence, and the Gendered Culture of Commerce in Cochabamba, Bolivia, 1870s–1950s," *Hispanic American Historical Review* 83, no. 1 (2003); Gina Hames, "Maize-Beer, Gossip, and Slander: Female Tavern Proprietors and Urban, Ethnic Cultural Elaboration in Bolivia, 1870–1930," *Journal of Social History* 37, no. 2 (2003); Laura Gowing, *Domestic Dangers: Women, Words, and Sex in Early Modern London* (Oxford: Oxford University Press, 1996); Mary E. Odem, *Delinquent Daughters: Protecting and Policing Adolescent Female Sexuality in the United States, 1885–1920* (Chapel Hill: University of North Carolina Press, 1995); and Melanie Tebbutt, *Women's Talk? A Social History of "Gossip" in Working-Class Neighbourhoods, 1880–1960* (Brookfield, VT: Scholar Press, 1995).

5. Tebbutt, *Women's Talk*, 1.

6. Chris Wickham, "Gossip and Resistance among the Medieval Peasantry," *Past and Present* 160 (1998): 5. Donald Ramos delineates horizontal and vertical communities created by the act of gossiping. For example, constructed communities could be bounded horizontally by gender or occupation, and the function of gossip would be intra-group. Vertically constructed communities would link different social groups, and the gossip would have an inter-group function ("Gossip, Scandal and Popular Culture in Golden Age Brazil," *Journal of Social History* 33, no. 4 [2000]: 888).

7. Sally Engle Merry, "Rethinking Gossip and Scandal," in *Toward a General Theory of Social Control, vol. 1, Fundamentals*, ed. Donald Black (New York: Academic Press, 1984), 272. Merry rejects a structural-functionalist view that gossip as an institution functions to maintain harmony and equilibrium in communities.

8. Twinam in *Public Lives, Private Secrets* discusses how elite Spanish Americans could conceal pregnancies out of wedlock and other indiscretions, thereby protecting their honor.

9. There is an abundance of historiography on insult and slander in Europe and North America: Peter N. Moogk, "'Thieving Buggers' and 'Stupid Sluts': Insults and Popular Culture in New France," *The William and Mary Quarterly* 36, no. 4 (1979); David Garrioch, "Verbal Insults in Eighteenth Century Paris," in *The Social History of Language*, ed. Peter Burke and Roy Porter (Cambridge University Press, 1987); Fay Bound, "'An Angry and Malicious Mind'? Narratives of Slander at the Church Courts of York, c. 1660–c. 1760," *History Workshop Journal* 56 (2003). For Latin America, see Sarah C. Chambers, *From Subjects to Citizens: Honor, Gender, and Politics in Arequipa, Peru, 1780–1854* (University Park: The Pennsylvania State University Press, 1999), 99–101; Richard Boyer, *Lives of the Bigamists: Marriage, Family, and Community in Colonial Mexico* (Albuquerque: University of New Mexico Press, 1995); Cheryl English Martin, "Popular Speech and Social Order in Northern Mexico," *Comparative Studies in Society and History* 32, no. 2 (1990); Gotkowitz, *Trading Insults*, 83–118; Hames, *Maize-Beer*, 351–64.

10. Gotkowitz, *Trading Insults*, 88.

11. Even sisters took each other to court when they felt dishonored. See *Contra Mónica Jiménez por el delito de calumnia en perjuicio de Juana Jiménez*, Oaxaca, 1893, Juzgado Criminal Segundo, AHMCO.

12. Tebbutt, *Women's Talk*, 3.

13. Gotkowitz, "Trading Insults," 83–118.

14. In one case involving a musician who had been hired to play in a pulquería and was murdered, neighbors testified that the female owner had a bad reputation because she tolerated drunkenness and scandal in her establishment. See *Contra Eulalia Caballero y Josefa Hernández por sospechas de homicidio en Manuel Roldán*, Oaxaca, 1882, Juzgado Criminal Segundo, AHMCO.

15. Raymond Williams argues that culture is something fluid that is constantly modified by real-life situations including popular culture. See his "Marxist Cultural Theory," in *Rethinking Popular Culture: Contemporary Perspectives in Cultural Studies*, ed. Chandra Mukerji and Michael Schudson (Berkeley:

University of California Press, 1991), 413–16. Also see Donald Ramos, "Gossip, Scandal and Popular Culture," 888.

16. Although couples did indeed seize opportunities to court, they did not engage in the same level of "heterosexual sociability" as did their New York counterparts, who had fun in ice-cream parlors, dance halls, and movie theaters. See Christine Stansell, *City of Women: Sex and Class in New York City, 1789–1860* (New York: Alfred A. Knopf, 1986). Also see Kathy Peiss, *Cheap Amusements: Working Women and Leisure in Turn-of-the-Century New York* (Philadelphia: Temple University Press, 1986).

17. *Contra Micaela Velasco por infanticidio y contra Francisca y Sixta Pérez más lino por inhumación clandestina*, Oaxaca, 1889, Juzgado Criminal Segundo, AHMCO.

18. *Contra Eligia Escobar y María Bazán por contusiones y falta de respeto a Tomás Bazán*, Oaxaca, 1850, Juzgado de Primera Instancia, AHMCO.

19. Stern, *The Secret History of Gender*; Johnson and Lipsett-Rivera, *The Faces of Honor*.

20. *Isabel Pérez de San Andres Ixtlahuaca pide que su esposo ya no la offender*, San Andrés Ixtlahuaca, 1853, Juzgado Foráneo, AHMCO.

21. *Contra Juana Hernández quien trata de suicidarle al ingerir fósforos*, Oaxaca, 1888, Juzgado Criminal Segundo, AHMCO.

22. *María Agapita Pérez acusa a su esposo y suegro de malos tratos y otros excesos*, Oaxaca, 1852, Juzgado de Primera Instancia, AHMCO.

23. *En averiguación de infanticidio de quien es acusada María Josefa Felix de Xoxocotlán*, Oaxaca, 1869, Juzgado Tercero de la Capital, AHMCO.

24. *Contra Demetrio de Jesús por rapto*, Oaxaca, 1869, Juzgado Primero Criminal, AHMCO.

25. *Instruida contra Pablo de la Cruz por estupro a Brígida Osorio*, Oaxaca, 1857, Juzgado de Letras, AHMCO.

26. The young women in the rapto cases could be described as *"era mundana"* or that she had carnally known other men.

27. *Contra Jesús García por rapto en Juana Alcazar*, Oaxaca, 1888, Primero Juzgado Criminal, AHMCO.

28. Love letter contained as evidence in *Contra Manuel Vivas por rapto en la joven, Josefa Calvo*, Oaxaca, 1899, Juzgado Primero de lo Capital, AHMCO.

29. *Francisca Soto acusa a su esposo José María Serna del delito de adulterio*, Oaxaca, 1882, Juzgado Criminal Segundo, AHMCO.

30. *Contra Sebastián Robles por adulterio a su esposa Micaela Quiróz*, Oaxaca, 1894, Juzgado Criminal Segundo, AHMCO.

31. Gowing, *Domestic Dangers*, 113.

32. Christiansen, *Disobedience*.

33. *Contra Higinia Cruz por injurias y difamación de le acusa Petrona García*, Oaxaca 1910, Juzgado Segundo Penal, AHMCO.

34. *Antonio Sánchez acusa de difamación a Encarnación Jiménez hecha publicamente a su esposa Isidora Ramírez*, Oaxaca, 1897, Juzgado Criminal Primero, AHMCO.

35. *Contra Manuela García por injurias a Manuela Ruiz*, Oaxaca, 1907, Juzgado Segundo Penal, AHMCO.

36. *Contra Isaura Chávez por injurias y difamación de que le acusa Carmen Castillo*, Oaxaca, 1909, Juzgado Segundo Penal, AHMCO.

37. *Contra Constantino Flores y Ysable Pacheco por injurias y difamación de que les acusa María Sánchez*, Oaxaca, 1910, Juzgado Segundo Penal, AHMCO.

38. Tebbutt, *Women's Talk*, 1–2.

39. *Contra José Inés Caballero y cómplices por rapto*, Oaxaca, 1873, Juzgado Tercero de la Capital, AHMCO.

40. In contrast, for Peruvian cases, Christine Hunefeldt found that in breach of promise and rapto cases, judges required a written contract of betrothal for the case to be pursued in court. See her *Liberalism in the Bedroom*.

41. *Contra Melquiadez Barzalobre por rapto en Juana Silva*, Oaxaca, 1872, Juzgado Criminal Primero, AHMCO.

42. *Contra Manuel Vivas por rapto en la joven, Josefa Calvo*, Oaxaca, 1899, Juzgado Primero de lo Capital, AHMCO. This case is discussed fully in chapter 6.

43. *Contra Faustina Medina por atentados contra el pudor y rapto en Francisca Martínez de que es acusada por Paula Jiménez*, Oaxaca, 1896, Juzgado Criminal Primero, AHMCO.

44. *Contra Carlos Gutiérrez por rapto en Bibiana Tapía*, Oaxaca, 1886, Juzgado Criminal Segundo, AHMCO.

45. *Contra Melquiadez Barzalobre por rapto en Juana Silva*, Oaxaca, 1872, Juzgado Criminal Primero, AHMCO.

46. *Contra José García por rapto y estupro en Narcisa Rafaela Cortés*, Oaxaca, 1886, Juzgado Primero Criminal, AHMCO.

47. *Contra José Arías por estupro violento en Carmen Carreño*, Oaxaca, 1897, Juzgado Criminal Primero, AHMCO.

48. *Contra Don Manuel Noriega por rapto y estupro en María Antonia López*, Oaxaca, 1854, Juzgado de Paz de Jalatlaco, AHMCO.

49. *Contra Franciso Mimiago por rapto de seducción en Primitiva Franco*, Oaxaca, 1886, Juzgado Primero Criminal, AHMCO.

50. *Contra Matías Hernández por rapto en Francisca Boza*, Oaxaca, 1887, Juzgado Criminal Segundo, AHMCO.

51. *Contra Teofilo Colmenares por rapto de seducción en la joven Francisca Silva*, Oaxaca, 1889, Juzgado Criminal Segundo, AHMCO.

52. This is not to be confused with economic inequality, which was an important reason that many parents disapproved of their children's choices for marriage. See Socolow, "Acceptable Partners."

53. *Contra Manuel Vivas por rapto en la joven, Josefa Calvo*, Oaxaca, 1899, Juzgado Primero de lo Capital, AHMCO.

54. *Contra Vicente Jiménez acusado del rapto de Atitana Cazonla*, Oaxaca, 1869, Juzgado Segundo de la Capital, AHMCO.

55. *Contra José Ruiz por rapto y estupro con fuerza en la joven Margarita Morales*, Oaxaca, 1885, Juzgado Primero Criminal, AHMCO.

56. *Contra Gabriel Flores acusado de conato de estupro en perjuicio de la niña Teofila N.*, Oaxaca, 1878, Juzgado Criminal Primero, AHMCO.

57. *Contra Aniceto Ramos por el delito de rapto hecho en Ángela Gabriela Ramírez,* Oaxaca, 1852, Juzgado Primero Criminal, AHMCO.

58. *Contra José Zárate y Carmen Ramírez acusado de ultraje a la moral,* Oaxaca, 1886, Juzgado Criminal Segundo, AHMCO. The two were fifteen- and fourteen-year-old cousins caught in the act of fornication near the river.

59. *Contra Ramona García y Concepción Vargas por haber entregado con engaños a una menor la cual violó el Señor Manuel Pérez Ortiz,* Xochimilco, 1897, Juzgado Criminal Segundo, AHMCO.

60. *Contra Benito Meixueire por rapto y Manuela Mendoza por complicidad en el delito,* Oaxaca, 1879, Juzgado Criminal Primero, AHMCO.

61. *Contra Gaspar Lázaro por rapto en Casimira Montaño,* Oaxaca, 1889, Juzgado Criminal Segundo, AHMCO.

62. *Contra Joaquín Chávez por rapto y fuerza,* Tlalixtac, 1869, Juzgado de Letras, AHMCO.

63. *Contra Inocente Zárate por rapto en Carmen Falledos,* Oaxaca, 1888, Primero Juzgado Criminal, AHMCO; *Contra Joaquín Chávez por rapto y fuerza,* Tlalixtac, 1869, Juzgado Criminal Segundo, AHMCO; *Contra Jesús Romero por rapto y estupro en Juana Paula Morales,* Oaxaca, 1853, Juzgado Segundo de la Capital, AHMCO; *Contra Isidoro Velasco por fuerza a María Estefana Martínez,* Oaxaca, 1889, Juzgado Criminal Primero, AHMCO.

64. Martínez Gracida, historian and politician of Oaxaca, notes that the Indian pueblos tolerate prostitution as a necessary evil but would punish prostitutes by cutting their hair to mark them as disreputable women. Women who procured male lovers for other women (madams) were sometimes imprisoned or had their hair burned in the plaza. See his *Las razas indígenas de Oaxaca,* 124. Socolow also argues that hair cutting was a way of shaming women ("Women and Crime," 49). In her study of republican Arequipa, Peru, Sarah Chambers notes that cutting a woman's hair was a "serious mark of shame" (*From Subjects to Citizens,* 178).

65. Lyman L. Johnson, "Dangerous Words, Provocative Gestures, and Violent Acts," in *The Faces of Honor: Sex, Shame, and Violence in Colonial Latin America,* ed. Lyman L. Johnson and Sonya Lipsett-Rivera (Albuquerque: University of New Mexico Press, 1998). Johnson leads off his article with the description of a case of a man who fatally wounded his coworker after the victim pulled a wood chip out of perpetrator's beard while they enjoyed drinks at a tavern.

66. *Contra Nicolás Flores por rapto y estupro en la joven Patrocinia Jiménez,* Oaxaca, 1885, Juzgado Primero Criminal, AHMCO; *Contra Manuel Máximo Rodrígues por rapto de seducción en Andrea Legaspe,* Oaxaca, 1886, Juzgado Primero Criminal, AHMCO.

67. *Contra Aniceto Ramos por el delito de rapto hecho en Ángela Gabriela Ramírez.* Oaxaca, 1852, Juzgado Primero Criminal, AHMCO.

68. *Contra Francisco García por rapto en la joven Dolores Chagoya,* Oaxaca, 1887, Juzgado Primero Criminal, AHMCO.

69. *Contra Rómulo N. por rapto,* Oaxaca, 1876, Juzgado Primero Criminal, AHMCO.

70. *Contra Gaspar Lázaro por rapto en Casimira Montaño*, Oaxaca, 1889, Juzgado Criminal Segundo, AHMCO.

71. *Contra José Martínez por rapto y estupro en la joven Soledad Blanco*, Oaxaca, 1887, Juzgado Criminal Segundo, AHMCO.

72. Taylor, *Drinking, Homicide, and Rebellion*.

73. *Contra Manuel Vivas por rapto en la joven Josefa Calvo*, Oaxaca, 1899, Juzgado Primero de lo Capital, AHMCO.

74. *Contra Catarino Santaella por rapto en Simona Camarillo*, Oaxaca, 1861, Juzgado de Letras; *Contra Domingo Sánchez acusado por Dionicia Selis de rapto en su hija Pascuala de León*, Oaxaca, 1867, Juzgado Tercero de la Capital, AHMCO.

75. *Contra Agustín Robles por rapto de que lo acusa Eduardo Fernández del Campo*, Oaxaca, 1908, Juzgado Segundo Penal, AHMCO.

Chapter Five

* A version of this chapter was published as "Disobedient Daughters and the Liberal State: Generational Conflicts over Marriage Choice in Working-Class Families in Nineteenth-Century Oaxaca, Mexico," *The Americas: A Quarterly Review of Inter-American Cultural History* 63, no. 4 (2007): 615–48.

1. *Contra Juan Noriega, por rapto de seducción en Primitiva Franco*, Oaxaca, 1885, Juzgado Primero Criminal, Archivo Histórico Municipal de la Ciudad de Oaxaca (AHMCO). Her mother claimed that Primitiva was thirteen, but the girl herself claimed to be sixteen, and since no baptismal record could be found in church archives, the court could not determine Primitiva's true age. Señora Teresa turned to the court three times. Six years earlier, her orphaned niece who lived with her also eloped with her sweetheart. In the file, Teresa claims that she surprised the couple on numerous occasions in "illicit relations." The case is interesting because another woman is charged as an accomplice to the rapto. Unfortunately, there is no record of the outcome in the file. See *Contra Benito Meixueire por rapto y Manuela Mendoza por complicidad en el delito*, Oaxaca, 1879, Juzgado Primero Criminal, AHMCO.

2. *Contra Franciso Mimiago por rapto de seducción en Primitiva Franco*, Oaxaca, 1886, Juzgado Primero Criminal, AHMCO. In this case, Primitiva claimed to be twenty years old, but by means of a physical exam that assessed pelvic and breast development, doctors determined that she was probably sixteen or seventeen years old. I discuss how men and women acted out masculinity and femininity in the scripts of rapto/seduction in "Runaway Daughters: Women's Masculine Roles in Elopement Cases in Nineteenth-Century Mexico" in *Mexico Uncut: Performance, Space, and Masculine Sexuality after 1810*, ed. Anne Rubenstein and Victor Macias González (Albuquerque: University of New Mexico Press, forthcoming).

3. Although lower-class parents had a harder time "sheltering" their daughters than did the elite, they still valued modest and respectable behavior among women. Some women in case testimony argued that even though they were poor, they never talked to male strangers on the street. For a discussion, see Nancy E. van Deusen, "Determining the Boundaries of Virtue: The Discourse

of *Recogimiento* among Women in Seventeenth-Century Lima," *Journal of Family History* 22, no. 2 (1997).

4. Mary Odem (*Delinquent Daughters*, 158) also argues against viewing the court system as a top-down model of social control. Instead, she conceives of the system as an arena where various actors debated and negotiated issues related to sexuality, filial obligation, and parental right.

5. Silvia M. Arrom, "Perspectives on the History of the Mexican Family," *Latin American Population History Bulletin*, no. 17 (1990); Sonya Lipsett-Rivera, "Introduction: Children in the History of Latin America," *Journal of Family History* 23, no. 3 (1998): 221–24; Potthast and Carrera, *Entre la familia*; Tobias Hecht, ed., *Minor Omissions: Childhood in Latin American History and Society* (Madison: University of Wisconsin Press, 2002).

6. Blum, "Conspicuous Benevolence."

7. Potthast and Carrera, *Entre la familia*, 10. See also Jean Jacques Rousseau, *Emile, or On Education*, translated by Allan Bloom (New York: Penguin, 1991), 37.

8. Potthast and Carrera, *Entre la familia*, 10.

9. Bianca Premo, "Minor Offenses: Youth, Crime, and Law in Eighteenth-Century Lima" in *Minor Omissions: Childhood in Latin American History and Society*, ed. Tobias Hecht (Madison: University of Wisconsin Press, 2002), 116–19.

10. Potthast and Carrera, *Entre la familia*, 8.

11. Ibid., 12.

12. Hecht, *Minor Omissions*, 244–47.

13. Potthast and Carrera, *Entre la familia*, 12. Ramos Escandón, "Entre la ley y el cariño"; Blum, "Conspicuous Benevolence."

14. French, "Prostitutes and Guardian Angels."

15. Potthast and Carrera, *Entre la familia*, 9.

16. For a concise overview, see Susan Migden Socolow, *The Women of Colonial Latin America* (New York: Cambridge University Press, 2000). See also Richard Boyer, "Women, *La Mala Vida*, and the Politics of Marriage" in *Sexuality and Marriage in Colonial Latin America*, ed. Asunción Lavrin, (Lincoln: University of Nebraska Press, 1989); Stern, *The Secret History of Gender*; Sandra Lauderdale Graham, "Honor among Slaves," in *The Faces of Honor: Sex, Shame, and Violence in Colonial Latin America*, ed. Lyman L. Johnson and Sonya Lipsett-Rivera (Albuquerque: University of New Mexico Press, 1998).

17. Arrom, *The Women of Mexico City*, 78–79.

18. Guy, "Lower-Class Families," 320.

19. Ramos Escandón, "Entre la ley y el cariño," 116.

20. Arrom, "Changes in Mexican Family Law," 305–6.

21. Ortiz-Urquidi, *Oaxaca, cuna de la codificación iberoamericana* (México: Editorial Porrúa, 1974), 385.

22. Ibid., 33–41. Ortiz-Urquidi notes that the text of the code has been lost, but he provides ample proof from the state's library and official letters that the code indeed existed.

23. Arrom, "Changes in Mexican Family Law," 117.

24. Arrom, *The Women of Mexico City, 1780–1850*, 310, fn. 110.

25. Ibid., 69. Arrom has argued that patria potestad is a misnomer in cases of mothers who gain parental authority after they are widowed because they receive all the obligations of the patriarch, but none of the privileges.

26. Ibid., 86–87.

27. Ibid., 88–89.

28. Ibid., 87.

29. See articles 80 and 85 from the 1827–1828 *Código Civil para Gobierno del Estado Libre de Oajaca*, reprinted in Ortiz-Urquidi, *Oaxaca*.

30. Arrom, *The Women of Mexico City, 1780–1850*, 92.

31. Article 90 from the *Código Civil*, in Ortiz-Urquidi, *Oaxaca*.

32. Article 94, ibid.

33. Article 246, ibid.

34. *Código Penal para el Estado de Oaxaca: Expedido por el Ejecutivo del mismo, en uso de la facultad que le concedió el Artículo 2 del Decreto núm. 19 de 17 de diciembre de 1887* (Oaxaca: Imprenta del Estado en la Escuela de Artes y Oficios, 1888), XI–XII, and *Código Penal para el Distrito Federal*.

35. Ortiz-Urquidi, *Oaxaca*, 5.

36. Seed, *To Love, Honor, and Obey*. Mark Szuchman ("A Challenge to the Patriarchs") also found that nineteenth-century Argentine couples were in conflict with parents about love matches.

37. *Contra Amando Fuentes y Eduardo Díaz; éste por rapto en Tomasa Fuentes y aquel por amagos y amenazas al citado Díaz*, Oaxaca, 1857, Juzgado Criminal Primero, AHMCO. The judge dismissed the charge of rapto because Tomasa chose to go to Eduardo and she was over sixteen years of age. The judge punished Amando for threatening his sister's suitor with a gun and fined him two pesos and sentenced him to two days in jail. "Amando" is, in fact, the name recorded in the court files.

38. Donna J. Guy, "The State, the Family, and Marginal Children in Latin America," in *Minor Omissions: Childhood in Latin American History and Society*, ed. Tobias Hecht (Madison: University of Wisconsin Press, 2002), 141–42.

39. Premo, "Minor Offenses," 116–17.

40. H. Congreso del Estado de Oaxaca, *Suplemento al número 37 del Periódico Oficial, Código Civil declarado vigente por el H. Congreso del Estado de Oaxaca*, 4th ed. (Oaxaca: Imprenta del Estado, 1904), Article 209.

41. *Contra Melquiadez Barzalobre por rapto en Juana Silva*, Oaxaca, 1872, Alcalde Primero Constitucional, AHMCO.

42. *Contra Jesús Pimentel por rapto de seducción en Porfiria Ramírez*, Oaxaca, 1886, Juzgado Criminal Segundo, AHMCO.

43. *Contra Basilio López por rapto y estupro en Luz García*, Oaxaca, 1887, Juzgado Criminal Segundo, AHMCO.

44. *Contra Gaspar Lázaro por rapto en Casimira Montaño*, Oaxaca, 1889, Juzgado Criminal Segundo, AHMCO.

45. *Contra Pioquinto Aguilar por rapto en Feliciana Sánchez*, Oaxaca, 1887, Primero Juzgado Criminal, AHMCO.

46. *Contra Aurelio García por robo sin violencia, rapto y estupro en perjuicio de Rosa Martínez*, Oaxaca, 1880, Juzgado Primero Criminal, AHMCO.

47. *Contra Eduardo Ramírez por rapto en Francisca Delgado*, Oaxaca, 1887, Juzgado Criminal Segundo, AHMCO, and *Averiguación del rapto de que se queja Perfecta Medina perpetrado en su hija Anita Nicolás*, Oaxaca, 1870, Juzgado de Letras, AHMCO.

48. *Contra José Inés Caballero y accomplices por rapto*, Oaxaca, 1873, Juzgado Tercero de la Capital, AHMCO.

49. *Contra José García por rapto y estupro en Narcisa Rafaela Cortés*, Oaxaca, 1886, Juzgado Primero Criminal, AHMCO.

50. In colonial Oaxaca, Chance (*Race and Class*, 160) found that masons were low-status artisans whereas artisan occupations like painters, silversmiths, and musicians had a much higher status.

51. Martínez-Alier (*Marriage, Class, and Colour*, 107) notes that Cubans in the nineteenth century cited maltreatment as one reason they eloped with their sweethearts.

52. Asunción Lavrin does not cite maltreatment as one of the reasons that minors eloped. See Lavrin, ed. *Sexuality and Marriage in Colonial Latin America* (Lincoln: University of Nebraska Press, 1989), 65–66. Seed (*To Love, Honor, and Obey*) and Gutiérrez (*When Jesus Came*) also do not cite maltreatment as a justification for eloping.

53. The first instance of a runaway daughter citing abuse at home as one reason she eloped appears in 1845. The next instance does not surface until 1867.

54. French, "Prostitutes and Guardian Angels."

55. Patricia Seed. *To Love, Honor, and Obey.* Shumway (*The Case of the Ugly Suitor*, 73–79) also found that romantic and paternal love informed *disenso* (prenuptial conflict) cases from Buenos Aires. Like the cases from Oaxaca, *porteño* parents complained that their children were too immature to responsibly choose life mates.

56. Richard Boyer, "Honor among Plebeians," and Lyman L. Johnson, "Dangerous Words."

57. Lawrence Stone, *The Family, Sex, and Marriage in England, 1500–1800* (New York: Harper and Row, 1977).

58. For a discussion of a rapto case and its love letters, see French, "'Te Amo Muncho.'" French beautifully reconstructs the tragic story of love turned violent as couple struggled over notions of honor, deceit, and trust.

59. *Contra Pedro Clerín por rapto en Eulalia Vásquez*, Oaxaca, 1872, Juzgado de Letras, AHMCO.

60. *Contra el gendarme Juan López por rapto en Arcadia Beníntes*, Oaxaca, 1887, Juzgado Primero Criminal, AHMCO.

61. *Contra José Martínez por rapto y estupro en la joven Soledad Blanco*, Oaxaca, 1887, Juzgado Criminal Segundo, AHMCO.

62. A vagrant could mean a jobless or homeless person but it was also a term used just to denigrate someone's reputation. The 1871 Penal Code dealt with

"Vagrancy and Begging" under "Crimes against the Public Order" and defined vagrants as "lacking property and rents, do not exercise an honest industry, art, or trade for a living, without having a legitimate impediment." *Código Penal para el Distrito Federal*, Article 854. Also see Piccato, *City of Suspects*, 171, and his discussion of *rateros* as vagrants before the law.

63. *Contra Manuel Vivas por rapto en la joven, Josefa Calvo*, Oaxaca, 1899, Juzgado Primero de lo Capital, AHMCO.

64. *Contra Manuel Mimiaga por rapto en Guadalupe Ogarrio*, Oaxaca, 1873, Juzgado lo Capital, AHMCO.

65. *Contra Victoriano Chávez acusado del rapto de María Asunción Quevedo*, Oaxaca, 1869, Juzgado Segundo de la Capital, AHMCO.

66. *Contra Aniceto Ramos por el delito de rapto hecho en Ángela Gabriela Ramírez*, Oaxaca, 1852, Juzgado Criminal Segundo, AHMCO.

67. *Contra Isaac Robles por rapto en Encarnación Arango*, Oaxaca, 1906, Juzgado Segundo Penal, AHMCO.

68. *Código Penal para el Estado de Oaxaca*, Article 807.

69. *Contra Julián y Dolores Serna el primero por contusiones a la segunda y contra ésta por faltas de aquel el cual es su padre*, Oaxaca, 1875, Juzgado Segundo del Partido, AHMCO.

70. Arrom, "Changes in Mexican Family Law," 305–17.

71. *Contra Nicolás Flores por rapto y estupro en la joven Patrocinia Jiménez*, Oaxaca, 1885, Juzgado Primero Criminal, AHMCO.

72. The court found that Narcisa had lost her virginity earlier but still sentenced her abductor to prison. See *Contra José García por rapto y estupro en Narcisa Rafaela Cortés*, Oaxaca, 1886, Juzgado Primero Criminal, AHMCO.

73. *Contra Gregorio Cruz por estupro que cometió en perjuicio de la menor Juana Guzmán*, Oaxaca, 1853, Juzgado de Primera Instancia, AHMCO; *Contra Manuel de la Cruz por estupro cometido en perjuicio de Policarpia Marea ambos de esta ciudad*, Oaxaca, 1855, Juzgado Criminal Segundo, AHMCO; *Contra Nicolás Flores por rapto y estupro en la joven Patrocinia Jiménez*, Oaxaca, 1885, Juzgado Primero Criminal, AHMCO; *Contra José García por rapto y estupro en Narcisa Rafaela Cortés*, Oaxaca, 1886, Juzgado Primero Criminal, AHMCO; *Contra José Rios Nataret por rapto y estupro en la menor Dolores Garcés*, Oaxaca, 1887, Primero Juzgado Criminal, AHMCO; and *Contra Inocente Zárate por rapto en Carmen Falledos*, Oaxaca, 1888, Primero Juzgado Criminal, AHMCO; *Contra Joaquín Chávez por rapto y fuerza*, Tlalixtac, 1869, Juzgado de Letras, AHMCO. Of those seven cases, four of the plaintiffs were fathers; one was a husband; one ama initiated the other case; and only one mother successfully had her daughter's suitor fined and imprisoned. Although statistically these numbers are not significant, it is interesting that only one mother had the court side with her against the male suitor.

74. Hunefeldt, *Liberalism in the Bedroom*, 196–97.

75. Martínez-Alier, *Marriage, Class, and Colour*, 135.

76. Stern, *Secret History of Gender*, 97–98.

77. Christiansen, *Disobedience*, 88.

Chapter Six

1. *Contra Manuel Vivas por rapto en la joven Josefa Calvo*, Oaxaca, 1899, AHMCO.
2. Ibid.
3. *En averiguación del rapto cometido en la persona de Francisca Pérez*, Oaxaca, 1872, Juzgado Primero de la Capital, AHMCO.
4. Middle- and upper-class Mexicans were disdainful of amasiatos or consensual unions, relationships maintained by poor Mexicans, not the elite. Hence, Luz Esther professed to be outraged that Manuel would suggest she be his amasia. See Pablo Piccato, *City of Suspects*, 114–15.
5. *Contra Manuel Canseco por conatos de rapto de seducción de que lo acusa Adela Valle*, Oaxaca, 1899, Juzgado Primero de lo Capital, AHMCO.
6. I found only one case where a woman was charged with rapto: a mother was charged with "abducting" a young woman for her son. Unfortunately, the case file only includes the original complaint but no supporting depositions. See *Contra Faustina Medina por atentados contra el pudor y rapto en Francisca Martínez*, Oaxaca, 1896, Juzgado Primero Criminal, AHMCO.
7. *Contra José Rios Nataret por rapto y estupro en la menor Dolores Garcés*, Oaxaca, 1887, Primero Juzgado Criminal, AHMCO.
8. In cases of sexual crimes, girls under the age of twelve were usually listed as niña (female child) or less frequently, doncella (maiden). In the Oaxacan cases examined for this study, after the age of twelve, girls or young women were identified as soltera (single), libre (free or single), or, rarely, as doncella.
9. *Contra Manuel de la Cruz por estupro cometido en perjuicio de Policarpia Marea ambos de esta ciudad*, Oaxaca, 1855, Juzgado Criminal Segundo, AHMCO. Doctors used the euphemism of *"bello en las partes genitales"* (beauty in the genitals) to signify puberty in women. In the defense lawyer's statement, in talking about the lack of facial hair in Indian men, he seems to equate "bello" with pubic hair in indigenous women.
10. Sueann Caulfield and Martha de Abreu Esteves, "Fifty Years of Virginity in Rio de Janeiro: Sexual Politics and Gender Roles in Juridical and Popular Discourse, 1890–1940," *Luso-Brazilian Review* 30, no. 1 (1993).
11. *Criminal de parte, por rapto y estupro en la persona de Enriqueta Selle y de su acusa Leonardo Selle*, Oaxaca, 1891, Primero Juzgado Criminal, AHMCO.
12. For a discussion of medical theses that investigated female genitalia and sexuality, see Rivera-Garza, "The Criminalization of the Syphilitic Body," 155–64.
13. Colonial Latin Americanists have contributed the most extensive research how the honor/shame complex patterned gender roles over time. See especially Lavrin, ed. *Sexuality and Marriage* and Johnson and Lipsett-Rivera, ed. *The Faces of Honor.*
14. Several scholars substantiate that the members of the working class believed that they possessed honor and regularly defended it. See van Deusen, "Determining the Boundaries of Virtue," Lavrin, ed. *Sexuality and Marriage*, and Johnson and Lipsett-Rivera, ed. *The Faces of Honor.*
15. Love letters contained in the case file *Contra Enrique Martínez por rapto en la jóven Carmen Llaguno*, Oaxaca, 1892, Juzgado Primero de lo Capital, AHMCO. Whether Enrique penned the letter himself, I cannot determine

with certainty. Some lovers used scribes or friends who could write. Enrique was literate enough to sign his name to his deposition.

16. *Contra Francisco Lorza por rapto y violación en María de los Santos González*, Oaxaca, 1884, Juzgado Primero de la Capital, AHMCO. In his contemporary field research in Bolivia, Jaime Luis Daza found that rock throwing was akin to flirting with a potential lover or a step in courtship, where the girl encouraged the boy's overtures by hurling a rock at him. See "The Cultural Context of Courtship and Betrothal in a Quechua Community of Cochabamba, Bolivia" (PhD diss., UCLA, 1983).

17. Van Deusen, "Determining the Boundaries of Virtue."

18. Christiansen, *Disobedience*.

19. Love letter contained as evidence in *Contra Manuel Vivas por rapto en la joven, Josefa Calvo*, Oaxaca, 1899, Juzgado Primero de lo Capital, AHMCO.

20. Studies by Martha Esteves and Sueann Caulfield substantiate this point. In their study of sexual politics in judicial and popular discourse in Brazil ("Fifty Years of Virginity"), they find that while the legal and popular interpretations of appropriate sexual behavior differed, there were also key points of commonality.

21. Twinam, *Public Lives, Private Secrets*.

22. *Contra Inocente Zárate por rapto en Carmen Falledos*, Oaxaca, 1888, Primero Juzgado Criminal, AHMCO.

23. See especially Lavrin, ed. *Marriage and Sexuality*, and Johnson and Lipsett-Rivera, ed. *The Faces of Honor*.

24. Seed, *To Love, Honor, and Obey*, 123–35.

25. Although it is irrefutable that colonial-era plebeians believed that they too possessed honor, some scholars have found that these individuals did not use the word "honor" in their testimonies, especially if they resided in cities with large numbers of elites (see, in particular, Johnson, "Dangerous Words"). Sonya Lipsett-Rivera ("A Slap in the Face of Honor") found that the word honor was more common used in colonial towns and villages far from the seats of power. For a complex study of the private and public aspects of honor, see Twinam, *Public Lives, Private Secrets*. The Oaxacan cases where participants used the word "honra" or its derivatives are: *Contra Amando Fuentes y Eduardo Díaz; este por rapto en Tomasa Fuentes y aquel por amigos y amenazas al citado Díaz*, 1857, Juzgado Criminal Primero; *Contra Victorio Rivera y hijo por rapto y seducción de la hija de Florencia García*, 1881, Juzgado Criminal Primero; *Contra Justo Martínez por rapto en Concepción Camacho*, 1881, Juzgado Criminal Primero; *Contra Mariano Cruz por rapto de seducción en Petrona Vásquez*, 1886, Juzgado Primero de lo Criminal; *Contra Jose Ríos Nataret por rapto y estupro en la menor Dolores Garcés*, 1887, Primero Juzgado Criminal; *Contra Francisco Cruz acusado por Néstora Cruz de los delitos de injurias, difamación, calumnia, atentado contra el pudor, estupro no violento y separación de su virginidad*, 1893, Primero Juzgado Criminal; *Contra José Martínez por rapto y estupro en la joven Soledad Blanco*, 1887, Juzgado Criminal Segundo; *Contra Crescencio Zaavedra por rapto y estupro en María Paula Robles*, 1870,

Juzgado de Letras; *Contra Manuel Mimiaga por rapto en Guadalupe Ogarrio,* 1873, Juzgado Primero de la Capital; *Contra Arcadio Ortega acusado de fuerza en Anastacia Delgado,* 1875, Juzgado Tercero de la Capital; *Contra Agustín Robles por rapto de que lo acusa Eduardo Fernández del Campo,* 1908, Juzgado Segundo Penal; *Contra El Preceptor Andrés Flores por haberse raptado a la menor e hija de la Señora Francisca Reyes,* San Sebastina Tutla 1890, Juzgado Criminal Segundo. All available at AHMCO.

26. *Contra Jesús García por rapto en Juana Alcazar,* Oaxaca, 1888, Primero Juzgado Criminal, AHMCO.

27. *Contra El Preceptor Andres Flores por haberse raptado a la menor e hija de la Señora Francisca Reyes,* San Sebastiana Tutla, 1890, Juzgado Criminal Segundo, AHMCO.

28. *Contra Pedro Escobar por estupro en Andrea Pacheco,* Oaxaca, 1876, Juzgado Primero Criminal, AHMCO.

29. *Criminal contra Reinaldo Ramírez por rapto y violación en Rosa Martínez Gracida,* Oaxaca, 1889, Juzgado Primero Criminal, AHMCO.

30. *Contra Cipriano López acusado del rapto y seducción,* Oaxaca, 1875, Juzgado Tercero de la Capital, AHMCO.

31. *Contra Arcadio Ortega acusado de fuerza en Anastacia Delgado,* Oaxaca, 1875, Juzgado Tercero de la Capital, AHMCO.

32. *Contra Mateo Pérez acusado de rapto y estupro en Herlinda Mendoza,* Oaxaca, 1886, Juzgado Criminal Segundo, AHMCO.

33. *Contra Crisóforo Ramírez y Genoveva García por rapto y robo,* Oaxaca 1908, Juzgado Segundo Penal, AHMCO.

34. Caulfield (*In Defense of Honor*) also found similar results. For a discussion of working-class honor and its alternate model for the working class, see Kathryn A. Sloan, "Runaway Daughters," in *Mexico Uncut: Masculinity and Social Space in Mexico after 1850,* ed. Anne Rubenstein and Victor Macías González (Albuquerque: University of New Mexico Press, forthcoming).

35. For a discussion of the runaway daughters who took on the masculine role in the rapto dramas, see Sloan, "Runaway Daughters."

36. Hayden White quoted in Gowing, *Domestic Dangers,* 232.

37. Gowing argues that "defending rather than witnessing in a suit opened the field for some special skills . . . instead of elaborating the plaintiff's story, they aimed to retell the contested events from a different angle . . . by placing the focal events in a new and transforming context" (*Domestic Dangers,* 236–37).

38. Código Penal de 1871, Article 34, Part 14. Note that dueling among upper-class Mexicans was unofficially condoned and only lightly, if at all, punished. For a discussion of real-life cases, see Pablo Piccato's essay "Politics and the Technology of Honor: Dueling in Turn-of-the-Century Mexico," *Journal of Social History* 33, no. 2 (1999): 331–54 and David S. Parker, "Law, Honor, and Impunity in Spanish America: The Debate over Dueling, 1870–1920," *Law and History Review* 19, no. 2 (Summer 2001): 311–38.

39. Stern, *Secret History of Gender.*

Conclusion Notes

1. Report of the Special Rapporteur, "Women and Violence," United Nations Department of Public Information, Feb. 1998.

2. José Manuel Valencia Toledo, "Guendaxheela (Las bodas de mi pueblo)," *Tona taati* (October 1, 2007). Available at http://www.tonataati.org/tradicion/tradicion2.html (last accessed on March 2, 2008).

3. Mary Jordan, "In Mexico, an Unpunished Crime," *Washington Post* June 30, 2002, A1.

4. As Latin American nations achieved independence, the honor code transformed when citizenship bestowed expanded rights and liberties on a wider cross-section of society. Privileges and offices were no longer hereditary, and honor became based more on merit. This is evidenced constantly in the rapto cases, as even the poorest litigant defended his or her honor as hardworking, circumspect residents of Oaxaca City. For a discussion highlighting the transformation of the honor code from colonial to republican Peru, see Chambers, *From Subjects to Citizens*, 161–88.

5. A Google search of "hymenoplasty" delivers several links to plastic surgeons that offer to rebuild the hymen. For an article about Muslim women seeking virginity reconstruction, see James Chapman, "Women Get 'Virginity Fix' NHS Operations in Muslim-driven Trend," *Daily Mail*, March 26, 2008. http://www.dailymail.co.uk/pages/live/articles/news/news.html?in_article_id=494118&in_page_id=1770&in_a_source (last accessed on March 26, 2008).

Bibliography

Archives and Collections

Archivo Histórico Municipal de la Ciudad de Oaxaca (AHMCO), Oaxaca City

Archivo General del Estado de Oaxaca (AGEO), Oaxaca City

Caroline and Erwin Swann Caricature and Cartoon Collection, (CESCCC), Library of Congress, Washington, DC

Hemeroteca Nacional, Universidad Nacional Autónoma de México (UNAM), Mexico City

Nettie Benson Library, University of Texas at Austin

Center for Southwest Research, Zimmerman Library, University of New Mexico Libraries, Albuquerque

Van de Velde Oaxaca Collection

Mexican Broadsides Collection (MBC)

Mexican Popular Prints Collection (MPPC)

Mexican Chapbooks Collection (MCC)

Newspapers and Periodicals

El Diario del Hogar, Mexico City

El Hijo del Trabajo, Mexico City

El Ideal Semanario para los obreros y los pueblo, Oaxaca

El Imparcial, Mexico City

El País, Mexico City

El Socialista, Mexico City

El Universal, Mexico City

La Mujer, Mexico City

The Mexican Herald, Mexico City

The Oaxaca Herald, Oaxaca

Periódico Oficial del Gobierno del Estado de Oaxaca, Oaxaca

Primary Sources

Blichfeldt, E. H. *A Mexican Journey*. Chautauqua, NY: The Chautauqua Press, 1919.

Brioso y Candiani, Manuel C. *Catecismo político de los oaxaqueños: Obra destinada a las escuelas de enseñanza primaria*. Oaxaca: Imprenta del Estado, 1889.

Carson, W. E. *Mexico: Wonderland of the South*. New York: MacMillan, 1914.

Carriedo, Juan Bautista. *Ensayo histórico-estadística del departamento de Oaxaca*. Oaxaca: Imprenta del Estado, 1889.

Castañeda Guzmán, Luis, and Manuel Esparaza, eds., *Cordilleras eclesiásticas de Oaxaca, 1820–1880*. Oaxaca: Carteles Editores, 2002.

Cerqueda, Juan Nepomuceno. *Colección de leyes y decretos del Estado Libre y Soberano de Oaxaca*. Oaxaca: Imprenta de Ignacio Rincon, 1861.

Código civil para Gobierno del Estado Libre de Oajaca. Oaxaca: Imprenta del Gobierno, 1828.

Código civil vigente en el Distrito y Territorios Federales: Edición anotada y concordada con la legislatura vigente, y la Nueva Ley sobre Relaciones Familiares. Colección de Códigos y Leyes Federales. New edition. Mexico City: Herrero Hermanos, Sucesores, 1920.

Código penal para el Distrito Federal y Territorio de la Baja California sobre delitos del fuero común y para toda la Republica sobre delitos contra la Federación. Ratified in 1870, first edition issued by the Mexican government in 1871. Mexico City: Tipografía de Flores y Monsalve, 1874.

Código penal para el Estado de Oaxaca: Expedido por el Ejecutivo del mismo, en uso de la facultad que le concedió el Artículo 2 del Decreto núm. 19 de 17 de diciembre de 1887. Oaxaca: Imprenta del Estado en la Escuela de Artes y Oficios, 1888.

Colección de leyes, circulares y resoluciones referentes al estado civil de las personas, para el uso de las oficinas del ramo en el Estado. Oaxaca: Imprenta del Estado, 1872.

Colección de leyes, decretos, reglamentos y disposiciones sobre Instrucción Pública: Dictadas por el Gobierno del Estado desde el año de 1824 a la fecha. Oaxaca: Secretaría del Gobierno Constitucional del Estado, Sección de Instrucción Pública, 1894.

de Esesarte, Juan A. *Oaxaca, Geografía especial del Estado: Para uso de la juventud*, edited by Cosme Sánchez Llanes. 3rd ed. Oaxaca: Imprenta de San-Germán, 1909.

de Iglesias, Manuel. *Reflexiones sobre el diálogo de los morenos comunicado en el conductor eléctrico número 23*. Oaxaca: Br. D. José María Idiaquez, 1820.

Dublán, Manuel. *Curso de derecho fiscal: Escrito en lecciones diarias para los alumnos juristas del Instituto de Oaxaca*. Oaxaca: Impreso por I. Candiani, Imprenta del Instituto, 1865.

Esparza, Manuel. *Gillow durante el Porfiriato y la Revolución en Oaxaca, 1887–1922*. Tlaxcala, Mexico: Talleres Graficos de Tlaxcala, 1985.

———. *Morelos en Oaxaca: Documentos para la historia de la Independencia*. Oaxaca: Archivo General del Estado de Oaxaca, 1986.

———. *Relaciones geográficas de Oaxaca, 1777–1778*. Mexico City: CIESAS, 1994.

Estado de Oaxaca. *Código penal para el Estado de Oaxaca*. Oaxaca: Imprenta del Estado, 1888.

Flores, Francisco A. *El himen en México: Estudio hecho con unas observaciones presentadas en la Cátedra en Medicina Legal*. Mexico City: Oficina Tipografía de la Secretaria de Fomento, 1885.

Gay, José Antonio. *Historia de Oaxaca*. Mexico City: Imprenta del Comercio de Dublán, 1881.

Guerrero, Julio. *La génesis del crimen en México. Estudio de psiquiatría social*. Mexico City: Librería de la Viuda de Ch. Bouret, 1901.

H. Congreso del Estado de Oaxaca. *Suplemento al número 37 del Periódico Oficial, Código Civil declarado vigente por el H. Congreso del Estado de Oaxaca*. 4th ed. Oaxaca: Imprenta del Estado, 1904.

Lara y Pardo, Luis. *La prostitución en México*. Mexico City: Librería de la Viuda de Ch. Bouret, 1908.

Ley reglamentaria de Instrucción Primaria: Expedida por el Ejecutivo del Estado en 10 de abril de 1893, y sus reformas hasta 1908. Oaxaca: Talleres de Imprenta de J. S. Soto, 1910.

Martínez Gracida, Manuel. *Efemérides oaxaqueñas, 1853–1892*. Mexico City: Tipografia de "El siglo XIX," 1892.

———. *Colección de "Cuadros sinópticos" de los pueblos, haciendas y ranchos del Estado Libre y Soberano de Oaxaca*. Oaxaca: Imprenta del Estado, a cargo de I. Candiani, 1883.

———. *Las razas indígenas de Oaxaca*. San Jacinto, Tacuba, D. F. [s. n.], 1932.

Mateos Alarcón, Manuel, ed. *Código Civil del Distrito Federal*. Mexico City: Librería de la Viuda de Ch. Bouret, 1906.

———. *La evolución del derecho civil mexicano desde la Independencia hasta nuestros dias*. Mexico: Tipografía Viuda de F. Díaz de León, 1911.

Molina Enríquez, Andrés. *Los grandes problemas nacionales, 1909*. Mexico City: ERA, 1981.

Montes de Oca, José María. *Vida de San Felipe de Jesús, Protomartir de Japón y patrón de su patría México*. Mexico City: Montes de Oca, 1801.

Navarrete, Demetrio M. *Lecciones de nomenclatura geográfica y geografía de la ciudad de Oaxaca y del Distrito del Centro: Para texto de las escuelas primarias de la Capital*.

Oaxaca (Mexico: State), and Juan Cerqueda Nepomuceno. *Colección de leyes y decretos del estado libre y soberano de Oaxaca* (Oaxaca: Imprenta de Ignacio Rincon, 1861).

Ortiz-Urquidi, Raúl. *Oaxaca, Cuna de la codificación iberoamericana*. Mexico City: Editorial Porrúa, 1974.

Paso y Troncoso, Francisco del. *Relaciones geográficas de Oaxaca*. Mexico City: Editorial Innovación, 1981.

Portillo, Andrés. *La hija del cielo: Estudios poéticos sobre el destino de la mujer*. Oaxaca: Imprenta de San German, 1899.

Ringrose, Hyacinthe, ed., *Marriage and Divorce Laws of the World*. New York: The Musson-Draper Company, 1911.

Roumagnac, Carlos. *Crímenes sexuales y pasionales: Estudios de psicología morbosa*. Vol. 1, *Crímenes sexuales*. Mexico City: Lib. de Bouret, 1906.

———. *Los criminales en México*. Mexico City: Tipografía "El Feníx," 1904.

Taylor, J. P., and George M. Howat, eds. *The Civil Code of the Mexican Federal District and Territories: A Translation, with an Appendix as to the Civil Codes of the Various Mexican States, Explanatory Notes, etc.* San Francisco: American Book and Print. Co, 1904.

Toussaint, Manuel. *Oaxaca*. Mexico City: Editorial "Cultura," 1926.

Unda, José S. *Prontuario de los delitos ligeros de que habla la sección 8 de tit. 3 del Código de procedimientos criminales*. Oaxaca: Imprenta del Estado, I. Candiani, 1887.

Secondary Sources

Agostoni, Claudia. "Médicos y parteras en la Ciudad de México durante el Porfiriato." In *Cuatro estudios de género en el México urbano del siglo XIX*, edited by Gabriela Cano and Georgette José Valenzuela, 71–96. Mexico City: UNAM, Programa Universitario de Estudios de Género, 2001.

Agostoni, Claudia, and Gabriela Cano, eds. *Modernidad, tradición y alteridad: La Ciudad de México en el cambio de siglo (XIX–XX)*. Mexico City: UNAM, 2001.

Alonso, Ana María. "Rationalizing Patriarchy: Gender, Domestic Violence, and Law in Mexico." *Identities* 2, nos. 1–2 (1995): 29–47.

———. *Thread of Blood: Colonialism, Revolution, and Gender on Mexico's Northern Frontier*. Tucson: University of Arizona Press, 1995.

Anderson, Benedict. *Imagined Communities: Reflections on the Origin and Spread of Nationalism*. London: Verso, 1983.

Antondo Rodríguez, Ana María. *El amor venal a la condición feminina en el México colonial*. Mexico City: INAH, 1992.

Arrom, Silvia M. "Changes in Mexican Family Law in the Nineteenth Century: The Civil Codes of 1870 and 1884." *Journal of Family History* 10, no. 3 (1985): 305–17.

———. "New Directions in Mexican Legal History." *The Americas* 50, no. 4 (1994).

———. "Perspectives on the History of the Mexican Family." *Latin American Population History Bulletin*, no. 17 (Spring 1990): 4–9.

———. *The Women of Mexico City, 1780–1850*. Stanford, CA: Stanford University Press, 1985.

Balimori, Diana A., and Stuart Voss. *Notable Family Networks in Latin America*. Chicago: University of Chicago Press, 1984.

Barabas, Alicia. "Rebeliones e insurreciones indígenas en Oaxaca: La trayectoria histórica de la resistencia étnica." In *Etnicidad y pluralismo cultural: La dinámica étnica en Oaxaca*, edited by Alicia Barabas and Miguel Bartolomé, 213–56. Mexico City: Consejo Nacional para la Cultura y las Artes, 1990.

Bartra, Roger. *The Cage of Melancholy: Identity and Metamorphosis in the Mexican Character*, translated by Christopher J. Hall. New Brunswick, NJ: Rutgers University Press, 1992.

Bastian, Jean-Pierre. "Modelos de mujer protestante: Ideología religiosa y educación femenina, 1880–1910." In *Presencia y transparencia: La mujer en la historia de México*, edited by Carmen Ramos-Escandón, 163–80. Mexico City: El Colegio de México, 1987.

Beals, Ralph L. *The Peasant Marketing System of Oaxaca, Mexico*. Berkeley: University of California Press, 1975.

Beezley, William H. *Judas at the Jockey Club and Other Episodes of Porfirian Mexico*. 2nd ed. Lincoln: University of Nebraska Press, 2004.

Beezley, William H., and Linda A. Curcio-Nagy, eds. *Latin American Popular Culture: An Introduction*. Wilmington, DE: Scholarly Resources, 2000.

Beezley, William H., Cheryl English Martin, and William E. French, eds. *Rituals of Rule, Rituals of Resistance: Public Celebrations and Popular Culture in Mexico*. Latin American Silhouettes. Wilmington, DE: SR Books, 1994.

Beltrán Garibay, Ira. "A State of Danger: Sexuality in Criminological and Judicial Discourse in Mexico 1900–1940." Paper presented at the Third International Colloquium on Gender and Mexican History, Salt Lake City, Utah, September 2005.

Ben-Amos, Ilana Krausman. "Reciprocal Bonding: Parents and Their Offspring in Early Modern England." *Journal of Family History* 25, no. 3 (2000): 291–312.

Benjamin, Thomas, and Mark Wasserman, eds. *Provinces of the Revolution: Essays on Regional Mexican History, 1910–1929.* Albuquerque: University of New Mexico Press, 1990.

Berry, Charles R. *The Reform in Oaxaca, 1856–76: A Microhistory of the Liberal Revolution.* Lincoln: University of Nebraska Press, 1981.

Bliss, Katherine Elaine. *Compromised Positions: Prostitution, Public Health, and Gender Politics in Revolutionary Mexico City.* University Park: The Pennsylvania State University Press, 2001.

Blum, Ann S. "Conspicuous Benevolence: Liberalism, Public Welfare, and Private Charity in Porfirian Mexico City, 1877–1910." *The Americas* 58, no. 4 (2001): 7–38.

Bound, Fay. "'An Angry and Malicious Mind'? Narratives of Slander at the Church Courts of York, c. 1660–c. 1760." *History Workshop Journal* 56, no. 1 (2003): 59–77.

———. "Writing the Self? Love and the Letter in England, c. 1660–c. 1760." *Literature and History* 11, no. 1 (2002): 1–19.

Boyer, Richard. "Honor among Plebeians." In *The Faces of Honor: Sex, Shame, and Violence in Colonial Latin America,* edited by Lyman L. Johnson and Sonya Lipsett-Rivera, 152–78. Albuquerque: University of New Mexico Press, 1998.

———. *Lives of the Bigamists: Marriage, Family, and Community in Colonial Mexico.* Albuquerque: University of New Mexico Press, 1995.

Brockington, Lolita Gutiérrez. *The Leverage of Labor: Managing the Cortés Haciendas in Tehuantepec, 1588–1688.* Durham, NC: Duke University Press, 1986.

Brown, Roger Lee. "The Rise and Fall of Fleet Marriages." In *Marriage and Society: Studies in the Social History of Marriage,* edited by R. B. Outhwaite, 117–36. New York: St. Martin's Press, 1981.

Bulnes, Francisco. *El verdadero Juárez y la verdad sobre la intervención y el imperio.* Mexico City: La vda de C. Bouret, 1904.

Burguière, André. "The Formation of the Couple." *Journal of Family History* 12, no. 1–3 (1987): 39–53.

Burns, E. Bradford. *Patriarch and Folk: The Emergence of Nicaragua, 1789–1858.* Cambridge, MA: Harvard University Press, 1991.

Butler, Judith. *Bodies That Matter: On the Discursive Limits of "Sex."* New York: Routledge, 1993.

———. *Gender Trouble: Feminism and the Subversion of Identity.* New York: Routledge, 1990.

Campbell, J. K. *Honour, Family, and Patronage: A Study of Institutions and Moral Values in a Greek Mountain Community.* Oxford: Clarendon Press, 1964.

Cano, Gabriela, and Georgette José Valenzuela, eds. *Cuatro estudios de género en el México urbano del siglo XIX*. Mexico City: UNAM, Programa Universitario de Estudios de Género, 2001.

Carmagnani, Marcello. "Local Governments and Ethnic Government in Oaxaca." In *Essays in the Political, Economic, and Social History of Colonial Latin America*, edited by Karen Spalding, 107–24. Newark, DE: University of Delaware, Latin American Studies Program.

Castillo, Debra A. *Easy Women: Sex and Gender in Modern Mexican Fiction.* Minneapolis: University of Minnesota Press, 1998.

Caulfield, Sueann. "The History of Gender in the Historiography of Latin America." *Hispanic American Historical Review* 81, no. 3–4 (2001): 451–92.

———. *In Defense of Honor: Sexual Morality, Modernity, and Nation in Early Twentieth-Century Brazil*. Durham, NC: Duke University Press, 2000.

Caulfield, Sueann, Sarah C. Chambers, and Lara Putnam, eds. *Honor, Status, and Law in Modern Latin America*. Durham, NC: Duke University Press, 2005.

Caulfield, Sueann, and Martha de Abreu Esteves. "Fifty Years of Virginity in Rio de Janeiro: Sexual Politics and Gender Roles in Juridical and Popular Discourse, 1890–1940." *Luso-Brazilian Review* 30, no. 1 (1993): 47–72.

Cavallo, Sandra, and Simona Cerutti. "Female Honor and the Social Control of Reproduction in Piedmont between 1600 and 1800: Selections from *Quaderni Storici*." In *Sex and Gender in Historical Perspective*, edited by Edward Muir and Guido Ruggiero, translated by Margaret A. Gallucci, 73–109. Baltimore: Johns Hopkins University Press, 1990.

Chambers, Sara C. *From Subjects to Citizens: Honor, Gender, and Politics in Arequipa, Peru, 1780–1854*. University Park: The Pennsylvania State University Press, 1999.

Chance, John. *Conquest of the Sierra: Spaniards and Indians in Colonial Oaxaca*. Norman: University of Oklahoma Press, 1989.

———. *Race and Class in Colonial Oaxaca*. Stanford, CA: Stanford University Press, 1978.

Chassen-López, Francie R. "Cheaper than Machines: Women and Agriculture in Porfirian Oaxaca, 1880–1911." In *Women of the Mexican Countryside, 1850–1990*, edited by Heather Fowler-Salamini and Mary Kay Vaughan, 27–73. Tucson: University of Arizona Press, 1994.

———. *From Liberal to Revolutionary Oaxaca: The View from the South, Mexico 1867–1911*. University Park: The Pennsylvania State University Press, 2004.

Chassen-López, Francie R., and Hector G. Martínez, "El desarollo económico de Oaxaca a finales del Porfiriato," *Revista Mexicana de Sociología* 48, no. 1 (1986): 285–305.

Chiñas, Beverly. *The Isthmus Zapotecs: A Matrifocal Culture of Mexico*. 2nd ed. Fort Worth, TX: Harcourt, Brace, Jovanovich, 1992.

Christiansen, Tanja. *Disobedience, Slander, Seduction, and Assault: Women and Men in Cajamarca, Peru, 1862–1900*. Austin: University of Texas Press, 2004.

Clagett, Helen L. *A Guide to the Law and Legal Literature of the Mexican States*. Washington, DC: The Library of Congress, 1947.

Clagett, Helen L., and David M. Valderrama. *A Revised Guide to the Law and Legal Literature of Mexico.* Washington, DC: Library of Congress, 1973.

Clendinnen, Inga. "Yucatec Maya Women and the Spanish Conquest: Role and Ritual in Historical Reconstruction." *Journal of Social History* 15, no. 3: 427–42.

Cook, Scott, and Martin Diskin, eds. *Markets in Oaxaca.* Austin: University of Texas Press, 1976.

Cope, R. Douglas. *The Limits of Racial Domination: Plebeian Society in Colonial Mexico City, 1660–1720.* Madison: The University of Wisconsin Press, 1994.

Cosio Villegas, Daniel, and Moisés González Navarro. *Historia moderna de Mexico: el Porfiriato: la vida social.* Mexico City: Editorial Hermes, 1973.

Davis, Natalie Zemon. "Boundaries and the Sense of Self in Sixteenth Century France." In *Reconstructing Individualism: Autonomy, Individuality and the Self in Western Thought,* edited by Thomas C. Heller, Morton Sosna, and David E. Wellbery. Stanford, CA: Stanford University Press, 1986, 53–63.

———. *Fiction in the Archives: Pardon Tales and Their Tellers in Sixteenth-Century France.* Stanford, CA: Stanford University Press, 1987.

Daza, Jaime Luis. "The Cultural Context of Courtship and Betrothal in a Quechua Community of Cochabamba, Bolivia." PhD diss., University of California, Los Angeles, 1983.

De Munck, Bert. "Free Choice, Modern Love, and Dependence: Marriage of Minors and *Rapt De Seduction* in the Austrian Netherlands." *Journal of Family History* 29, no. 2 (2004): 183–205.

Deutsch, Sandra McGee. "Gender and Sociopolitical Change in Twentieth-Century Latin America." *Hispanic American Historical Review* 71, no. 2 (1991): 259–306.

Diaz, Arlene J. *Female Citizens, Patriarchs, and the Law in Venezuela, 1786–1904.* Lincoln: University of Nebraska, 2004.

Díaz, Maria Elena. "The Satiric Penny Press for Workers in Mexico, 1900–1910: A Case Study in the Politicization of Popular Culture." In *Molding the Hearts and Minds: Education, Communications, and Social Change in Latin America,* edited by John A. Britton, 65–91. Wilmington, DE: Scholarly Resources, Inc., 1994.

Donovan, Brian. "Gender Inequality and Criminal Seduction: Prosecuting Sexual Coercion in the Early 20th Century." *Law and Social Inquiry: Journal of the American Bar Foundation* 30, no. 1 (2005): 61–88.

Dore, Elizabeth, ed. *Gender Politics in Latin America: Debates in Theory and Practice.* New York: Monthly Review Press, 1997.

———. "The Holy Family: Imagined Households in Latin American History." In *Gender Politics in Latin America: Debates in Theory and Practice,* edited by Elizabeth Dore, 101–17. New York: Monthly Review Press, 1997.

———. "One Step Forward, Two Steps Back." In *Hidden Histories of Gender and the State in Latin America,* edited by Elizabeth Dore and Maxine Molyneux, 3–32. Durham, NC: Duke University Press, 2000.

Dore, Elizabeth, and Maxine Molyneux, eds. *Hidden Histories of Gender and the State in Latin America.* Durham, NC: Duke University Press, 2000.

Dubinsky, Karen. *Improper Advances: Rape and Heterosexual Conflict in Ontario, 1880–1929.* Chicago: The University of Chicago Press, 1993.

Engelstein, Laura. "Morality and the Wooden Spoon: Russian Doctors View Syphilis, Social Class, and Sexual Behavior, 1890–1905." In *The Making of the Modern Body: Sexuality and Society in the Nineteenth Century*, edited by Catherine Gallagher and Thomas Laqueur, 169–208. Berkeley: University of California Press, 1987.

Farr, James R. *Authority and Sexuality in Early Modern Burgundy, 1550–1730*. New York: Oxford University Press, 1995.

Ferguson, Eliza Earle. "Reciprocity and Retribution: Negotiating Gender and Power in Fin-De-Siècle Paris." *Journal of Family History* 30, no. 3 (2005): 287–303.

Findlay, Eileen J. Suárez. "Courtroom Tales of Sex and Honor: *Rapto* and Rape in Late-Nineteenth Century Puerto Rico." In *Honor, Status, and Law in Modern Latin America*, edited by Sueann Caulfield, Sarah C. Chambers, and Lara Putnam, 201–22. Durham, NC: Duke University Press, 2005.

————. *Imposing Decency: The Politics of Sexuality and Race in Puerto Rico, 1870–1920*. Durham, NC: Duke University Press, 1999.

Fischer, Brodwyn. "Slandering Citizens: Insults, Class, and Social Legitimacy in Rio De Janeiro's Criminal Courts." In *Honor, Status, and Law in Modern Latin America*, edited by Sueann Caulfield, Sarah C. Chambers, and Lara Putnam, 176–200. Durham, NC: Duke University Press, 2005.

Flores Ruiz, César. *El régimen penitenciario en el Estado de Oaxaca*. PhD diss., UNAM, Mexico City, 1967.

Foucault, Michel. *Discipline and Punish: The Birth of the Prison*. Translated by Alan Sheridan. New York: Pantheon, 1977.

————. *The History of Sexuality*. Vol. 1, *An Introduction*. Translated by Robert Hurley. New York: Pantheon, 1978.

Franco, Jean. *Plotting Women: Gender and Representation in Mexico*. New York: Columbia University Press, 1989.

Frank, Patrick. *Posada's Broadsheets: Mexican Popular Imagery, 1890–1910*. Albuquerque: University of New Mexico Press, 1998.

French, William E. "Prostitutes and Guardian Angels: Women, Work, and the Family in Porfirian Mexico." *Hispanic American Historical Review* 72 (November 1992): 529–55.

————. "Rapto and Estupro in Porfirian and Revolutionary Chihuahua." Paper presented at the IX Reunión de Historiadores Mexicanos e Norteamericanos, October 1994.

————. "'Te Amo Muncho': The Love Letters of Pedro and Enriqueta." In *The Human Tradition in Mexico*, edited by Jeffrey M. Pilcher, 123–36. Wilmington, DE: Scholarly Resources Inc., 2003.

Freud, Sigmund. *Sexuality and the Psychology of Love*. New York: Collier Books, 1963.

Fuchs, Rachel G. "Seduction, Paternity, and the Law in Fin de Siècle France," *Journal of Modern History* 72, no. 4 (2000): 944–89.

García Canclini, Néstor. *Transforming Modernity: Popular Culture in Mexico*. Translations from Latin America Series. Austin: University of Texas Press, 1993.

Garner, Paul. "The Politics of National Development in Late Porfirian Mexico: The Reconstruction of the Tehuantepec National Railway 1896–1907." *Bulletin of Latin American Research* 14, no. 3 (1995): 339–56.

———. "Oaxaca: The Rise and Fall of Sovereignty." In *Provinces of the Revolution: Essays on Regional Mexican History, 1910–1929*, edited by Thomas Benjamin and Mark Wasserman, 163–84. Albuquerque: University of New Mexico Press, 1990.

Garrioch, David. "Verbal Insults in Eighteenth-Century Paris." In *The Social History of Language*, edited by Peter Burke and Roy Porter, 104–19. New York: Cambridge University Press, 1987.

Gayol, Sandra. "'Honor Moderno': The Significance of Honor in Fin-De-Siècle Argentina." *Hispanic American Historical Review* 84, no. 3 (2004): 475–98.

Gonda, Susan. "Strumpets and Angels: Rape, Seduction, and the Boundaries of Consensual Sex in the Northeast, 1789–1870." PhD diss., UCLA, 1999.

González Domínguez, María del Refugio. "Notas para el estudio del proceso de la codificación civil en México (1821–1928)." In *Libro del Cincuentenario del Código Civil*, edited by José Arce y Cervantes, Héctor Fix-Zamudio, Jorge A. Sánchez-Cordero Dávila. Mexico City: UNAM, Instituto de Investigaciones Jurídicas, 1978.

Gotkowitz, Laura. "Trading Insults: Honor, Violence, and the Gendered Culture of Commerce in Cochabamba, Bolivia, 1870s–1950s." *Hispanic American Historical Review* 83, no. 1 (2003): 83–118.

Gowing, Laura. *Domestic Dangers: Women, Words, and Sex in Early Modern London*. Oxford: Oxford University Press, 1996.

Graham, Sandra Lauderdale. "Honor among Slaves." In *The Faces of Honor: Sex, Shame, and Violence in Colonial Latin America*, edited by Lyman L. Johnson and Sonya Lipsett-Rivera, 201–28. Albuquerque: University of New Mexico Press, 1998.

Gramsci, Antonio. *Selections from the Prison Notebooks, 1929–1935*. New York: International Publishers, 1971.

Grandin, Greg. *Blood of Guatemala: A History of Race and Nation, 1760–1940*. Stanford, CA: Stanford University Press, 1994.

Greenberg, James. *Santiago's Sword: Chatino Peasant Economies and Religion*. Berkeley: University of California Press, 1981.

Guardino, Peter. *The Time of Liberty: Popular Political Culture in Oaxaca, 1750–1850*. Durham, NC: Duke University Press, 2005.

Gutiérrez, Ramón. *When Jesus Came, The Corn Mothers Went Away: Marriage, Sexuality, and Power in New Mexico, 1500–1846*. Stanford, CA: Stanford University Press, 1991.

Gutmann, Matthew. *The Meanings of Macho: Being a Man in Mexico City*. Berkeley: University of California Press, 1996.

Guy, Donna J. "Lower-Class Families, Women, and the Law in Nineteenth-Century Argentina." *Journal of Family History* 10, no. 3 (1985): 318–31.

———. "Parents Before the Tribunals: The Legal Construction of Patriarchy in Argentina." In *Hidden Histories of Gender and the State in Latin America*, edited by Elizabeth Dore and Maxine Molyneux, 172–93. Durham, NC: Duke University Press, 2000.

———. *Sex and Danger in Buenos Aires: Prostitution, Family, and Nation in Argentina*. Lincoln: University of Nebraska Press, 1991.

———. "The State, the Family, and Marginal Children in Latin America." In *Minor Omissions: Childhood in Latin American History and Society*, edited by Tobias Hecht. Madison: University of Wisconsin Press, 2002.

———. "Women, Peonage, and Industrialization: Argentina, 1810–1914." *Latin American Research Review* 16, no. 3 (1981): 65–89.

Halberstam, Judith. *Female Masculinity*. Durham, NC: Duke University Press, 1998.

Halperín Donghi, Tulio. "1880: Un nuevo clima de ideas." In *El espejo de la historia: Problemas argentinos y perspectivas latinoamericanas*. Buenos Aires: Sudamericana, 1987.

Hames, Gina. "Maize-Beer, Gossip, and Slander: Female Tavern Proprietors and Urban, Ethnic Cultural Elaboration in Bolivia, 1870–1930." *Journal of Social History* 37, no. 2 (2003): 351–64.

Hardach-Pinke, Irene. "Managing Girls' Sexuality among the German Upper Classes." In *Secret Gardens, Satanic Mills: Placing Girls in European History, 1750–1960*, edited by Mary Jo Maynes, Birgitte Soland, and Christina Benninghaus, 104–14. Bloomington: Indiana University Press, 2005.

Hecht, Tobias, ed. *Minor Omissions: Childhood in Latin American History and Society*. Madison: University of Wisconsin Press, 2002.

Heywood, Colin. *A History of Childhood*. Cambridge: Polity Press, 2001.

Higgins, Michael James, and Tanya L. Coen. *Streets, Bedrooms, and Patios: The Ordinariness of Diversity in Urban Oaxaca. Ethnographic Portraits of the Urban Poor, Transvestites, Discapacitados, and Other Popular Cultures*. Austin: University of Texas Press, 2000.

Holloway-Ramírez, Susan. "Seducers as Agents of Social Change: A Selected History of the Discourse of Seduction in European and Canadian Writing." PhD diss., University of Manitoba, 2002.

Houlbrooke, Ralph. *Church Courts and the People during the English Reformation, 1520–70*. New York: Oxford University Press, 1975.

Hunefeldt, Christine. *Liberalism in the Bedroom: Quarreling Spouses in Nineteenth-Century Lima*. University Park: The Pennsylvania State University Press, 2000.

Hurl-Eamon, Jennine. "Domestic Violence Prosecuted: Women Binding Over their Husbands for Assault at Westminster Quarter Sessions, 1685–1720." *Journal of Family History* 26, no. 4 (2001): 435–54.

Ibarra, Ana Carolina. *Clero y política en Oaxaca: Biografía del Doctor José de San Martín*. Oaxaca: Instituto Oaxaqueño de las Culturas, 1995.

Iturribarría, Jorge Fernando. *Oaxaca en la historia: De la época precolumbina a los tiempos actuales*. Mexico City: Editorial Stylo, 1955.

Jackson, Robert H., ed., *Liberals, the Church, and Indian Peasants: Corporate Lands and the Challenge of Reform in Nineteenth-Century Spanish America*. Albuquerque: University of New Mexico Press, 1997.

Johnson, Lyman L. "Dangerous Words, Provocative Gestures, and Violent Acts." In *The Faces of Honor: Sex, Shame, and Violence in Colonial Latin America*, edited by Lyman L. Johnson and Sonya Lipsett-Rivera, 127–51. Albuquerque: University of New Mexico Press, 1998.

Johnson, Lyman L. and Sonya Lipsett-Rivera, eds. *The Faces of Honor: Sex, Shame, and Violence in Colonial Latin America*. Albuquerque: University of New Mexico Press, 1998.

Jordan, Mary. "In Mexico, an Unpunished Crime." *Washington Post*, June 30, 2002.

Journal of Family History, special issue on children in the history of Latin America, 16, no. 3 (1991).

Kellogg, Susan. "Hegemony out of Conquest: The First Two Centuries of Spanish Rule in Central Mexico." *Radical History Review* 53: 27–46.

———. *Weaving the Past: A History of Latin America's Indigenous Women from the Prehispanic Period to the Present*. New York: Oxford University Press, 2005.

Kowalewski, Stephen A., and Jacqueline J. Saindon, "The Spread of Literacy in a Latin American Peasant Society: Oaxaca, Mexico, 1890–1980," *Comparative Studies in Society and History* 34, no. 1 (1992): 110–40.

Kuznesof, Elizabeth Anne. "Gender Ideology, Race, and Single Parenthood in Urban Mexico, 1750–1850." In *State and Society in Spanish America during the "Age of Revolution,"* edited by Victor Uribe, 149–72. Wilmington, DE: SR Books, 2001.

———. "The History of the Family in Latin America: A Critique of Recent Work." *Latin American Research Review* 24, no. 2 (1989): 168–86.

———. "The House, the Street, Global Society: Latin American Families and Childhood in the Twenty-First Century," *Journal of Social History* 38, no. 4 (2005): 859–72.

———. *Household Economy and Urban Development: São Paulo, 1765–1836*. Boulder, CO: Westview Press, 1986.

———. "Raza, clase e matrimonio en la Nueva España: Estado actual del debate." In *Familias Novohispanas: Siglos XVI al XIX*, edited by Pilar Gonzalbo Aizpuru, 373–88. Mexico City: El Colegio de México, 1991.

Kuznesof, Elizabeth Anne, and Robert Oppenheimer. "The Family and Society in Nineteenth-Century Latin America: An Historiographical Introduction," *Journal of Family History* 10, no. 3 (1985): 215–34.

Larson, Jane E. "Women Understand So Little, They Call My Good Nature 'Deceit': A Feminist Rethinking of Seduction." *Columbia Law Review* 93, no. 2 (1993): 374–472.

Lavrin, Asunción, ed. *Sexuality and Marriage in Colonial Latin America*. Lincoln: University of Nebraska Press, 1989.

Leneman, Leah. "Seduction in Eighteenth and Early Nineteenth-Century Scotland." *The Scottish Historical Review* 78, no. 205 (1999): 39–59.

Lewin, Linda. "Some Historical Implications of Kinship Organizations for Family-Based Politics in the Brazilian Northeast." *Comparative Studies in Society and History* 21, no. 2 (1979): 262–92.

Lipsett-Rivera, Sonya. "De Obra y Palabra: Patterns of Insult in Mexico, 1750–1856," *The Americas* 54, no. 4 (1998): 511–39.

———. "The Intersection of Rape and Marriage in Late-Colonial and Early-National Mexico." *Colonial Latin American Historical Review* 6, no. 4 (1997): 559–90.

———. "Introduction: Children in the History of Latin America." *Journal of Family History* 23, no. 3 (1998): 221–24.

———. "A Slap in the Face of Honor: Social Transgression and Women in Late-Colonial Mexico." In *The Faces of Honor: Sex, Shame, and Violence in Colonial Latin America*, edited by Lyman L. Johnson and Sonya Lipsett-Rivera, 179–200. Albuquerque: University of New Mexico Press, 1998.

Lomnitz, Larissa, and Marisol Pérez Lizaur. "The History of a Mexican Urban Family." *Journal of Family History* 3, no. 4 (1978): 392–409.

López Casillas, Mercurio. *José Guadalupe Posada: Illustrator of Chapbooks*, translated by Gregory Dechant. Mexico City: Editorial RM, 2005.

Lyons, Martyn. "Love Letters and Writing Practices: On *Escritures Intimes* in the Nineteenth Century." *Journal of Family History* 24, no. 2 (1999): 232–39.

Macías, Ana. *Against All Odds: The Feminist Movement in Mexico to 1940*. Westport, CN: Greenwood Press, 1982.

Malinowski, Bronislaw, and Julio de la Fuente. *Malinowski in Mexico: The Economics of a Mexican Market System*, edited by Susan Drucker-Brown. London: Routledge and Kegan Paul, 1982.

Mallon, Florencia. "Exploring the Dimensions of Democratic Patriarchy in Mexico: Gender and Popular Resistance in the Puebla Highlands, 1850–1876." In *Women of the Mexican Countryside: 1850–1996*, edited by Heather Fowler-Salamini and Mary Kay Vaughan, 3–26. Tucson: University of Arizona Press, 1994.

———. *Peasant and Nation: The Making of Postcolonial Mexico and Peru* (Berkeley: University of California Press, 1995).

Martin, Cheryl English. "Popular Speech and Social Order in Northern Mexico." *Comparative Studies in Society and History* 32, no. 2 (1990): 305–24.

Martínez-Alier, Verena. "Elopement and Seduction in Nineteenth-Century Cuba." *Past and Present* 55 (May 1972): 91–129.

———. *Marriage, Class and Colour in Nineteenth Century Cuba: A Study of Racial Attitudes and Sexual Values in a Slave Society*. 2nd ed. Ann Arbor: University of Michigan Press, 1989.

Martínez Vásquez, Victor Raúl, ed. *La Revolución en Oaxaca, 1900–1930*. Oaxaca: Instituto de Administración Pública de Oaxaca, 1985.

Mathews, Holly F. "Sexual Status in Oaxaca: An Analysis of the Relationship between Extradomestic Participation and Ideological Constructs of Gender." PhD diss., Duke University, 1982.

Maynes, Mary Jo, Birgitte Soland, and Christina Benninghaus, eds. *Secret Gardens, Satanic Mills: Placing Girls in European History, 1750–1960*. Bloomington: Indiana University Press, 2005.

McCaa, Robert. "Gustos de los padres, inclinaciones de los novios y reglas de una feria nupcial colonial: Parral, 1770–1810." *Historia Mexicana* 40, no. 4 (1991): 579–614.

————. "Marriageways in Mexico and Spain, 1500–1900." *Continuity and Change* 9, no. 1 (1994): 11–43.

McCreery, David. "This Life of Misery and Shame: Female Prostitution in Guatemala City, 1880–1920." *Journal of Latin American Studies* 18, no. 2 (1986): 333–53.

Mead, Karen. "Gendering the Obstacles to Progress in Positivist Argentina, 1880–1920." *Hispanic American Historical Review* 77 (November 1997): 645–75.

Melhuus, Marit. "Power, Value, and Ambiguous Meanings of Gender." In *Machos, Mistresses, Madonnas: Contesting the Power of Latin American Gender Imagery*, edited by Marit Malhuus and Kristi Anne Stolen, 230–59. London and New York: Verso, 1996.

Mernissi, Fatima. *Beyond the Veil: Male-Female Dynamics in Modern Muslim Society*. Bloomington: University of Indiana Press, 1987.

Merry, Sally Engle. "Rethinking Gossip and Scandal." In *Toward a General Theory of Social Control*. Vol. 1, *Fundamentals*, edited by Donald Black, 271–302. New York: Academic Press, 1984.

Montes González, Soledad, and Julia Tunon, eds. *Familias y mujeres en México: Del modelo a la diversidad*. Mexico City: El Colegio de México, 1997.

Moogk, Peter N. "'Thieving Buggers' and 'Stupid Sluts': Insults and Popular Culture in New France." *The William and Mary Quarterly* 364 (1979): 524–47.

Morris, Rosalind C. "All Made Up: Performance Theory and the New Anthropology of Sex and Gender." *Annual Review of Anthropology* 24 (1995): 567–92.

Murphy, Arthur D. "City in Crisis." *Urban Anthropology and Studies of Cultural Systems and World Economic Development* 20 (Spring 1991): 1–15.

Murphy, Arthur D., and Alex Stepick. *Social Inequality in Oaxaca*. Philadelphia, PA: Temple University Press, 1991.

Nader, Laura. *Harmony Ideology: Justice and Control in a Zapotec Mountain Village*. Stanford, CA: Stanford University Press, 1990.

Nelson, Lise. "Bodies (and Spaces) do Matter: the limits of performativity." *Gender, Place, and Culture* 6, no. 4 (1999): 331–53.

Odem, Mary E. *Delinquent Daughters: Protecting and Policing Adolescent Female Sexuality in the United States, 1885–1920*. Chapel Hill: University of North Carolina Press, 1995.

Overmyer-Velázquez, Mark. *Visions of the Emerald City: Modernity, Tradition, and the Formation of Porfirian Oaxaca, Mexico*. Durham, NC: Duke University Press, 2006.

Parcero, María de la Luz. *Condiciones de la mujer en México durante el siglo XIX*. Mexico City: Instituto Nacional de Antropología e Historia, 1992.

Parker, David S. "Law, Honor, and Impunity in Spanish America: The Debate over Dueling, 1870–1920." *Law and History Review* 19, no. 2 (2001): 311–38.

Pastor, Rodolfo, and Elías Trabulse. *Fluctuaciones económicas en Oaxaca durante el siglo XVII*. Mexico City: El Colegio de México, 1979.

Paz, Octavio. *The Labyrinth of Solitude: Life and Thought in Mexico*. Translated by Lysander Kamp. New York: Grove, 1961.

Peiss, Kathy. *Cheap Amusements: Working Women and Leisure in Turn-of-the-Century New York*. Philadelphia, PA: Temple University Press, 1986.

Penyak, Lee Michael. "Criminal Sexuality in Central Mexico, 1750–1850." PhD diss., University of Connecticut, 1993.

Pérez-Rayón Elizundia, Nora. "La crítica política liberal a fines del siglo XIX. *El Diario del Hogar*." In *Modernidad, tradicion y alteridad: La Ciudad de México en el cambio de siglo (XIX–XX)*, edited by Claudia Agostoni and Gabriela Cano, 115–42. Mexico City: UNAM, 2001.

Piccato, Pablo. *City of Suspects: Crime in Mexico City, 1900–1931*. Durham, NC: Duke University Press, 2001.

———. "Politics and the Technology of Honor: Dueling in Turn-of-the-Century Mexico." *Journal of Social History* 33, no. 2 (1999): 331–54.

———. "Politics and the Technology of Honor: Dueling in Turn-of-the-Century Mexico." *Journal of Social History* 33, no. 2 (1999): 331–54.

Potthast, Barbara, and Sandra Carreras, eds. *Entre la familia, la sociedad y el Estado: Niños y jóvenes en América Latina (siglos XIX–XX)*. Madrid: Iberoamericana, 2005.

Premo, Bianca. "Minor Offenses: Youth, Crime, and Law in Eighteenth-Century Lima." In *Minor Omissions: Childhood in Latin American History and Society*, edited by Tobias Hecht, 114–38. Madison: University of Wisconsin Press, 2002.

Putnam, Lara. *The Company They Kept: Migrants and the Politics of Gender in Caribbean Costa Rica, 1870–1960*. Chapel Hill: University of North Carolina Press, 2002.

Putnam, Lara, Sarah C. Chambers, and Sueann Caulfield. "Introduction: Transformations in Honor, Status, and Law Over the Long Nineteenth Century." In *Honor, Status, and Law in Modern Latin America*, edited by Sueann Caulfield, Sarah C. Chambers, and Lara Putnam, 1–26. Durham, NC: Duke University Press, 2005.

Radkau, Verena. *"Por la debilidad de nuestro ser": Mujeres del pueblo en la Paz Porfiriana*. Mexico City: Centro de Investigaciones y Estudios Superiores en Antropología Social, Secretaría de Educación Pública, 1987.

Ramírez, Alfonso Francisco. *Historia de la Revolución Mexicana en Oaxaca*. Mexico City: Instituto Nacional de Estudios Históricos de la Revolución Mexicana, 1970.

Ramos, Donald. "Gossip, Scandal, and Popular Culture in Golden Age Brazil." *Journal of Social History* 33, no. 4 (2000): 887–912.

Ramos Escandón, Carmen. "Entre la ley y el cariño: Normatividad juridica y disputas familiares sobre la patria potestad en México (1873–1896)." In *Entre la familia, la sociedad y el estado: Niños y jóvenes en América Latina (siglos XIX–XX)*, edited by Barbara Potthast and Sandra Carreras, 115–41. Madrid: Iberoamericana, 2005.

———. "Mujeres positivas: Los retos de la modernidad en las relaciones de género y la construcción del parámetro femenino en el fin de siglo mexicano, 1880–1910." In *Modernidad, tradición y alteridad: la Ciudad de México en el cambio de siglo (XIX–XX)*, edited by Claudia Agostoni and Gabriela Cano. Mexico City: UNAM, 2001.

──────. "Señoritias porfirianas: Mujer e ideología en el México progresista, 1880–1910." In *Presencia y transparencia: La mujer en la historia de México*, edited by Carmen Ramos Escandón, 143–61. Mexico City: El Colegio de México, 1987.

Rivera-Garza, Cristina. "The Criminalization of the Syphilitic Body: Prostitutes, Health Crimes, and Society in Mexico City, 1867–1930." In *Crime and Punishment in Latin America*, edited by Carlos Aguirre and Gilbert M. Joseph, 147–80. (Durham, NC : Duke University Press, 2001).

──────. "She neither Respected nor Obeyed Anyone: Inmates and Psychiatrists Debate Gender and Class at the General Insane Asylum La Castañeda, Mexico, 1910–1930." *Hispanic American Historical Review* 81 (August–November 2001): 653–88.

Rodríguez Sáenz, Eugenia. *Hijas, novias y esposas: Familia, matrimonio y violencia doméstica en el Valle Central de Costa Rica (1750–1850)*. San José, Costa Rica: EUNA, 2000.

──────. "¿Víctimas inocentes o codelincuentes? Crimen juvenil y abuso sexual en Costa Rica en los siglos XIX y XX." In *Entre la familia, la sociedad y el estado: Niños y jóvenes en América Latina (siglos XIX–XX)*, edited by Barbara Potthast and Sandra Carreras, 173–202. Madrid: Iberoamericana, 2005.

Roldán Vera, Eugenia. "El niño enseñante: Infancia, aula y Estado en el método de enseñanza mutual en Hispanoamérica independiente." In *Entre la familia, la sociedad y el Estado: Niños y jóvenes en América Latina (siglos XIX–XX)*, edited by Barbara Potthast and Sandra Carrera, 51–88. Madrid: Iberoamericana, 2005.

Romero Frizzi, María de los Angeles. *Lecturas históricas del estado de Oaxaca*, Vol. 3, Siglo XIX, *1877–1930*. Mexico City: Instituto Nacional de Antropología e Historia, 1990.

Rousseau, Jean Jacques. *Emile, or On Education*, translated by Allan Bloom. New York: Penguin, 1991.

Rowe, William, and Vivian Schelling. *Memory and Modernity: Popular Culture in Latin America*. New York: Verso, 1991.

Ruiz Cervantes, Francisco José. *La revolución en Oaxaca: El movimiento de la soberania, 1915–1920*. Mexico City: Fondo de Cultura Económica, 1986.

──────, ed. *Manifiestos, planes, y documentos políticos del Oaxaca revolucionario (1910–1920)*. Oaxaca: Casa de la Cultura Oaxaqueña, 1987.

Ruiz Cervantes, Francisco José, and Anselmo Arellanes Meixueiro. *Aspectos del movimiento obrero en Oaxaca: Fuentes*. Oaxaca: Casa de la Cultura Oaxaqueña, 1986.

Sánchez Silva, Carlos, "Don José Zorrilla Trápaga (1829–1897): El 'Tenorio oaxaqueño.' In *Formación empresarial, fomento industrial y compañías agrícolas en el México del siglo XIX*, edited by Mario Trujillo Bolio and José Contreras Valdez, 67–90. Mexico City: CIESAS, 2003.

──────, ed. *Historia, sociedad y literatura de Oaxaca: Nuevos enfoques*. Oaxaca: Fondo Editorial IEEPO, 2004.

Scott, Joan Wallach. *Gender and the Politics of History*. New York: Columbia University Press, 1988.

———. "Gender: A Useful Category of Historical Analysis." *American Historical Review* 91, no. 5 (1986): 1053–75.

Seed, Patricia. *To Love, Honor, and Obey in Colonial Mexico: Conflicts Over Marriage Choice, 1574–1821.* Stanford, CA: Stanford University Press, 1988.

———. "Narratives of Don Juan: The Language of Seduction in 17th Century Hispanic Literature and Society." *Journal of Social History* (Summer 1993): 745–68.

Shadle, Brett L. "Bridewealth and Female Consent: Marriage Disputes in African Courts, Gusiland, Kenya." *The Journal of African History* 44, no. 2 (2003): 241–62.

Sharpe, J. A. *Early Modern England: A Social History, 1550–1760.* Baltimore, MD: E. Arnold, 1987.

Shorter, Edward. "Illegitimacy, Sexual Revolution, and Social Change in Modern Europe," *Journal of Interdisciplinary History,* 2, no. 2 (1971): 237–72.

Shumway, Jeffrey M. *The Case of the Ugly Suitor and Other Histories of Love, Gender, and Nation in Buenos Aires, 1776–1870.* Lincoln: University of Nebraska, 2005.

———. "'The Purity of My Blood Cannot Put Food on My Table': Changing Attitudes Towards Interracial Marriage in Nineteenth-Century Buenos Aires." *The Americas* 58, no. 2 (2001): 201–20.

Sloan, Kathryn A. "Disobedient Daughters and the Liberal State: Generational Conflicts over Marriage Choice in Working Class Families in Nineteenth-Century Oaxaca, Mexico." *The Americas* 63, no. 4 (2007): 615–48.

———. "Runaway Daughters and Dangerous Women: Work, Sexuality, and Gender Relations among the Working Class in Porfirian Oaxaca, Mexico." PhD diss., University of Kansas, 2002.

———. "Runaway Daughters: Women's Masculine Roles in Elopement Cases in Nineteenth-Century Mexico." In *Mexico Uncut: Masculinity and Social Space after 1810,* edited by Anne Rubenstein and Victor Macias González. Albuquerque: University of New Mexico, forthcoming.

Smout, T. C. "Scottish Marriage, Regular and Irregular, 1500–1940." In *Marriage and Society: Studies in the Social History of Marriage,* edited by R. B. Outhwaite, 204–36. New York: St. Martin's Press, 1981.

Socolow, Susan M. "Acceptable Partners: Marriage Choice in Colonial Argentina, 1778–1810." In *Sexuality and Marriage in Colonial Latin America,* edited by Asunción Lavrin, 209–51. Lincoln: University of Nebraska Press, 1989.

———. "Women and Crime: Buenos Aires, 1757–97." *Journal of Latin American Studies* 12, no. 1 (1980): 39–54.

———. *The Women of Colonial Latin America.* New York: Cambridge University Press, 2000.

Sousa, Lisa Mary. "Women and Crime in Colonial Oaxaca: Evidence of Complementary Gender Roles in Mixtec and Zapotec Societies." In *Indian Women of Early Mexico,* edited by Susan Schroeder, Stephanie Wood, and Robert Haskett, 199–216. Norman: University of Oklahoma Press, 1997.

Speckman Guerra, Elisa. *Crimen y castigo. Legislación penal, interpretaciones de la criminalidad y administración de justicia (Ciudad de México, 1872–1910).* Mexico City: El Colegio de México, 2002.

———. "De amor y desamor: ideas, imagenes, recetas y códigos en los impresos de Antonio Vanegas Arroyo." *Revista de Literaturas Populares* 1, no. 2 (2001): 68–101.

———. "Las tablas de la ley en la era de la modernidad." In *Modernidad, tradición y alteridad: La Ciudad de México en el cambio de siglo (XIX–XX)*, edited by Claudia Agostoni and Gabriela Cano, 241–70. Mexico City: UNAM, 2001.

———. "Los jueces, el honor y la muerte. Un análisis de la justicia (Ciudad de México, 1871–1931)," *Historia Mexicana*, 220 (2006): 1411–66.

Spores, Ronald. *The Mixtec in Ancient and Colonial Times*. Norman: University of Oklahoma Press, 1984.

Spurling, Geoffrey. "Honor, Sexuality, and the Colonial Church." In *The Faces of Honor: Sex, Shame, and Violence in Colonial Latin America*, edited by Lyman L. Johnson and Sonya Lipsett-Rivera, 45–67. Albuquerque: University of New Mexico Press, 1998.

Stansell, Christine. *City of Women: Sex and Class in New York City, 1789–1860*. New York: Alfred A. Knopf, 1986.

Stepan, Nancy Leys. *"The Hour of Eugenics": Race, Gender, and Nation in Latin America*. Ithaca, NY: Cornell University Press, 1989.

Stephen, Lynn. "Sexualities and Genders in Zapotec Oaxaca." *Latin American Perspectives* 29, no. 2 (2002): 41–59.

———. *Zapotec Women*. Austin: University of Texas Press, 1991.

Stern, Steve J. *The Secret History of Gender: Women, Men, and Power in Late Colonial Mexico*. Chapel Hill: University of North Carolina Press, 1995.

Stone, Lawrence. *The Family, Sex and Marriage in England, 1500–1800*. New York: Harper and Row, 1977.

———. *Uncertain Unions and Broken Lives: Marriage and Divorce in England, 1600–1857*. New York: Oxford University Press, 1995.

Szuchman, Mark. "A Challenge to the Patriarchs: Love among the Youth in Nineteenth-Century Argentina." In *The Middle Period in Latin America: Values and Attitudes in the 17th–19th Centuries*, edited by Mark Szuchman, 141–66. Boulder, CO: Lynne Rienner Publishers, 1989.

Tamayo, Jorge. *Oaxaca en el siglo XX*. Mexico City: Editora de El Nacional, 1956.

Taylor, William B. *Drinking, Homicide, and Rebellion in Colonial Mexican Villages*. Stanford, CA: Stanford University Press, 1979.

———. *Landlord and Peasant in Colonial Oaxaca*. Stanford, CA: Stanford University Press, 1972.

Tebbutt, Melanie. *Women's Talk? A Social History of "Gossip" in Working-Class Neighbourhoods, 1880–1960*. Brookfield, VT: Ashgate, 1995.

Torres Septién, Valentina. "Un ideal femenino: Los manuales de urbanidad: 1850–1900." In *Cuatro estudios de género en el México urbano del siglo XIX*, edited by Gabriela Cano and Georgette José Valenzuela, 97–128. Mexico City: UNAM, Programa Universitario de Estudios de Género, 2001.

Traffano, Daniela. "En torno a la cuestión indígena en Oaxaca: La prensa y el discurso de los políticos." In *Historia, sociedad y literatura: Nuevos enfoques*, edited by Carlos Sánchez Silva, 123–34. Oaxaca: Fondo Editorial IEEPO, 2004.

Twinam, Ann. "Honor, Sexuality, and Illegitimacy in Colonial Spanish America." In *Sexuality and Marriage in Colonial Latin America*, edited by Asunción Lavrin, 118–55. Lincoln: University of Nebraska Press, 1989.

———. "The Negotiation of Honor." In *The Faces of Honor: Sex, Shame, and Violence in Colonial Latin America*, edited by Lyman L. Johnson and Sonya Lipsett-Rivera, 68–102. Albuquerque: University of New Mexico Press, 1998.

———. *Public Lives, Private Secrets: Gender, Honor, Sexuality, and Illegitimacy in Colonial Spanish America*. Stanford, CA: Stanford University Press, 1999.

Vargas, Lucrecia Infante. "Igualdad intelectual y género en *Violetas de Anahuac*: Periódico literario redactado por señoras, 1887–1889." In *Cuatro estudios de género en el México urbano del siglo XIX*, edited by Gabriela Cano and Georgette José Valenzuela, 129–56. Mexico City: UNAM, Programa Universitario de Estudios de Género, 2001.

Van Deusen, Nancy E. "Determining the Boundaries of Virtue: The Discourse of *Recogimiento* among Women in Seventeenth-Century Lima." *Journal of Family History* 22, no. 2 (1997): 373–89.

Varley, Ann. "Women and the Home in Mexican Family Law." In *Hidden Histories of Gender and the State in Latin America*, edited by Elizabeth Dore and Maxine Molyneux, 238–61. Durham, NC: Duke University Press, 2000.

Vaughan, Mary Kay. "Modernizing Patriarchy: State Policies, Rural Households, and Women in Mexico, 1930–1940." In *Hidden Histories of Gender and the State in Latin America*, edited by Elizabeth Dore and Maxine Molyneux, 194–214. Durham, NC: Duke University Press, 2000.

———. *The State, Education, and Social Class in Mexico, 1880–1928*. Dekalb: Northern Illinois University Press, 1982.

Verba, Ericka Kim. "Las Hojas Sueltas (Broadsides): Nineteenth-Century Chilean Popular Poetry as a Source for the Historian." *Studies in Latin American Popular Culture* 12 (1993): 141–58.

Vergara Quiroz, Sergio, ed. *Cartas de mujeres en Chile, 1630–1885: Estudio, selección documental y notas*. Santiago, Chile: Editorial Andrés Bello, 1987.

Voekel, Pamela. *Alone before God: The Religious Origins of Modernity in Mexico*. Durham, NC: Duke University Press, 2002.

Walters, Jonathan. "Invading the Roman Body: Manliness and Impenetrability in Roman Thought." In *Roman Sexualities*, edited by Judith P. Hallett and Marilyn B. Skinner, 29–46. Princeton, NJ: Princeton University Press, 1997.

Warren, Richard. *Vagrants and Citizens: Politics and the Masses in Mexico City from Colony to Republic*. Wilmington, DE: Scholarly Resources, 2001.

Waterbury, Ronald. "Non-revolutionary Peasants: Oaxaca Compared to Morelos in the Mexican Revolution." *Comparative Studies in Society and History* 17, no. 4 (1975): 410–42.

Whitecotton, Joseph. *The Zapotecs: Princes, Priests, and Peasants*. Norman: University of Oklahoma Press, 1984.

Wickham, Chris. "Gossip and Resistance among the Medieval Peasantry." *Past and Present* 160 (August 1998): 3–24.

Williams, Raymond. "Base and Superstructure in Marxist Cultural Theory." *Rethinking Popular Culture: Contemporary Perspectives in Cultural Studies,* edited by Chandra Mukerji and Michael Schudson, 407–23. Berkeley: University of California Press, 1991.

Winter, Marcus C. *Lecturas históricas del estado de Oaxaca,* vol 1, *Epoca prehispánica.* Mexico City: Instituto Nacional de Antropología e Historia, 1990.

Wolf, Eric. *Sons of the Shaking Earth: The People of Mexico and Guatemala—Their Land, History, and Culture.* Chicago: University of Chicago Press, 1959.

Wright-Rios, Edward. "Piety and Progress: Vision, Shrine, and Society in Oaxaca, 1887–1934." PhD diss., University of California, San Diego, 2004.

Index

Catholic Church: colonial courts of, 6, 40; liberalism and, 28; as official religion, 23–24; power of, 8, 55; secret marriage and, 6, 145; sexuality and, 54–55; women and, 50

Cazonla, Atitana, 123

Cervantes, Adelaida, 124

Chagoya, Dolores, 126–27

chapbooks, 11, 63–64

charities, 7

Chávez, Isaura, 117

Chávez, Joaquín, 125

Chávez, Victoriano, 148

child abuse, 2, 73, 170, 180. *See also* abuse, domestic

childhood: in Greco-Roman tradition, 137–38; in Latin America, 132–35

children: abuse of, 2, 73, 170, 180; patria potestad and, 132–36, 139, 149; the Porfiriato (1876–1911) and, 73; spoiling of, 66–72

church courts, 6, 40

Church of the Soledad, 18, 156

científicos (scientists/officials), 49–54, 56

Civil Code (1827–1828), of Oaxaca State, 136–39

Civil Code for the Federal District and the Territory of Baja California (1870), 136–37

civil law: civil marriage, 1, 6, 41, 173–74; development of, 135–36

class structure: in Oaxaca City, 28–29

Clerín, Pedro, 146

cochineal, 16, 18–19

cocina en el bolsillo, La (*Pocket Kitchen*), 64

Colección de cartas amorosas, no. 1 (broadsheet), **93**

Colección de cartas amorosas, no. 4 (broadsheet), **94**

Colección de cartas amorosas series (broadsheet), 92–95

Colmenares, Teofilo, 122–23

communal traditions, 8, 31

Comte, Auguste, 49, 51

consensual unions (amasiato): acceptance of, 21–23, 41, 54, 85, 132, 152, 166, 173; economic aspects of, 122; legal aspects of, 38, 119, 120–21, 153, 170

Correo de las Señoras, El, 51

corridos (ballads), 64, 83

Cortés, Hernán, 16

Cortés, Narcisa Rafaela, 121, 143–44

courts: church, 6, 40; depositions, 8, 63, 157, 163, 175; in Oaxaca City, 9, 94, 149–51

courtship: broadsheets on, 92–102; gestures and scenes of, 123–29; in indigenous communities, 22; in Oaxaca City, 9, 10, 29; private v. public, 118–20; rapto and, 9, 33–34; in working-class neighborhoods, 103–29

Covarrubias, Miguel, 22

crimen de la tragedia de Belen Galindo, El (broadsheet), **84**

crimes, sensational, 65–68

criminal records, 8

Cruz, Francisco, 46–47

Cruz, Higinia, 116

Cruz, Manuel de la, 162–63

Cruz, Mariano, 1–4, 182–83

Cruz, Néstora, 46–47

Cruz, Pablo de la, 112–13

Cuba, colonial, 7

"Cubanita, La" (broadsheet), 96–98

Darwin, Charles, 56. *See also* Social Darwinism

defense attorneys, 9

deflowering. *See* estupro

Delgado, Anastacia, 62, 94–96, 172

Delgado, Francisca, 143

Delgado, Juan, 172, 175–76

depósito (place of temporary custody), 141–42

Diario, El, 44–45

Díaz, Eduardo, 140

Díaz, Porfirio: Juárez Maza and, 51; Oaxaca State and, 10; presidency of, 7, 16, 26–31, 44, 49, 139

Diego, Juan, 35

Discursos patrióticos (*Patriotic Speeches*), 64

divorce, 136

domestic violence, 5–6

dowries, 34, 55

egalitarianism, 23–24

Ejemplo: El hijo desobediente (broadsheet), **72**

Ejemplo: Infame hija que da muerte á sus queridos padres (broadsheet), **71**

elopement: marriage and, 177, 180–81; rapto and, 1–2, 9, 12, 21–22, 29, 33–35, 58, 94

emancipation: of minors, 2, 139–45, 152–53, 160, 169–70

encomiendas (land grants), 16

endogamous marriage, 7, 181

Escobar, Eligia, 108–9

¡Espantoso crimen nunca visto! (broadsheet), **75**

Espantoso parricidio (broadsheet), **71**

Esther, Luz, 158–60
estupro (deflowering): estupro inmaturo,
    60, 138; legal aspects of, 9, 34, 41, 46
Evangelicalism, 8

Falledos, Carmen, 103–5, 128, 168, 175
family honor: legal aspects of, 10, 39,
    41, 134; scripted roles and, 36; sexual
    honor and, 5–6, 34–35, 58–59, 63, 116,
    155–77; societal aspects of, 1, 148, 182
family structure: liberalism and, 8, 10, 41,
    130–32; the Porfiriato (1876–1911) and,
    7, 117, 174
fandangos (dances), 28, 102, 110
federalism, 24–25
Felix, María Josefa, 111
Fernández, Margarita, 128
Flores, Andrés, 171
Flores, Constantino, 117
Flores, Francisco A.: El hímen en México,
    59–60
Flores, Nicolás, 150–51
Franco, Primitiva, 122, 130–31
Fuentes, Amando, 140
Fuentes, María, 87
Fuentes, Tomasa, 140

Gaceta Callejera, 73, 76
Gaona, Enrique, 43–44
Gaona, Rodolfo, 43–46, 77–78, 79
Garcés, Dolores, 161–62
García, Aurelio, 143
García, Fernando, 125
García, Francisco, 126–27
García, Genoveva, 173
García, Jesús, 113–14, 170–71
García, José, 121, 143–44
García, Luz, 142
García, Petrona, 116
García, Ramona, 124
gender ideologies: Hispanic v. Indian, 5,
    35–38, 54; of modern Mexico, 9, 12;
    normative values and, 5, 9, 12, 35–38,
    54; three-gender system, 37; women
    and, 21–22, 31, 177
Generation of 1880 (Argentina), 50
Gillow, Eulogio, 28
godparenthood, 83, 150–51
González, Juan, 98
González, Juana, 46–47
gossip: as community surveillance, 9, 29,
    107–8, 128; as normative force, 105–6;
    rapto and, 106; reputation and, 112–15;
    slander and, 105–6
Greco-Roman tradition, 137
Guacamaya, La, 64

Guadalupe Bejarano en las bartolinas de
    Belén (broadsheet), 74
Guanajuato, 16
Guardino, Peter, 23
"Güera Chabela, La" (broadsheet), 84
Guerrero, Julio, 53–54, 66
Guillén, Manuel, 53
Gutiérrez, Carlos, 120

Hardwicke's Marriage Act of 1753
    (England), 40
Hernández, Herlinda, 108
Hernández, Juana, 110
Hernández, Mariana, 125
Hernández, Matias, 122–23
Hernández, Refugio, 113
Hernández, Teresa, 156
hidalgo (leader), 19
Hidalgo y Costilla, Miguel, 23
Hijo del Trabajo, El, 48
hijo desobediente, El (broadsheet), 72
hímen en México, El (Flores), 59–60
honor: code of, 9; family honor, 1, 5–6, 10,
    34, 36, 39, 41, 63, 134, 148, 182; female,
    35, 145; honor killings, 83–84, 102;
    male, 35, 78; moral lessons on, 83–87;
    reputation and, 36, 47, 58, 147; seman-
    tics of, 170–76; sexual, 5–6, 34–35,
    58–59, 63, 116, 155–77; slander and,
    115–17; work ethic and, 111, 115, 174
¡Horrible asesinato! (broadsheet), 82
Horrible Crimen (broadsheet), 70
Huitzilopochtli, 66
humor: in popular culture, 87–92
hymens: elastic, 59, 164, 181; hymeno-
    plasty and, 181–82; statistical analysis
    of, 53, 165; virginity and, 35, 47, 58–59,
    163

Imparcial, El, 44–45
infanticide, 108
infidelity, 56, 83, 96, 108–9
inheritance laws, 55
in-laws: in popular culture, 83; role of in
    couple's life, 110–11
intergenerational conflict, 4, 10, 38, 131
international sign language, 94, 94
Isthmus of Tehuantepec, 22
Iturbide, Agustín, 24

Jalatlaco, 13
Jesús, Demetrio de, 112
Jiménez, Bonifacia, 158
Jiménez, Encarnación, 117
Jiménez, Francisco, 150–51
Jiménez, Patrocinia, 150–51